Walking Towards Hope

Experiencing Grace in a Time of Brokenness

Walking Towards Hope

Experiencing Grace in a Time of Brokenness

Paul M. Beckingham

CASTLE QUAY BOOKS
CANADA

Published by: Castle Quay Books
500 Trillium Drive, Kitchener, Ontario, N2G 4Y4
Tel: (800) 265-6397   Fax (519) 748-9835
E-mail: info@castlequaybooks.com
www.castlequaybooks.com

Copy-editing by Janet Diamond
Cover Design by John Cowie, *eyetoeye design*
Printed at Essence Publishing, Belleville, Ontario

Library and Archives Canada Cataloguing in Publication

Beckingham, Paul M., 1952-
      Walking towards hope: experiencing grace in a time of brokenness / Paul M. Beckingham.

Includes index.
ISBN 1-894860-24-1

      1. Beckingham, Paul M., 1952- 2. People with disabilities--Religious aspects--Christianity. 3. Hope--Religious aspects--Christianity. 4. People with disabilities--Biography.   5. Brain-damage--Patients--Biography. 6. Christian biography. 7. Missionaries--Biography. I. Title.

RC387.5.B42 2004   270'.092   C2004-905540-2

To
Mary,
Hannah, Naomi, Leah,
David, and Aaron.
One family on a journey—
Walking—together—towards hope.

TABLE OF CONTENTS

FOREWORD

"Because he loves me," says the LORD,
"I will rescue him; I will protect him,
for he acknowledges my name.
He will call upon me, and I will answer
him; I will be with him in trouble,
I will deliver him and honor him"
(Psalm 91:14–15).

I have rarely been so moved as when reading this book. Paul Beckingham was my friend at Regent College, Vancouver, and I knew him then as an extraordinarily gifted Christian leader. He was superb with youth: indeed, he had been youth director of the tough London City Mission. He was the pastor of one of the dynamic churches in the Vancouver area, Marineview Chapel. And he was a very gifted evangelist. Our practice at Regent was to take teams out for a week or more of intentional evangelism in Canadian cities and universities, and he and Richard Sharp, now ambassador at large of Operation Mobilisation USA, were major stars. They were the best evangelists I had the privilege of working with. After gaining his M.Div., Paul went with the Canadian Baptist Ministries as a missionary to Kenya.

9

I next saw him when he was well into his recovery from an automobile accident so horrific that fifteen bones were smashed, and he sustained massive injuries to his skull. It was so horrific that several surgeons refused to operate. So horrific that three times he passed away and was resuscitated during the hours of surgery. I say he was well into his recovery when I next saw him, but that is an exaggeration. His concentration was very short, his limp profound, his exhaustion and pain obvious. But he had started on the long road back to life from the very edge of the grave.

The book is superbly written. It enables the reader almost to get inside the experience of the patient. Paul had been a major achiever, and after the accident had to settle for disabilities that would accompany him to the grave. How could such a man cope with these outstanding injuries? How could his wife and family handle the radical change in husband and father? This book lets us in on the story. It is a story of anger, pain and disability. A story of incoherence, despair and the closest possible brush with death. It tells of love, sacrifice and gradual recovery, still incomplete years after the fateful crash that day on the Limuru road when Paul the missionary had his car reduced to a mangled wreck by an enormous Kenyan military vehicle—whose driver wandered back, looked at the scene and has not been heard of since. It is a story of astounding heroism in him, and in his wife Mary. A story of prayer and, most of the time, deep faith. But supremely this book carries a message of hope which could be of inestimable value to those who are struggling with disability and disaster. The theme of hope is interwoven with almost every chapter. He has clearly read widely on the subject—Moltmann's book, among others, has been a blessing to him. But his greatest teacher has been his own experience of hope in the crucible of sustained and intolerable anguish.

He tells of the sustainable development he longs to see take root in Kenya, which could change the lives of penniless people like Daniel, injured in the car with him. He gives a moving account of his return to Kenya after years of partial recovery, to lay some of the ghost of the past. He gives us postcards from Kenya—stories of those who made an indelible impact on him during his missionary service. He has absorbed something of the African attitude to time—"hurry kills." So there is a wonderfully reflective note to this book, and the effect is both beautiful and challenging. The authentic Christian conviction comes out of the twisted chaos of his accident: Satan meant it for evil, but God meant it for good. And you can see the goodness of God beginning to unfold as the story develops. Of course it is costly grace: there is no cheap story of victory here. The book's subheading says it all "Experiencing grace in a time of brokenness." And a long time it was.

There is a fascinating account of his neurological tests with a top Jewish neuropsycholgist who was both compassionate and utterly honest. He believed that there were certain things that Paul could still achieve to a high standard, but never the complex multi-task skills that he had once had. Nor would he ever complete the doctorate on which he had set his hopes. The book leaves him in a "Don't know" attitude to the future, teaching in Carey Theological College, Vancouver. And lo and behold on the title page I read "Dr. Paul Beckingham"! He got there after all. Now that is some story. A story of faith in the dark, hope in a hopeless situation, vast courage and determination, and a character that has clearly been refined by the whole experience. I suspect that Paul's greatest influence will prove not to have been in the hey-day of his strength and abilities, but in the impact his life continues to make on countless people after the accident. Read it—and pass it on. It will change you.

REV. DR. MICHAEL GREEN
Oxford University

PREFACE

He has broken my strength in midcourse,
He has shortened my days.
"O my God," I say, "take me not away
in the midst of my days—
you whose years endure
throughout all generations!"
(Psalm 102:23–24, ESV)

My mind goes back to the days when Paul Beckingham, as an Englishman turned Canadian like myself, a home mission leader now studying theology to equip himself for wider work, was a member of my fellowship group at Regent College. Energetic and exuberant, with an arresting testimony to God's work in his life thus far, the gifts and instincts of a pastoral pioneer were already apparent in him and he was a huge asset in our group process. I remember too how he helped us to move house in heat that was almost killing me; he manhandled cases of books with an ease and speed that were almost debonair. It is wrenching to think how much less he is, in human terms, today than he was then.

What does a horrific accident, that leaves you permanently disabled in body, and with brain damage as well, do to your sense of

13

who you are before God? Having endured just such an accident, Paul here tells of his partial recovery over five years in such a way as to answer that question as far as he can. He was a missionary in Kenya when it happened; he is back in Vancouver now, limited in body and mind for the rest of his earthly life. His story, unselfconsciously and even cheerfully told, is about God and an honest man who now grows, not upwards into further achievement, but downwards into increasing realism about the restrictions under which he must live. His book is not a prettied-up presentation for pious purposes, but simply the plain record of a brave man and his brave wife breasting wave after wave of trouble with God-given guts. The story will stabilize you even as it shakes you, for the goodness and glory of God are in it along with everything else.

It is not beyond God to get himself glory in the life of someone he loves by weakening that person. There was an earlier Paul to whom God gave a thorn in the flesh; had he not done so we might never have had the second letter to the Corinthians, the biblical classic on, among other things, weakness taken in stride by faith. There is Joni Eareckson, quadriplegic magnificent, without whose superb books and advocacy for the disabled any number of us would be poorer. In this apostolic succession of God-sent weakness, Paul Beckingham now stands. It is a safe and even privileged place to be.

My guess is that you have never read anything like this narrative before. My amazement is that it exists at all. My plea is: don't miss it! I covet for you what it gave to me.

REV. DR. JAMES I. PACKER
Regent College
Vancouver, BC

INTRODUCTION

This personal narrative of the author is remarkable indeed. For after all he has suffered mentally, emotionally, and relationally, he is still able to give us such a lucid, detailed, and deeply personal narrative of his journey of hope. He is like Lazarus, speaking to us again, as risen from the dead! His normalcy was shattered, and unconsciously he shatters our understanding of "being normal" too. So if you want to remain cocooned in the complacency of your own egotistic "cabin," then this is definitely not a book you should read; put it back quickly on the shelf! But if you are open to big questions, of why we suffer, how we cope with tragedy, what is hope, and of how we re-live through a shattered life, then this will become a wonderful companion beside you, "walking towards hope."

Years before the car accident that has radically changed Paul Beckingham's life, vividly I remember the narration of his childhood's hardships, when he came as a theological student, into my college office. He had suffered poverty and a dysfunctional family life. As a young teenager he remembered carrying his grandfather's ashes on his bicycle from the mortuary, giving him years of adult responsibility that robbed him of his childhood. This is all dismissed in this more recent narrative, because however "high" or "low" this childhood terrain may have been, it was nothing in comparison to the magnitude of the mountain ranges of pain, a shattered body, and a traumatized brain that the author has had to traverse since his road accident in Nairobi.

The development of medicine, especially of neuro-physiology, both advance and yet complicate the recovery from injury, as the author narrates. For post-traumatic shock is now a very common injury with the dramatic increase of road traffic and road accidents. Brain injury is so much better understood, so that patients like the author now understand the permanent disabilities that change their personalities, skills and professional aptitudes. Ironically then, in a culture that never was more self-conscious of the central importance of professional roles and skills, in the church as in society at large, there is intensified the frustrations imposed upon the handicapped. For it not just injury that handicaps us, it is also the cultural values imposed upon us, that we blindly accept as "normal." The detailed understanding of this, and of the growing acceptance of such mental limitation by the author, is perhaps the most insightful part of this narrative, still in process.

As readers, some will fully enter into the depths of the author's sufferings, for they have been there too. Others of us can only see it through a glass dimly, for thankfully we have been spared such tortures of body and mind. But as it is so wisely described, an individual's tragedy becomes a collective tragedy, affecting a wife, five children, and indeed the wider circles of a mission organization, as well as a network of friends and colleagues. What happens to us as human beings, has social consequences. A whole ecological network is affected too. As the apostle Paul reminds us, when one suffers then the whole "body" suffers too! So if we have a healthy gift of empathy and compassion, we shall all read this remarkable story of how careless driving affects lives permanently! And yet it is also, where devoted health-givers performed amazing skills of surgery, nursing, and therapy. But behind it all, the story speaks of a loving God who can redeem and give us hope to walk again in his companionship.

Dr. James M. Houston
Regent College
Vancouver, BC

AUTHOR'S INTRODUCTION

*I have much to write to you, but I
do not want to use paper and ink.
Instead, I hope to visit you and talk
with you face to face, so that our joy
may be complete* (2 John 12).

Writing these pages has caused me to make frequent soul safaris—interior visits to untamed places. Frederick Buechner, pastor, writer, and repository of spiritual wisdom, describes this kind of journey as a "stopover" in *A Room Called Remember*.[1]

He carefully distinguishes two kinds of remembering. First, he identifies fleeting remembrances—those kinds of recollections that, unbidden, come back to tease us. They scrawl pictures on the vacant screens of our minds—the forms of people and events that have been half-forgotten for years.

Then, there are those images, events, and personalities from earlier days and previous experiences that we intentionally call to mind. It is this kind of deliberate remembering that takes place in the interior space within each of us known as "a room called remember."

From such a room we intentionally bring to mind selected people who have touched our lives deeply. To capture their stories in print involves a release of scrambled emotions. For me, the memory of each person is nestled in a tumult of contradictory feelings, still alive and uncomfortably raw to this day. As I write these words, I feel my heartbeat quicken as my chest tightens and my shoulders begin to hunch, restricting my breathing to a shallow gasp. Old anxieties combine with present uncertainties to make me feel numb and powerless, feeble and helpless, once more.

Recalling the vivid details of how these people touched (and some of them actually saved) my life is to renew my deep acquaintance with these wonderful characters—personalities driving the events that create stories quite unforgettable. Without such people in our lives we would have few stories to tell—and none of lasting value. In their absence, a vacuum of dumb silence would shroud their unspoken voices, invisible faces, and stillborn heartbeats held prisoner within the subdued hush of songs unsung. Without them, life would be reduced to a seemingly endless repetition of lacklustre routine punctuated by the humdrum-ho-hum of a heavy-footed army of unfulfilled days.

These larger-than-Texas characters with their spontaneous investment in my life shape memories with their dramatic energy, vivid colour, and fine focus. When I deliberately recall their textured richness, I am instantly reconnected with the faces of friends in unlikely situations. These remembered people weave in and out of my life to form a glad refrain in a song of faithful friendship. They become central to my story as it unfolds in these pages, for they describe the person I am and am becoming. Reflecting upon such poignant realities, I welcome each of them into my memory bank in order to celebrate them here.

In those milestone moments, I gladly relive their warm friendship. For their love, prayers, and practical support, and for their tender encouragement, I am forever in their debt. By being present to me, they continue to bless unfolding seasons opening for my family since that day we were overtaken by a life-transforming auto accident and, in its tow, came the long years of recovery. But you never truly recover from events that turn you into a different sort of person. You simply try to cope a little better, one day at a time.

Such friends encompass the globe. From the Limuru Road in Nairobi, they extend through Kenya, linking hands over Canada, the US, and Europe. They include people of faith who build community by participating in local church life. They enrich their faith communities in far away places like Britain, Malaysia, and Japan. Thinking of them today, I hold them in my memory like vivid postcards from precious former places. Like the biblical writer thinking of faraway friends, I, too, have often felt *I have much to write to you, but I do not want to use paper and ink. Instead, I hope to visit you and talk to you* (2 John 12). That might, one day, become possible and it is a hope that I cherish. And that thought brings me to the richly layered subject of hope.

The loss of hope can cripple the soul and wound the heart with its devastation. I know, because it happened to me. I didn't choose for it to come about that way but, nonetheless, it did. Re-emerging hope is as important as it is tender—so hope and its recovery form the strong subplot of this story. At times hope emerges as the main theme. It is a profoundly precious commodity as Robert Rasmussen accurately notes:

> I doubt we could live long without hope. Of course we could keep our hearts beating and our lungs breathing. But I'm talking about *living!* Devastation distinguishes itself by the complete absence of hope, strengthened by love.... He created us to be a people of hope. And hope permeates the Sanctuary. It flows through us. As we are aware of our life in Christ, we gain more than enough hope to help us wait through any situation.[2]

That is the kind of hope I hold out to you in the same way that it came to me—as a free gift. It arises from the sanctuary of God's presence deep within our personal pain. I pray that you are able to receive it, and that it will grow tall wherever you plant it in your life.

Hope arrives in the stories of other survivors of loss, catastrophes of every kind. I love the courage and dogged determination they display as they reveal the depth of their injuries, challenges, and dreams, and their determination to walk their unknown path of recovery. I know that for each of them the act of writing becomes as healing as it is challenging. A significant contributor to this kind of writing is Claudia Osborn who, in her book *Over My Head,* shares the details of just what recovery from a traumatic brain injury (TBI) has meant for her. For me, she has been a quiet inspiration. She was a young doctor prior to her injury and writes movingly and with insight about her condition and her struggle towards a recovery from the losses she has suffered. She powerfully explains the size of the challenges she faces:

> It is a daunting task for me to make my thoughts clear. My difficulty in telling this story was compounded by the deficits in my memory, language, and organizational skills. I have no memory of being injured.... My first bid for independence was, as all baby steps are, unsure and teetering. [3]

Claudia speaks accurately for many of us who have, like her, suffered similarly. I trust that as I also share with you in what I have written, my story, too, may offer real hope to other TBI survivors who bravely struggle each day as they fight for the recovery they long for—and as their families struggle with them.

However, a notable dimension of recovery has been missing from many TBI survivors' stories I read. None of them has sketched a path towards a *spiritual* recovery—the healing of the wounded spirit. I did not start out that way either, when I began to write. Oddly, my goal was quite different.

I intended, instead, to do some preparatory work in the area of brain injury as a foundation for a piece of research I was designing. Through my research, I wanted to discover some appropriate pastoral care interventions that pastors, chaplains, and hospital visitors might bring to TBI survivors and their families. However, when I sat down to begin, I found that all I could write about was my own accident, my own brain injury, my family's struggle alongside me.

The details just poured out of me. My problem was never "What shall I write about today?" It was "How can I get away from the computer long enough to get a good night's sleep?" I found myself getting out of bed in the middle of the night to write more. Of course, each morning was a struggle for me to get up and remain wakeful throughout the new day. I was driven by a desperate need to write, a need to make sense of my life in the face of absurd circumstances.

Somewhere deep inside, I knew that this book was not just so much publishing fodder. I did not write to publish. I wrote frantically for therapy—for my own healing. I wrote with tears rolling off my cheeks and hitting the page. I often turned away from my writing to sit in deep silence, moved beyond words by the things I felt I needed to write. Many times, I wrote with a sense that God Himself was watching over my shoulder as I wrote. He comforted me in my inner pain and alienating isolation—all evidence of a broken spirit.

Does that mean that, pontiff-like, I claim to be writing *ex cathedra*, without mistake or fault? Clearly not. It simply means that I hope what I have written will assist others in their pain. It may help you, too. If it does, and that is my prayer, then I join you in thanking the Father of Love who meets us precisely in our pain. He carries us always, but He is especially close when we are deeply hurt. The hope He brings is central to my story—and that is how my narrative unfolds.

Hope, however, remains an unsolved paradox. As creatures of time, we look forward to the future, and yet the future will for each of us end in death. Such a realization can sometimes deliver its own terrible sense of ultimate hopelessness, and many feel and express this conclusion. Cynicism springs up easily like a garden of weeds, overgrown and out of control. The fireweed of hopelessness chokes the life out of the fruit, shrubs, and flowers that we have planted, tended, and nurtured. The usual "answers" to the world's problems—better education, economic development, science and technology—promise much yet ultimately seem to deliver little. Time traps us in days and weeks and the ultimate futility of life's untimely ending.

The person of faith is not immune to such feelings of despair. However, his or her vision stretches eagerly forward to focus far beyond the endpoint of this life. Hope ultimately has an eschatological focal point. Hope looks beyond the trials and pain of the present without ignoring them or disregarding their reality. It reaches forward to a time when the promise it anticipates will be received in faith. In the meantime, life is nurtured by the inbreaking of hope into our present experience as a foretaste of much more that is to come.

Hope is no simple matter. Hope becomes an issue for those who wrestle with its future promise, while facing a problematic present filled with personal violation, robbery, and loss that painful circumstances deliver daily. Glenn Tinder notes this well when he says, "Hope is not an easy and natural attitude for creatures who must, with the capacity for looking far ahead, inhabit mortal time."[4]

As I read stories of survivors of tragedy and their slow recovery of hope, I sense that they have experienced hope's complex, multi-layered reality. At many points, all of our personal life stories reflect this kind of thickly layered density, behaving like perfume. Life events might, for example, form a perfumed top note that holds a light floral tone, refreshing and sweet. Beneath it lurks a middle note, cast of a deeper mixture, spreading a more thoughtful depth across the body of the fragrance. Finally, a bass note with its darker oils lingers long within our memory, undergirding life's more transient moments. With the body's heat, and over time, all perfumes change—they mellow and develop. Sometimes they turn sour through abrasive or lengthy contact with the skin's acidity.

The story that will unfold in these pages covers a similar span of emotional responses to lived experience. Behind and beneath them lie deeper spiritual realities. I touch on these realities lightly. Like an anchor, spirituality often lies submerged as it does its stabilizing work in dangerous waters. Sharp and ugly barnacles habitually cling to an anchor as pain attaches to faith. Yet grace is magnetically drawn towards pain. It was so once upon a cross; it is so now at the crossroads in our lived experience where faith and pain intersect.

I thank the God of Grace for so many hands that helped us through our wretched times of pain. Whether they were folded in prayer or bruised in the effort to free us from the car wreckage, many hands were grazed as, with sleeves up-rolled, they worked in practical ways on our behalf.

In these pages, you will stagger with us through our personal sacred journal of a broken spirit—and finally—a healed heart. We welcome you to join us as our private walking partners along our journey of faith. And as our pain connects with yours, I pray that you may also come to know the reality of a hope restored—the kind of hope that emerges when God encounters and embraces you with the depth of His personal love for you. May you, too, experience grace in a time of brokenness.

DR. PAUL M. BECKINGHAM
Carey Theological College
Vancouver, BC

PROLOGUE

A Life Interrupted

This day was about to end horribly for me—for us all. Thankfully, I was utterly unaware that this unfolding reality was soon to hit me hard.

I did not know it when we visited the Elephant Orphanage, but I was about to drive a car carrying four people head-on into an oncoming truck—a military truck—a military tank carrier, to be precise. It was pulling an extra-wide load. The driver, however, was not hauling a tank on this Kenyatta Day. Instead, he had a large container loaded onto his extra-wide trailer.

Mary and Aaron were not prepared either for what would almost immediately happen to them. They were soon to be unbelievably traumatized. Mary would need to nurse her awkwardly broken collarbone before the day was done and, in shock herself, would have to calm her screaming son.

We were to eat out that night at a favourite hotel. Instead, in a few short minutes, Daniel would be hauled unconscious from our car wreck with his thigh badly broken. My wrecked body would reveal fifteen broken or displaced bones, two fractures of the skull, a severe brain injury, a foot needing to be reattached, and a heart that was about to stop three times. Huge blood loss would leave its ugly trail inside the car and out. It would be an hour and a half before my comatose and shattered body could be peeled from the mangled metal we once referred to as "our car." It seems that some days don't end quite as well as you might expect.

Life before the accident ended abruptly, and forever. Later—much later—I would begin to fight back, to reject this before-and-after analysis. I remember, one day, coldly deciding never to allow this event to become my defining moment. And why? Simply because it is not the single event from which I choose to draw my life's significance or meaning. My life held meaning before—and will beyond—this accident, or other terrible, invasive events that may afflict me.

I choose not to allow these interruptions to impose their diminishing definitions upon who I am—upon the larger person I might still become. I will invite healthier events than these to bring their definitions to my life. Instead, I will let praiseworthy people and laudable values gift me with real reasons to carry on living. With hands open and outstretched, I receive hope and a renewed sense of a future as godly gifts, and in my heart I will dare to dream. With all the energy I have left I will work to see pain redeemed and trust restored. I want to soar with eagles, to rise up on wings, and to become more of the person I truly am, in the grace of God.

Today, He draws alongside me, and tomorrow I know He will carry me home and wipe away every tear, ease every pain, and fill every sigh. Why? Because He loves me, because He loves me, because He loves me. And more than that, I am persuaded He also loves *you*! His love lasts from eternity to eternity. It is rich and real and deeper than your deepest need.

CHAPTER ONE

The Prognosis

EASTER 1999

*Where then is my hope? Who can see
any hope for me?* (Job 17:15).

"I'm afraid there is no more that I can do for you..."
The words hung there before me, dark and menacing, sus-
pended in the air for the longest time. They bounced like gunfire
glancing off the walls on an otherwise pleasant spring morning. I
fought to take them in while, outside, the birds sang boldly
unaware in the sunshine. Inside, those words of finality rang oddly
hollow, groaning unmusically. Surely, I told myself, they held no
truth. How could they? If life moved forward and the earth still
spun as it appeared to—but before my blurred eyes my world had
ground abruptly to an ugly halt. Everything but my head now
seemed to have stopped spinning.
The young surgeon, pleasant and smiling, appeared to be his
normal self. The building we stood in remained unchanged since

our entry just a few moments earlier. Yet nothing was the same any more. The rooms remained bright and airy, a pleasant place to be, but to me, at that moment, it seemed to be the most unpleasant place on earth. Somehow, in slow motion, everything was changing before me. Surely I had misheard this young doctor. But his warm and serious eyes now stared me down with the hard facts.

I am fighting to take it in, struggling to process it all, trying to make some kind of appropriate response. Silence. Like a man turned mute, I remain utterly speechless, but inside I want to scream. I want to yell to any who will hear me, "But I'm a *man*, damn it! I am *not* useless!" Too many years of learning to always give the polite response, however, has done its work of socializing me. They have turned me into Mr. Most-of-the-Time-Nice. These lessons in good manners cause me now to smile benignly back, staring dumbly as I fight to make broken sense of it all. The doctor sees only my uncomprehending, stupid smile.

But to me, it is my best-composed beam of serenity—my caring, pastoral smile. I'm a pastor by training and by inclination. I want to protect this poor doctor from the shock of having to give his patient—me!—the bad news. I truly do not want him to become upset like I am. I plunge into deep inner pain, and I do not know what on earth to do with it. I have not learned how to express this kind of pain and anger in ways that feel safe to me. So, I simply say nothing, trying to let his grim prognosis sink in without letting my hurt spill over in any ugly or embarrassing ways.

He continues to talk, this smart and gentle doctor, keeping it simple all the time. He professionally avoids any signs of affect in his voice. His tone is smooth and even, like an airline pilot calmly telling his passengers that there is some kind of technical hitch, as the plane spins and falls without a trace from a cloudless sky.

"Your foot is very swollen," he continues calmly. "You are having a severe arthritic attack. This will likely happen to you again and again. It will become more intense and more frequent. There is no more that I can do until I need to amputate. Your talus bone is dying."

I respond again with my intensely active silence—active because I am desperately trying to put all of this craziness together. I feel the way I did the first time I tried to juggle. I know myself to be a complete klutz. The beanbags and brightly coloured balls just hit the floor, rolling away from me at speed. So, I silently sit without utterance, but not without the clamour of rapid conversation buzzing inside my overactive head. I cannot multi-task to hear, absorb, process, and respond to this doctor's inquisitive look as he patiently awaits my answer. I am travelling at half speed through a fog, and I cannot work it all out in order to shape some kind of adequate or reasoned response in the brief time it takes for the doctor to deliver his news to me.

He waits for my reply in what feels like a short eternity of silence. I can feel myself sinking into shock, boxing in slow motion, tying to defend myself with hands tied firmly behind my back. Inside, I am buffeted and bruised. Externally, my foot throbs, silently screaming at me through waves of unbearable pain.

"But," he goes on, breaking the prolonged hiatus of silence, speaking now in a tone that turns words of potential hope into cheap and throw-away verbiage, "I am prepared to refer you to a foot reconstruction surgeon." And, like an automaton I hear myself give my hollow, knee-jerk, "thank you," to which he throws back an automatic, "You're welcome."

Quite suddenly, it seems, we're out of the consultation room, and I am back on my crutches. Clumsily, and painfully slowly, I navigate my way around the outer reception area, absorbing the pressure of crutches as they push up and under my aching shoulders. As we head back to our car, his words still do not make any sense to me. A shadow of dark despair gathers somewhere deep inside me and I fear it will utterly overwhelm me. I thrash like a drowning man in lapping waves that splash above my ears. Sinking slowly, my arms flail wildly at the water all around me, but I am helpless to save myself.

There will follow for me a dizzying sequence of eleven nights of sleepless pain. Finally, exhausted and frightened, I decide to visit my own family doctor. I feel utterly spent and hopelessly dejected. As a smiling Dr. Terri walks confidently into the treatment room, the chill around me begins to thaw. Her warm eyes beam at me and her deep knowing look unnerves me completely, for I sense in her an oasis of care and understanding for my dry, desert soul. The expression of care in her eyes almost brings me to tears. She is so very kind, and kindness given freely in a time of need can sweep your feet from under you.

Dr. Terri had been my first visitor some many months earlier in the Vancouver hospital where I was barrier nursed. I remember being truly puzzled that she should even remember who I was. But she did, caring enough to make a special trip to see me. I was so profoundly moved back then, and here, today, she was about to make me feel that way again.

"Ah," she says with real warmth and total credibility, "there's no reason for you to be in pain any longer."

Somewhat shocked and taken aback, I stutter, "B-b-but...I-I thought there was nothing that could be done!"

"Oh no! You have plenty of options outside of surgery." I staggered inwardly, taken aback by the strange thought that hope might still exist for me when the surgical experts seemed to have given up on me so recently. Maybe, after all, I had not come at last to the end of the particular road that I so dreaded.

"Many of my senior patients," Dr. Terri continued, "suffer with arthritis in their hands—they are bent and completely twisted out of shape. But even they don't have to be in the unnecessary pain or discomfort that you are presently experiencing."

Smiling and calm, she writes me a prescription for some powerful anti-inflammatory medication. As I stand to leave, she smiles warmly and hands me the note, together with several packs of pills—the complimentary testers that pharmaceutical reps donate to their general practitioners.

"Try these," she says, "I think they will work well for you."

Dr. Terry's hunch proved to be astonishingly accurate. That

night, I swallowed my first dose of the new drugs and, oh, what utter joy! I quickly fell into a deep and unbroken sleep—my first full night of pain-free slumber in more than ten days. My body ached for this kind of life-renewing therapy. Like a pampered child I sank into the welcome folds of my bed, and drifted off as if floating upon a cloud of safety towards some distant, sweet, and unknown place.

My journal shows that this was about a year and a half after *The Accident,* but it felt in those days that an agonizing lifetime had slowly passed before me. In many ways it had. When hope evaporates, time passes interminably slowly before your tired eyes—like a reluctant conveyor belt stacked with only the rejects remaining after all you once hoped for had been lost or spoiled. Meaningless bric-a-brac and worthless trinkets were now the very best that life seemed able to offer me. All reverts to empty vanity and useless frill when you lose your grip on hope.

Glenn Tinder, thinker, man of faith, and writer, has it right when he recognizes hope's centrality to all that we are, all that makes us truly human. He says:

> Hope is as necessary to life as light and air. Fear weakens and paralyzes us. These are matters of common experience. Hopelessness is a kind of death; one is immobilized by the dark and threatening visage of the future. But hope enlivens us. When viewed with hope, the way ahead is open and inviting. Hope draws us into the future and in this way it engages us in life.[5]

Many people—folks of all kinds—tell me that there has to be more to life than all that their present experience encompasses. With desperation they exclaim, *Surely there has to be something more than this!* Sometimes, they speak with hope, more often in tones of desperation. Many times, in bitter cynicism they throw doubt upon the hopeful outcome they desire. In such soured comments I hear the hollow cry of a broken spirit. Through its absence they begin to see that hope is vital to life itself—a profound spiritual reality.

Hope for your heart, this godly value, the deep inner expectation that something better waits in store for you, is sometimes mediated through ordinary human agencies. Many dying urchins on the streets of Calcutta testify to that truth as David Aikman accurately records:

> What Mother Teresa did not say, but that was obvious, was that she and her sisters had brought the reality of Christ's love to her "incurable" patients so powerfully that the imminent sense of heaven became inescapable to them. And it was the anticipation of heaven—the hope—that brought them such joy at the very end of their lives.[6]

God sometimes uses ordinary people—not only outstanding saints—to bring you His extraordinary hope for the future. In dark and distressing times, you might begin to ask deep and agonizing questions—the ones that simply have no easy answers. As hope starts to slip away when the answers come too slowly, you cry out, audibly or voicelessly in a frozen silence of fear: *Where then is my hope? Who can see any hope for me?* (Job 17:15).

When a friend—or stranger—clearly sees real hope in store for you and tells you truthfully, it can be for you a gentle ray of sunshine breaking, at last, through thick layers of fog. Hope thaws the ice of cold fear that entraps you, and you begin to feel love's affectionate embrace. You know with new certainty that you are treasured with a Love that will not let you go.

But it would be many months—even years—before that kind of warm embrace would comfort my family. For far longer than anyone should, they would fight to make sense of the unthinkable that was about to happen to them. You cannot prepare for a loss so big; you can only pray for the power to heal.

CHAPTER TWO

Just Another Day in Paradise

NAIROBI, KENYA: ON KENYETTA DAY

May your unfailing love rest upon us, O LORD, even as we put our hope in you (Psalm 33:22).

They did not seem to be wildly excited. In fact, my kids looked positively bored—and rather disbelieving. "Today is our *Family Fun Day*," I announced one morning, standing in our Kenyan kitchen. Lightly and in a carefree tone I added, "and you guys are going to have fun—whether you like it or not!" I said it through a breezy smile, but my unwilling gang seemed less than impressed and not at all amused.

Predictably, they neither jumped in joyous anticipation nor leaped around the house in busy activity to get ready. Instead, they prepared sluggishly to go out for the day. They showed about as much excitement as they would for a visit to the dentist for a filling or a root canal.

It seems that parents are a divinely appointed trial to their offspring, at least during those teenage years. On the other hand, teenagers also serve their own divine purpose. They are the ultimate test of their parent's sanity—and of their determination to smile at all times. These trials come frequently to both sides of the generational divide. When they do, it feels like a less-than-sparkling party and neither side is ready to dance. Teenagers put parents under strenuous and microscopic examination. On such parental evaluations, I rarely achieve the A grade that I would like—but a mere passing grade would sometimes be nice to get.

Whatever happened, I sometimes wonder, to those darling little children we used to have? They seemed to hang on every word and longed to learn new things from us. They would get excited about outings and new ideas. And then they became teens and I became rather redundant. It is odd how such a thing can happen in the blink of an eye. I am told that one day soon, we—my growing teens and I—will understand each other better as they graduate into adulthood and I enter my dotage. I can hardly wait—I just hope that I am still able to sit up and take nourishment when the day finally arrives!

Our fast-growing kids had reached the ages of ten, twelve, fourteen, sixteen and seventeen. Not surprisingly, then, it was not easy to get a unanimous decision—about almost anything. Maybe if I asked, "Do you guys want vanilla or chocolate ice cream?" I might receive a solid "Yes!" for chocolate. But few other questions would receive such a swift and affirmative response.

It should have been easier by now. After all, we had one less child at home to cast her vote. Our eldest daughter, Hannah, had just graduated from high school at seventeen. We all missed her terribly now that she was working away from home as an *au pair* in Paris, trying to improve her French language skills. Here in Nairobi, it still seemed no easier to arrive at a majority vote, even without the complication of her additional voice. To get a unanimous decision on my suggestions was tough—and today would be no exception.

A public holiday, like today's Kenyatta Day, meant that each family member held firmly to his or her own ideas of exciting things to do. Teens have very firm notions about what makes for a fun day, and each teenager seems to differ from their brothers and sisters.

As for anything that Dad suggests, well—maybe not! Mom had come up with a great idea, a way for us to be together and to go out and have some fun. A family outing to the Elephant Orphanage sounded like a lot of fun to both Mary and me. But to our gang that day, it painted a clear picture: a long, dusty drive in a hot van on bumpy Kenyan roads. Such journeys promised one thing only—great discomfort for all. Our guys were not convinced that this would be as enjoyable as their parents claimed. Besides, none of their friends would be coming along for the ride. So, if by some miracle it finally turned out to be fun, they would never openly admit it to Dad.

But eventually, we persuaded them to climb up into the sweltering van, though few were smiling on those hot and sticky seats. The van was airless and blistering, smelling of dust and melting vinyl. Each child sat as far from the others as possible; it was just too searing to get near anybody else. Despite our high hopes for this trip, the looks on our kids' faces told a different story. They were determined that whatever happened today, fun would play no part in it.

Some weeks later, as our offspring looked back to this day trip, they would arrive at their first unanimous conclusion in family history. They told me that they made a vow—they would never, ever go on another family fun day with me. Not ever! They were not about to enjoy the way these daylight hours would end; neither would I. This day would bring us to a complete agreement on that point, at least. It is odd to think that sometimes it takes a life-threatening event to produce a strong measure of consensus.

So we set off, at last. With high parental expectations—and gentle groans from teenagers—we bumped along towards the Elephant Orphanage, nestled on the edge of Nairobi's sprawling urban slums.

There were no elephants at the Elephant Orphanage that day. Mary and I wondered if already the whole day had suddenly come unglued. Yet, some interesting moments were still in store for us. Alongside the Nairobi Game Park, we watched with rapt attention as the game wardens led out two small orphaned rhinos, each weighing half a ton. Like their cousin elephants, young rhinos require their mother's protective shade. Usually, they will walk along beneath their mother's shelter. The larger animals act as a mobile umbrella, protecting their young ones from the fierce African sun. Like my own teens, these sizable young animals are prone to sunburn, though it is hard to imagine that their armoured skin might be so sensitive.

I recall once meeting a Hell's Angel at a campground somewhere in the south of England. He stood awkwardly, pacing the parched yellow grass near his parked motorbike. His arms were a screaming pink, sautéed vigorously under the midday sun. Mary had handed him some baby cream and we watched, transfixed, as this brute of a man sat quietly allowing Mary to tenderly apply that balm to his sunburned arms. We watched as he winced in pain. Rhinos are the bikers of the animal kingdom—big and vulnerable all at once. They, too, can be grilled like raw meat under African skies.

These young orphaned animals are cared for by experienced Kenyan game wardens who are careful not to domesticate these wild beasts. Eventually, they return the orphans to their natural habitat in the game park. This vast and rolling territory of yellow grassland is fenced only where it butts up against the city's black-top roads. The flimsy fences keep the more dangerous animals away from the centre of population—mostly.

These vast plains sit at an altitude of 5,500 feet, stretch for miles, and the animals are free to follow their chosen migratory trails across the length of East Africa. They can move from near the capital to fan out farther through the Great Rift Valley into the open plains of the Masai Mara. They travel down into Tanzania's Serengeti each year when their migratory reflex calls out to move them on. The skilled Kenyan caregivers raise their charges to live once more in the freedom and challenge of their rolling veldt environment.

The wardens do all they can to ensure the orphans develop no dangerous dependencies on man. To do so would be to deliver them into the hands of greedy poachers who stalk and slay these threatened rhinos. It is hard to imagine how such magnificent and scarce animals can be butchered simply for their large horns, their carcasses left rotting where they lie. Such is the mythical lure of the aphrodisiac qualities purported to be contained in rhino horns. Even greater is the economic pull and artistic attraction of carving ornate—and hugely expensive—dagger handles from their strong and heavy horn fibres for customers in countries nearby.

On that Kenyatta Day, we watched as two young rhino orphans were coaxed out of their enclosures. The wardens led them towards a muddy hollow supporting some small bushes in the shade of low-growing trees about the size of a man. There, they lay down contented, cool and wet in the red, sloppy soil. Under the wardens' watchful eyes, we came in close to watch them.

Kenyans in safari uniform began to smear the animals' rough skin with great daubs of red mud. Visitors to the orphanage followed suit, applying their own mudpacks to the orphans' leathery armour plating. Some of us were not so convinced that those muesli-looking mudpacks would clear their wrinkles. But these were not cosmetic treatments from animal estheticians—they were precautionary, medical applications from concerned wardens. Patting on the mud, a natural sunblock quickly formed to shield them from the sun, to freshen and safeguard their wrinkled skin.

"No!" Suddenly, the warden's voice rang out sharply. I looked up but it was clear that he was not talking to me. "Please don't touch their horns!" he said, turning to give his firm instruction to Aaron, my ten-year-old son.

Aaron was crouching low, cheek-to-cheek with a young rhino. He found it just too hard to keep his hands off the living horn that protruded from the beast's long snout. It was so smooth, so precious, and so alive—and so very big.

"They don't like that, *Mtoto*, and I don't want this one to charge you!" he said, more emphatically now. He was not smiling as he spoke; he was insistent and serious. His look showed real concern for my son's immediate safety.

Aaron began to think that the warden might, after all, be right about the dangers of hanging onto the young rhino's fast-developing horn. It is made from a dense kind of material that is the same substance as congealed hair—but far prettier, harder, and a lot more precious. Maybe it was the thought of a half-ton baby rhino rolling over him that finally deterred Aaron. He gingerly withdrew his hand—slowly and exceedingly carefully. Soon, Aaron was happy again, taking up the less adventurous task of gently applying handfuls of red mud and watching them dry before his eyes in great fat cakes and wads on the rhino's heaving belly.

The wet clay of the mudpies spread like a red dye over the enormous body of the baby rhino. In the heat of the day it dried almost instantly to a dull and dusty mud-tone gray. Aaron crouched close to this animal that had all the power of a small truck—one without brakes and rather questionable steering. He looked small and vulnerable as he crouched beside it. I kept a watchful eye on him, and my eyesight was much better than the rhino's.

These armoured quadrupeds suffer from exceptionally poor vision—but they enjoy an acutely developed olfactory gland that allows them outstanding powers of smell. Frequently, they will enter a tented camp to stomp out a small campfire whose smell has alerted them to a bonfire. They hate fires, so they often act as the African volunteer fire department, watching and responsive to careless visitors on camping safaris.

Long moments of rapt fascination with these unique beasts had now passed by in the heat of the open air. We began to feel dull pangs of hunger. We had brought some food for a picnic bag lunch to give our gang, for the sugar fix they would need to get through the day. It was dispatched in double-quick time. Fortified by the fresh tropical fruit and bread buns, we felt much better, ready to make a short tour of some penned animals nearby.

An evil looking collection of hyenas stared at us with wicked intent from behind the wire walls of their enclosure. Large, heavy-set scroungers, these scavengers paced up and down their lair, leaving a sharp and distinctly nasty odour behind them. Monkeys and antelopes wandered in their own safe spaces or drank from makeshift pools set in the floor of their pens.

Despite their fascination with the wild, my brood was rapidly tiring of this outing, their energy drained by the equatorial heat. The older kids had seen enough already. They wanted to move on to a freer part of the day where they could meet up with friends, hang out, and have real fun. We began to think about heading for home.

Our route back into town took us alongside Nairobi's Wilson Airport, the city's smaller commercial airfield. I parked our van next to the East African Aero Club building and brightly offered the children a quick tour of the property. I was hoping that my suggestion might stall their complaints about this further delay before reaching home.

Once inside the club, I managed to secure from a club member the last of seven signatures I would need to submit my application for membership. That was my real purpose for stopping there, for I was looking forward to taking a course of flying lessons. I felt a mounting excitement about that prospect—and not a little fear. Soon, I hoped to turn my student pilot's licence into the real thing.

Why? I pondered that question a lot—especially when the fear of flying gripped me. I am not sure that I understand my own reasons very well. Well, I really did not need to fly for the sake of my work. I was trying, maybe, to make an old dream come true. But I told myself that it might be very useful to take off from Nairobi to land in some far-flung place like Dadaab, set in the desert along the border with Somalia, to do my mission work. Besides, where better to fulfill my childhood ambition than in the most perfect climate on earth, here in Kenya? The thought of flying gave me considerable trepidation, but even more fascination. I love a challenge—and this test of character would be big enough for me.

But our fun day clock was now quickly ticking by and the children became rapidly tired. They showed their screaming boredom with loud complaints. They wanted no more new sights to see—they wanted home. It was barely mid-afternoon—so much, I thought, for a family fun day! We had spent just half a day together in the rising heat—not too bad, I guess. It was time to get back promptly to the cool of our house.

Upon our arrival home, Ebony and L.J. bounded over to welcome us enthusiastically. Our two German shepherd guard dogs gave us great joy—always playful and full of energy. Their excitement on seeing us gave rise to affectionate whimpers and wagging tails that shook their bodies in a playful frenzy. On a ten-point scale, their devotion to us scored at least a fifteen. It was like meeting long-lost cousins again after years of separation, though we had been away for barely half a day.

John, our gardener, swung open the big steel gates to our property. They clanked and scraped, scarring quarter circles in the uneven blacktop at the start of our driveway. The bottom locking bolts gouged small trenches describing the sweeping curve of the gates' swinging action. As we drove up the short drive to the house, a young Kenyan boy's waving hand revealed that Daniel Kariuki had arrived. He patiently awaited our return; he had come to play with Aaron.

Daniel, a sixteen-year-old Kikuyu boy, stood just a little smaller than Aaron who had just turned ten. Poor nutrition had retarded Daniel's growth. Like Aaron, he was still in elementary school, but only sporadically. He attended only when his mother could afford to pay for school fees and buy the necessary supplies. Even with the fees paid, on many occasions Daniel was not allowed into school. He was unable to afford a pencil and a new notebook. For just a few cents worth of basic materials his education was arrested.

Once, on discovering Daniel's predicament, Aaron took some money from his piggy bank to buy what Daniel needed. It did not amount to any great financial investment, but Aaron was able to do for Daniel what Daniel could not do for himself. His kindness became the vehicle to carry Daniel back to class. Daniel smiled shyly at the prospect of continuing his education; Aaron discovered that kindness is its own reward. Truly this proved to be a mutually beneficial arrangement and Aaron learned to give the gift of learning back to Daniel.

Daniel loved to come over and play with Aaron. They first met at a youth event we held at our home. We invited children and youth from the local Kenyan church where we attended to come to our property for food and a day of fun. More than forty Kenyan teenagers and younger children arrived.

Our kids organized the event and put together an exciting program with some low-key input from Mom. They wanted the African kids to mix together with other missionary kids from the mission school where they attended. Despite the large number of invitations that we gave out, only two other missionary kids arrived. With five of our own, that made just seven white kids in total. They spread themselves thinly among the forty-six local young Kenyans.

That smiling afternoon remains a vibrant memory, happy for all who came. It unfolded with bursts of laughter and bounding youthful energy. It came alive with games and singing. The joy of making new friends filled the house with life. The telling of stories and sharing in each other's life experiences began in earnest in the shade of our banana trees. Africans and North Americans sat together sipping cold drinks, chuckling and sharing tales from two continents and wisdom from different worlds. Trust was beginning to be built. Youngsters contributed to each other's lives and put together new friendships as we quietly watched the energetic activity unfold in our yard.

This opportunity, missed by the kids who opted not to come, became our very rich gain. As time went on, many of these friendships would deepen and mature. Some of our Kenyan visitors that day were to become a rich part of our lives.

In the days that followed, many of these young Kenyans came to visit our home, but the one who came most frequently was Daniel. A poor village boy, Daniel's mother was alone and struggling to raise a family of six children. With no paid employment, money was stretched tight—and then some.

What little financial support she had came by selling her vegetables beside the road to passersby. She tried hard to grow small crops on the patch of waste ground she called her *shamba*—her farm. She could grow some corn and sweet potatoes, spinach, and carrots. If she guarded them well from the hungry hands of illicit harvesters, she might even be able to cultivate some small sweet bananas.

Life for *Mama* Daniel and her six growing children presented mountainous challenges. Just staying alive through poverty, drought, and sickness became for them a fundamental goal.

Whenever Daniel arrived at our place, I would set down a large sandwich before him, his eyes wide at seeing so much food. I would often fry him a two-egg sandwich with the yolks cooked hard, African-style. Cooking it that way fends off the high risk of salmonella that soft yolks carry in a hot climate. Then, when supper was ready, often just a short time after he had finished his sandwich, Mary invited Daniel to join us to eat again. A great sense of satisfaction washed over us as we quietly watched Daniel enjoying this rare feast of food in abundance. Before he left, we always gave him a small gift for Mama—maybe a bag of sugar, some *Ugali* flour, or *Kimbo* cooking fat.

Sometimes, Daniel would look through our small collection of videos. Aaron showed him how to load the VCR and switch it on. Oddly, there was only one movie that Daniel would habitually choose to watch—*Mrs. Doubtfire*. The irony of a poor village boy in Kenya loving the antics of Robin Williams and American life in faraway California boggled my mind—but love it he did.

I wanted to explain to Daniel that this really was not the cultural heart of North America. But how could I begin to explain these concepts to him? English was his third language. He had learned Kikuyu on his mother's knee, Swahili at his preschool, and then English at primary school. Besides the considerable linguistic difficulties involved in trying to broach the subject, I might, in the end, be quite wrong. Maybe this movie really is a high point in our Western culture. For some Westerners it may, indeed, be as high as it gets. Perhaps it is too easy to be pretentiously highbrow and unnecessarily critical—after all, I enjoy the humour and pathos of that movie too.

On one of the several nights that Daniel slept over with us, Mary ran him a bubble bath—and his "seventeen-tooth smile" revealed his boundless joy. He splashed happily in a tub full of floating toys, and called us in to see him in the bath overflowing with bubbles and battleships in contest with Aaron, as they played together in happy innocence. Here, he played in a space where there were no mud floors, roaming rats, or leaks in the roof. Here, Daniel had no need to collect black garbage sacks and cardboard boxes to line the cold and leaky tin walls of the hut he called home.

When he was done, and the last of the bubbles had popped, Aaron loaned him a pair of fleecy pajamas. Daniel, his face a picture of joy, eagerly climbed into the top bunk above Aaron. Mary began reading them a bedtime story as each of the boys snuggled down cozily, eyelids drooping heavily after a happy day of playing together. Leaning over each of them in turn, she planted a gentle kiss on their brow, folded the sheets up to their ears, and God blessed them in the way only a mom can do. I don't know how Daniel felt that night, but as I watched him, cozy and at rest, I sensed that he laid his head on the breast of Jesus to catch the heartbeat of God's love.

Playing together was always exhilarating fun for Aaron and Daniel. Their play was in the exaggerated measure of a child's epic imagination. The vibrant colours of bougainvillea stood at their backs as they scampered out their energy with whoops of delight. With the shade of big trees overhead, they made full use of the large garden. It became for them a magical territory for running, hiding, and playing, and those activities were never burdensome. It seemed to me that if the spirit should so take them they could fly in an instant.

Some mousebirds, frantic builders of nests, perched proudly in the branches above them, dangling their long straight tail feathers. Nearby, groups of chattering superb starlings flashed sparks of iridescent gold through the filtered light of the equatorial African sky. It formed a moving picture—a video version of a Monet masterpiece—ever changing, always captivating.

Standing in the trees, aloof and distant from the noise below, those mythical ibis birds craned their necks to watch the boys at play. From the serenity of the quiet thorn trees overarching the young lads, the ibis birds sat like ancient Egyptian guards looking down upon a timeless scene of pyramids, deserts, and happy self-absorbed children at play. A primal holiness, a sense of the touch of God, seemed to be all around that place on tranquil days like this. In just a few moments, could we but see it then, all of this would change—irreversibly and forever.

I do not remember how I prayed at the end of that day. As I recall the idyllic scene in the garden that afternoon, I think that a fitting benediction—a perpetual blessing—on those timeless moments deep with joy might sound like this: *May your unfailing love rest upon us, O LORD, even as we put our hope in you* (Psalm 33:22).

There is a firm link between the act of praying and the gift of hope, as Henri Nouwen accurately reflects upon this invisible connection. He puts it this way: "Every prayer is an expression of hope. A man who expects nothing from the future cannot pray.... For this man life stands still."[7]

Soon there would be no better place than prayer—indeed no other place at all—for us to invest our hope. The reality of the Lord's unfailing love was about to become to us more than merely a sentimental hymn at vespers. Putting our hope in Him would be for us an act of desperate trust in the face of a sudden, unthinkable calamity. When life itself is threatened there are few places to turn, and none with guarantees. The prayer of faith would sound astonishingly like the prayer of panic, lest God be deaf to our anguished cries for mercy and grace.

CHAPTER THREE

Quiet Kenyan Afternoon

*Yet this I call to mind and therefore I
have hope: Because of the LORD's
great love we are not consumed, for
his compassions never fail*
(Lamentations 3:21–22).

I am astonished by the sheer variety of feelings that such a cata-strophic event as ours will evoke. All such events, though, have one thing in common—they run very deep within our consciousness. Some sensations never fully fade, even when we think they have gone. Deep emotions like fear, pain, and sadness—or some other combina-tion of powerful feelings—will catch us off guard completely. They surprise us with their immediacy, their harsh poignancy. When we recall a person, a place, or a particular event, those feelings come surging back, still distressing and powerful to wound us again. They lack none of their vibrant energy, their directness, so that years later they can still disturb and desperately unsettle us.

Sometimes, I call to mind—in slow, deliberate ways—other pain-filled incidents from years ago—and they still make me shudder.

Though separate and distinct from this event, they continue to have an impact upon it. Those old and unhealed feelings spill over into this new devastation, to multiply the pain and the present loss immeasurably.

One such earlier event occurred long before our brokenness on the Limuru Road, but the lingering feelings connect the two events for me. From that event, pain's razor edge, though now a little blunted, still cuts me deeply—it still draws fresh blood from the scarred veins of my emotions. It all happened to me some years ago, in an earlier chapter of my life.

I remember that vivid sense of shock—it slammed me hard when, ill prepared, I received the devastating news that tragedy had struck Mary's family. It took place more than a decade before we ever set out for Kenya. Yet, the profound effect of that abrupt and cold intrusion of bad news lingers with me still. Logged in my memory, it nestles just below the surface of my carefree laughter. It takes little scratching in that spot for the flood to return. Here it comes—the horror, disbelief, and profound sense of robbery, the untenable questions, dumb denial, and deep regrets. These are horribly familiar to fellow sufferers of sudden, unforeseen loss.

On the Limuru Road we were about to discover that our earlier experience would become a preparation—inadequate at best—for the unanticipated events that, even now, began to unfold just over the near horizon. Something unforeseen was unravelling progressively at the quiet start of a crescendo of chaos now rumbling towards us. Like an unstoppable lava flow, this latest loss event was ready to explode like an angry wave in our uninformed faces.

It approached us steadily, silently, and invisibly. We, meantime, chatted lightheartedly in our car on the short journey to Kithogoro village with Daniel. I sang a little song and whistled the tune. It had been in my mind all day. It was a carefree gesture on that public holiday. Little had we imagined as we watched Daniel eating his supper that this would be our last meal together in Kenya. For Daniel, there would be no more bubble baths, no more sleepovers, no more playing in our yard under the mythical gaze of the ibis birds. All these friendly and familiar sights would disappear forever before this day had ended.

Years earlier, I remember wishing about Mary's family tragedy, "I would give my right arm for the power to turn back the clock for just one nanosecond." Even now, more than thirteen years later, I sit here writing about it and longing so much to change it all. I want to make it somehow better. I want to replay the evil events of that earlier event, to rewrite them, redirect them, and rob them of their sting.

I want to bring those members of my wife's family back to life and out of the dark places where loss and tragedy lurk. Like a video king, I wish I could fast-forward the action of the movie I replay so often to move it further on, to catapult it to a new and happy ending. I want to propel their lives—the lives of people I love and care for—into happy normalcy and a peaceful resolution of their crisis. I wish for them what I have wanted so much for myself in these past days—for pain to be healed and hope to be restored.

I am a sucker, I freely admit, for happy endings because I have, I guess, lived through just too much sadness, too many miserable endings that make no sense to anyone.

I replay that phone call from the past—the one that delivered that earlier bad dream to us and turned it into a living nightmare. I recall the bruising pain of that disastrous news. It was like a solid, forceful punch to my chest. As I think about it, it was much more like a kick below the belt—some illegal, dirty move. Tragedies do not, alas, box according to the Queensberry Rules. Instead, they fight dirty—always. That earlier boxing bout—our tragic news— still evokes a fearful sense of impotence in me—a practical paralysis in the face of overwhelming odds.

There is within tragedies a crippling helplessness—the awareness that we are able to do precisely nothing. Paralysis—and at exactly the time when your whole inner being screams for urgent action. You experience two self-contradictory truths: an urgent need and an impossible reality. They describe a tension that ultimately tears you

47

apart. You respond with a desperate urge to do something—any-thing—to ease the torment of this tragic mess. And you know that you are paralyzed and unable to move towards a solution that will make anything right again, in the end.

I am a man and so I want to fix the problem. That is what men do—they fix things. They repair, they tinker and they botch. They get things working again any which way they can. Some throw money at a problem. Some sweat and toil at it until everything works again, sort of. Some perfectionist technicians work away until everything is even better than before. Whatever—however—they fix things. And my impulse, too, is to fix, fix, fix—even if I never finish a single job that I begin. Inevitably, of course, I have far more zeal to mend things than I have know-how or experience or ability. No matter, I will tinker away, nonetheless. If worst comes to worst, I might even take a peek at the instruction manual or dare to ask for help.

Today, however, there is no instruction manual, no help that seems adequate. In times of tragedy there never is. Somebody stole the manual, burned it, or rewrote it in a foreign language—in some kind of hieroglyphic nonsense-script. It has become unintelligible and unusable. That is precisely why tragedy is tragedy. It is this absence of help—its utter inaccessibility—that turns an emergency into a disaster. And so I am stuck—completely stuck and facing cat-astrophic loss.

Stuck is an awful place to be at a time like this. I am over-whelmed by a sense of utter helplessness, and it unquestionably defeats me. I detest this feeling of absolute vulnerability with an unutterable loathing, and I hate it as much as I dread it. That is what makes these emergencies so hugely uncomfortable for a very long time after they are over—they are never *over*. They throw us into a head-on collision with our inadequacies and—ultimately—with our own mortality. Mortality—that time when there will, after all, be no fix-it answers and death shall win again. That old robber, death, will have plundered life's storehouse once more.

And so I dumbly held the phone that day, so long ago. The crushing weight of deep inner anguish pressed heavily upon my chest. Frantically, the urge to help wailed on me—but, palms sweaty in anticipation of battle, I could do nothing. My pulse raced, and I was ready to leap into action—any action. Alarm bells clanged inside my head, and red lights flashed before my eyes. But there I was—stuck; nowhere to go, no one to see, and nothing to do. Nothing could be done except to choke back the bitter taste of tragedy. What was done was done—and I was neatly sidelined. I stood there wrestling with feelings of explosive response, but with nowhere to explode safely.

Thoughts like this inevitably lead to a sense of awful letdown, desperate disappointment. They bring us to the entrance gates of low-grade and chronic depression. There is an in-built sense of inadequacy about it all. Fight or flight gives over instead to hopeless thoughts of what might have been—and then all those "if onlys" come flooding in.

The "if only bird" flutters close by, overhead. We hear the flit-flit of its wings as it brushes past our ears. It leaves its haunting song of "if only, if only…" as it chirrups its endless echo down our tortured memories. *If only* cruelly intensifies it all. *If only* focuses our thoughts on the stark contrast—the points of difference—between what now really is and what once should have been, could have been or might have been, that now just cannot be. The hollow rattle of pain—the bones of a hope that died—rings from these futile feelings, and worry arrives to outstay its brief welcome in our lives.

At that moment of pain's impact, all those years ago, I turned at last to prayer. Why, I wonder, is prayer so often a measure of last resort—even for those who believe in it and make it their habit? "Why bother to *pray*," somebody asks, "when you can *worry*?" But sometimes prayer is all that is left when loss robs us of all that we once loved. Prayer is the effective antidote to worry—prayer and prayer-filled action.

So on that day—and still to this day—I pray. Prayer is still my only real response to the things I cannot handle. I gather myself and my world that makes little sense before a loving God. I ask Him to demonstrate the depth of His care for me—to do for me the things I cannot do for myself or for others.

Perhaps you understand that prayer is so much more than merely an SOS to God. But some situations call for exactly that kind of mayday signal to the One who hears. Why do I tell you all this? Because, today, I think I can understand—just a little bit—the kinds of feelings that lay in store for some of my friends, neighbours, and colleagues on that national day of celebration in East Africa. As that public holiday steadily approached its catastrophic close for us, these sorts of feelings would entrap them, too. This kind of praying would be needed to begin releasing them from the burden of friendship and the shock of loss.

Just around time's corner, on this Kenyatta Day in Nairobi, my associates and friends are about to be pulled out of their customary activities. Their family fun and the routine rhythms of their day will snap abruptly, and for what? Only to feel confusion, shock, and pain for the sake of the Beckingham family, and also for themselves as they are brought face to face with old and unresolved loss-events that they had buried somewhere in the deep recesses of the past.

Through our pain, they will soon be forced to relive their own losses—those earlier angst-filled events experienced long before. Competing and unfixed feelings will project their pain far beyond this day. They will echo their sorrow down long timelines on their journey of faith. Someday, those memories will form the fabric of their lived experience as they share their lives with others. At last, those pain-events will be woven into the rich and bittersweet blend of patterns that we call experience.

Perhaps such feelings will form a central part of their deep gift of friendship to others in distress. One day, they may offer it to others found walking through times of concentrated need.

We felt so tired on this quiet Kenyan afternoon. The day at the Elephant Orphanage was so much shorter than I had hoped. The dry, hot day had sucked away our energy like a desert breeze drying up the moisture of a mud pool. Supper—for most of the family—was done. Daniel was happy and stuffed with Mary's home-cooked food. I quietly hoped that he would soon have enough nourishment inside him to stimulate his long-overdue growth spurt. Daniel's strictly limited stature denied that his body belonged to a growing sixteen-year-old boy.

Mary and I had made our own plans for later that evening. They stretched out ahead of us like a leisurely African sky. They involved laughter, conversation, and relaxing in pleasant company. We were going to eat out with good friends, our next-door neighbours, Fraser and Diane Edwards. They, like us, were missionaries from Canada. Fraser headed up the work of a Canadian child sponsorship organization in East Africa. Having them live next door to us proved to be a bonus. They freely shared many years of experience living as missionaries in East Africa and, prior to that, in Papua New Guinea.

Daily, they helped us in all kinds of ways. If it was broken, Fraser could fix it; if it was puzzling, Diane could explain it. If they couldn't, they knew who could. They had become more than just a talking missionary manual on how to live in new and strange situations. They had become our friends. Tonight, we would go out to share a meal together, have fun and forget, if only briefly, the pressures and burdens of our calling, and the dangers of living and working in East Africa. That was our plan. It seemed good to us then—it seems even better now.

It was "Missionary Monday" at the Grand Regency Hotel. At this fine hotel, one of the smartest in Kenya, they did a "couple's special"—a two-for-one deal every Monday. It was the *only* place to be, and the place was always full—of missionaries. People on limited incomes, but with no limit to their imagination, dined out, and dined in style. They had discovered fine living at value prices.

Usually, they were there to celebrate a birthday, anniversary, or some other important occasion. Maybe, like us, they just needed a break for an evening, once in a while.

The buffet at the Grand Regency boasts five-star cuisine. Even better, the desserts sport all kinds of chocolate in abundance. Frequently, Mary would start her meal with dessert—some decidedly decadent, chuckling-with-chocolate confection. It is her odd way to begin a meal. With so small an appetite she rarely finds room to manage her dessert after even a modestly small main course. To lose a chocolate dessert would ruin her fun, leaving her feeling cheated out of all she had anticipated. A good night out is thus spoiled for want of a little chocolate. So, whatever works: dessert to start. After months of keeping closely to a local diet of beans, spinach and lentils, those desserts are the stuff that dreams are made of—especially for Mary. I can take them or leave them—though I usually I took them, and seconds, to boot.

Even more than the delicious food, I prized the live music. As a trumpet player, I am no less than a jazz king in the daydreamed improvisations of my own imagination. Like many other trumpet players, I often long to join the band and play along. The four-piece Kenyan jazz combo sported a blend of Western and African numbers, and soon I found my feet tap-tappitee-tapping along. The young African drummer magically wove a complex pattern of beats, meandering through a complexity of rhythms. Smiling and relaxed, he made it look too easy. The intoxicating fun of the music proved to be a perfect antidote for stress. Looking forward to our evening out, how could we anticipate the manner in which we would spend it? We would not be entering a five-star hotel tonight.

Still, we looked ahead eagerly to a Grand Regency dinner in the company of Fraser and Diane, whose dry and punchy sense of humour we so enjoyed. But first, we needed to get Daniel safely home.

"Mary, I'm feeling tired. Do you mind coming for the ride?"

"Sure, I'll be right along."

In our hurry, we left the washing of dishes at home until later. In typically *wazungu* (European) fashion, we felt pressed for time. *Ah, Bwana, in hurry, hurry there is no blessing,* says the old Swahili proverb. *You run fast never to arrive,* says another. We had good reason to run, however, on this occasion. On the equator the sun sets rapidly. It is dark—really dark—somewhere between 6:30 and 7:00 p.m. with only half an hour or so of variance depending on the season. It is better to play safe and simply reckon always on that earlier time for sunset. That night, we had good reason to be anxious about the onset of darkness.

A few weeks earlier, at church one Sunday morning, Daniel walked across the sanctuary to talk to Mary. The day before he had been playing with Aaron at our home. He had chosen, on that occasion, to return to his home rather than sleep over.

"Mama," he said quietly, "yesterday I had to walk home naked...." His voice tailed off in shame.

"Why?" Mary asked in puzzled astonishment.

"When I entered my village," he continued softly, "it was already dusk. I was attacked at the entrance to my village. They beat me. They stole my clothes so I was naked. They took the gift you gave me for my Mama."

Mary stared in silence, dumbly trying to take it all in. Why his clothes? Mary struggled to understand. They were only rags, second-hand clothes from Europe. The thrift stores there ship the stuff they cannot sell. It arrives in large bundles to be spread higgledy-piggledy in the open-air markets, picked over by eager hands. Each item has that rich, stale smell that thrift stores gather to themselves. Collars might be stained and worn, and buttons are often missing. Items sell for mere pennies among the local people.

So busy have these markets become that they are hailed as one of the few thriving sectors of the Kenyan economy. Clothes change hands for a pittance but at incredible turnover rates. Pennies quickly add up, and the newspapers have declared the *mitumba*—second-hand clothing—business to be worth millions of Kenyan shillings each year. Daniel's clothes were purchased as *mitumba* from such a market. Worn and torn, this was the "treasure" they beat him for, in order to pinch the shirt right off his back.

"I am so sorry," Mary offered. "Next time we will make sure you get home before darkness comes."

Today was that next time, and it was already 6:00 pm. Time to get going quickly. Hurriedly, we bundled Aaron and Daniel into the back of our car. Mary climbed into the front passenger seat to ride shotgun beside me. I enjoyed driving with Mary beside me because it gave us some moments in our busy schedule to unwind, some time to talk as we journeyed together. The sun, though sinking fast, was still up and we aimed to get Daniel home in good time. Kithogoro village was a short, ten-minute ride away from our house. Even with rush-hour traffic it never took long to get there.

I could not know it then but a future day would come, long after this car journey, when I too would say, *Yet this I call to mind and therefore I have hope: Because of the* LORD'*s great love we are not consumed, for his compassions never fail* (Lamentations 3:21–22).

The Limuru Road was about to teach us this lesson for this time and place and for the far-off places at other times where life would lead us, for life itself is a journey. The short trip to the village would take us off in many different directions in life. It was about to set us on a different kind of excursion—one to last a lifetime. This was the beginning of a journey not measured in miles alone, but in self-discovery, spiritual insights, and depth of pain.

It was also the beginning of an interior journey—part of our journey of faith, leading us along pathways where hope would be dashed and any sense of a future lost. Winding through backwoods leading to quieter trails, a hope and a future—unexpected and startling—might one day be recovered. Recovery from the angry noise of injury begins in an ultimate solitude, places of quiet stillness. Such places will terrify people like me, those addicted to the diversionary pleasure of background noise that helps us—in the short term, anyway—to avoid facing our pain.

At times, on our journey, we have been aware of a silent Travelling Companion walking closely beside us. At other times, God's silence felt like abandonment, as if He left us alone on the path. But silence is not absence; it is a quiet invitation to be with Him, to rest in His peace. Other pilgrims have felt this deep quietude on their journey of faith. With insight and accuracy, Ken Gire writes about the devotional life, putting it this way:

> When we live our lives within an inner stillness, the way a weaned child rests against its mother, we get a sense not only of oneness with the Father but a certainty of His purpose for our life.[8]

Love's silence is not hostile after all—it is an invitational silence of comfort, presence, and peace. Before I would ever come to discover such tranquility and healing for myself, I would need to take some unwelcome steps, walking bloodied and barefoot along the glass-splintered path of personal pain.

CHAPTER FOUR

The Ending of the Day

*What strength do I have, that I
should still hope? What prospects,
that I should be patient?* (Job 6:11).

What happened next? I wish I could tell you those rapidly unfolding details with an absolute certainty. The problem is those events unhinged me from reality as I lay unconscious, trapped, and near to death. Every fact I've learned about those split seconds of impact and the week that followed depend entirely upon the eye-witness accounts of others. I have no reliable personal recollection of that life-altering instant of collision.

I have had to learn the narrative of that time. The script I store and rehearse rests upon detailed descriptions presented to me. Despite knowing that I don't really know them, I'm still inclined to think that I can accurately remember all of the details of my story.

You may reasonably doubt it, but in my mind I can see much of the accident that I never saw drawn in magnificent Technicolor.

Like a familiar movie, I run it through my psyche. Mary maintains that because I've heard those graphic details countless times they now form a kind of pseudo-memory. It can trick me into thinking that this borrowed memory is truly mine.

It seems that I have taken these verbal reports and translated them into virtual memory, stored in a video format. Yet I can only tell you what happened next in the ways I've heard them from Mary, Aaron, Daniel, and others who were there. I trust their version because they were people who made themselves available to me, to all of us, and who saw what I will now describe.

I remember packing the four of us—two adults and two young boys—into the spare car from our mission fleet as we set off to take Daniel home. On that day, for some unusual reason that I don't remember, we had the use of the extra fleet vehicle—a small, well-kept Toyota Corolla.

"This is better than our gas-guzzling van for short journeys," Mary said. We were delighted to economize in a country where gas prices doubled those back home. It was also one of the best vehicles in the fleet—good paintwork and a smooth runner—but not for much longer. About another three minutes, to be precise. That is how long it would take us to drive it to destruction.

Initially, there was some argument about where Aaron should sit.

"Aaron, come sit over here," I said, directing him into one of the rear seats. Stubborn and tired, he deliberately climbed in on the wrong side of the car, pouting and refusing to budge. This would be awkward because later, at his final destination, Daniel would have to access the sidewalk by first climbing over Aaron to safely exit the vehicle.

"OK Aaron," I said with resignation, "but son, you're making things difficult," I added in a chiding tone. "No matter," I thought, "we'll proceed as we are. We can sort it out later."

Fathers can—and I often did—feel aggrieved by sons who overrule them, but it was getting darker and this was not a "see hill-take hill" battle I wanted to fight just then.

Setting off towards the tall gates at the end of our drive, we followed our unremarkable routine. I pulled to a halt at the end of our drive before entering the road. Aaron jumped out to open the steel gates and then close them, creaking behind us. Our attentive dogs crouched beside them but Aaron was careful to block their intended escape. On that particular evening we did not need time-wasting chases down our street to catch them. Nothing should distract us from getting Daniel securely home. Already the sounds of cicadas, bullfrogs, and the first night birds could be heard mingling in a magical cacophony, announcing the ending of the day and the sudden imminent appearance of darkness at the start of a long African night.

With Aaron jumping safely back inside the car, we ambled past the hedges of tropical plants, alive with spectacular chameleons shyly displaying their three-horned crowns. Over-hanging branches from umbrella thorn trees were bending low just above us, weighed down by the multiple decoy nests of weaver birds, built to confuse predators searching in vain for eggs in those empty nests. Under the tree's umbrella shelter, domestic workers gathered in small groups sitting just outside the garden gates. They gossiped and laughed together in these off-duty moments, sharing news of their day's work in animated conversation in Swahili or their tribal tongue.

We turned along the sharp dogleg bend in the road passing the German school, bringing us to a T-junction with the busy Limuru Road where you have to turn left or right. Our route would take us left and north onto the Limuru Road, running uphill and out of the city into the ascending Kikuyu tribal homelands. We joined the road near the entrance to Village Market, an upscale and recently constructed shopping centre aimed at relieving the expatriot community of some of their hard currency.

Waiting for a gap to open up in the busy traffic before we could join the flow meant that a full two minutes had elapsed by then since leaving home. Sixty short seconds to go to the end of life as we then knew it—but blissfully unaware, we were not counting down but chatting happily. Even if my life depended on it, I soon would be unable to count aloud or in my head, for many weeks to come.

Like a trusty compass, the Limuru Road flowed north waving farewell to Nairobi, and we knew its wavy bends, hills, and valleys with fond familiarity, having driven it daily for two-and-a-half years. Soft shoulders edge the sides of its broken blacktop that measures only sixteen feet wide. Typical of most roads at that time in Kenya, the unprotected outside edging butted up against unstable soil. This soft shoulder of dirt was washed away by the seasonal rains, and the road surface broke and crumbled into deep drainage ditches that formed sharp sloping valleys in the worn earth. At dusk or later, many a vehicle's nearside wheels will hit these hidden hollows, rolling over into the ditches or fields below, resulting in death or injury. Drivers looking for a more secure road surface attempt to dodge the legendary potholes. Almost every vehicle vies for a commanding road position by travelling in the middle of the road. They ride the crest in the centre of the road and then play "chicken" with the oncoming cars heading towards them, abruptly breaking left at only the last possible moment. This game creates more losers than winners and the stakes are hideously high.

The African outlook on safety is generally quite different from the orderly rules of the road governing European and North American safety conventions. It seems many Nairobi drivers observe just three rules of the road. Rule 1: If you cannot see it, it does not really exist. That means you can go around a blind bend in the middle of the road, and even on the wrong side of the road, with complete impunity because with nothing seen, nothing really exists to come towards you. Rule 2: If somehow a vehicle should suddenly come into view, then you should sound your horn loudly to make it disappear. Rule 3: If it should decide not to disappear, then you should flash your lights rapidly and repeatedly, and then drive straight towards it. Like magic, it will disappear, at last—perhaps.

When working within this different kind of world view, avoiding a collision actually requires no skill or forward planning. After all, if it is the will of Allah and it is your time to die, then nothing will prevent it. If it is not your day to die, nothing can cause your death—a perfect justification for crazy driving.

In a Western mindset, you might, for example, dangerously decide to overtake another vehicle on the outer edge of a blind bend. Without warning, an oncoming car unexpectedly appears at closing range and is about to ram you head-on. You stand on the gas and blast your horn. Then flashing your lights you wildly zigzag back into your own lane, cutting off the car you have passed, but escaping the oncoming vehicle by barely a spray paint's whisper. The oncoming driver has, by now, put his brakes to the ultimate road test, while the driver you passed—behind you, now—has left an extravagant amount of rubber tread smeared all over the road. They decorate many metres of blacktop, at the precise place in the road where you forced him to give way to allow you to squeeze back into his lane an inch ahead of his front bumper. It is a kind of crazy driving that many have attempted, and regretted, at some time in their early driving careers.

Though we might never admit to it, many of us in the West were probably scared witless by such crazy antics. Some of us, afterwards, might have needed to stop to be sick or to change our shorts. At moments like these, even die-hard atheists have caught themselves whispering a heartfelt prayer under their breath: "thank you, dear God—thank you—thank you!" Such is the level of rejoicing for unlikely travelling mercies gratefully received. Some of us might vow to the Lord to never again be so foolish. We might bargain with God: "Oh Lord, if you would just let me *live* I will do anything, ANYTHING, for you, for the rest of my days here on earth." Such is the extremity of our need in such scary moments.

Kenyan drivers, on the other hand, often reach a different conclusion. Their non-Western logic runs along distinctly African lines: "Mm," a driver thinks, "it worked okay that time, so it will probably work next time—I can safely try it again." Thus is born the habitually risk-taking driver. He is one who is about to surprise many an unsuspecting Westerner trying to share the road in more conventional ways than this Kenyan driver pursuing his East African *modus operandi*.

New missionaries suddenly discover themselves to be on more than simply a steep learning curve. They find themselves behind the wheel of a car on a blind bend with road rules that no longer work in any sure or predictable ways. They drive themselves crazy trying to work out for themselves the imprecise nature of these unwritten rules.

Add to this mix of small cultural differences the national collection of elderly and infirm vehicles, and some drivers who insist upon operating them like Formula One competitors. Now stir into this volatile muddle the magic of the *matatu*—the local Kenyan bus.

The *matatu* might be a VW microbus, or a home-built superstructure mounted on the chassis of a Toyota Land Cruiser. With a maximum capacity of, say, fourteen passengers the *matatu* will streak along at top speed with at least twenty people. They can carry an assortment of live chickens, goats, and incredible amounts of luggage including farm produce, furniture, barrels, mattresses, and bags—all tied down in a man-made mountain atop the bus. Arrays of goods and chattels serve to double the vehicle's height, lending the *matatu* all the stability of a novice stilt walker skating on ice.

Like an early warning system, the vehicle's stereo blares out a distorted megabass signal. Long before you see a *matatu*, you will hear its throbbing beat rumbling towards you. I am told that raucous music is no longer legal and that *matatus* are much quieter these days. But on that particular Kenyatta Day *matatus* were neither quiet nor illegal and impossibly loud music still ruled the airwaves.

As we turned onto the Limuru Road that evening, we neatly sandwiched ourselves between a couple of *matatus*. It would be only a few metres before the *matatus* would stop at a designated pickup point outside the shopping centre. Their horns announced their shrill arrival—a signal designed to drum up business from tired passersby trudging on foot to their homes.

With a reckless lack of restraint, *matatus* habitually lurch across all parts of the road in self-regulated chaos. You quickly learn to give them a wide berth. Like it or not—and most drivers do not—they rule the roads. Their gaudy paintwork will carry a huge slogan like *No Fear of Death*, or *Kiambu Gangstas*, or *Kiss Me Before You Die*. Their dark prophecies sometimes prove to be horribly accurate.

Like mercury steeply rising in a thermometer perched in the fire, the increasing daily death toll is baldly reported in the Kenyan newspapers. Accounts of road carnage multiply. It is almost impossible to pick up a newspaper on any given day without finding another horror story recounting the gruesome details of some appalling road accident. The consequent loss of life that comes in its wake is staggering. Usually a *matatu* will feature somewhere in the details of the story. Sometimes it is a larger bus, the kind that links Nairobi to other cities like Mombassa, Eldoret or Kisumu, some hours distant. The number of people dying daily on Kenyan roads beggars the imagination of Westerners.

We were about to discover a hard truth: the biggest single danger to missionaries worldwide is not civil war, land mines, or political insurrection. It is driving a vehicle. More missionaries meet their deaths in that way than in any other. This being a well-documented reality, you might expect that missions would insure their personnel fully against such eventualities. However, unbelievable as it sounds, some of them operate according to the same fatalistic principles that motivate those Kenyan Muslim drivers: *If it is the will of Allah....*

And so it is evening. Time in Africa passes slowly, for according to the proverb, "There is no hurry in Africa..." except for *matatus*. It is the numinous time of transition from light to overarching darkness. Darkness is about to win as it always prevails at the end of every day, but the hope of dawn is not far off. Light waits to win through with bright hope beating in its wings. Its promise is secure that darkness must be defeated, but not quite yet.

Now is the beginning of dusk, the gathering of gloom, and persistent dimness steadily growing. Day is being bundled gently into the dark shroud of night. Nighttime gathers up the day within its four-cornered cape. Already the sounds around us are changing. The singing of birds softens and dies, giving itself over to the brittle clatter of creepy-crawlies. The throaty belching of invisible hippos will now be breaking out beyond the city in the long grasses near the streams and watering holes. Mosquitoes are abuzz seeking bare skin to pierce. Sleeves and pant legs are now worn long to cover up bare wrists and ankles. Visitors and locals will hide these juicy targets from blood-seeking mozzies.

The explosive sounds of the African night erupt everywhere. Like a starting pistol, they are the clear signal that the sunset race is on. We have to get Daniel back to Kithogoro village before darkness descends to deliver its hidden dangers. They cloak themselves beyond the deepening shadows.

The Limuru Road was not especially busy during the early evening on that Monday. Steady traffic moved freely along the narrow road that serves as a main artery pumping workers home from the city. The larger highway a mile or so west carries more traffic, but the smaller road we take is known as a regular travel route for drivers preferring to avoid the hazards of the highway.

Large trees overhang our route at many points and the late afternoon light illuminates them with a clarity loved by photographers. At this time of day, the contrast between light and dark is stark and crisp. Shadows push forward dark and long against the clear light, offering a final burst of fire before falling from the sky. At this part of the road, we had once stopped to examine some distinctive roadkill that caught our attention. Two animals lay crushed and flattened—nothing unusual, except that these skins looked intriguingly like those of young leopard cubs. Leopards are shy and deadly animals, yet here they were so close to the busy city.

Hardly had our journey begun when we were stuck behind a *matatu*. This is an awkward and unpredictable place to be stuck.

Maybe there is only one worse place to be—inside the *matatu*. An eyewitness reported later that a small car was also travelling ahead of the *matatu*. Though a mere detail, it is the kind of feature that you remember as an eyewitness. The road sweeps past the Roslyn River Garden Nursery making a right-hand arc that rises steeply uphill. The back of the *matatu* effectively billboarded our forward view while the angle of the bend combined with the uphill slope to cut off my vision completely. I slowed slightly to improve my viewpoint.

Our conversation turned to planning our night out.

"Mary, would you like to drink with your meal? I'm happy to drive," I said. On the odd occasion when we had a glass of wine with a meal we designated which of us would stick to ginger ale in order to drive.

"Actually," Mary said, "we can both have a drink tonight. We are travelling with Fraser and Diane, and Fraser will be driving."

It is amazing what some people will have to live down. The annals of history record some decidedly odd one-liners as the last words and final farewell of the rich and famous. As they step blithely across the threshold into eternity, they leave behind a legacy of warped words of wisdom for the rest of us to puzzle over. Never lacking a due sense of the historical moment, I was about to add to this dubious collection of witticisms. Smiling warmly, I looked across at Mary and muttered, "Mm...Mary, I quite like you after you have had a glass of wine."

In the forty-five minutes that followed, Mary would be troubled by those words. She would be on her way to the hospital, leaving me for dead trapped inside a car wreck. Planning whether she should bury me in Kenya, Canada or Britain, her mind would turn to my funeral service. I wonder if she chose the hymns and set the Order of Service despite her claim that she was too numb to do so.

But she did pray that nobody would ask her, "Tell me Mary, your husband was a Baptist pastor and missionary, so he must have left you some precious last words. They will probably be a great comfort to you for many years to come. What were they? Please share them with us."

Mm...Baptist minister—glass of wine—words of connubial affection. Maybe at the close of the day, this particular saint only had feet of clay. Over the next ten days—and through the next two-and-a-half years of uncertain recovery—he would risk losing one of his clay feet. Without that leg to stand on, people might discover that, like them, he was vulnerable and weak.

I made my lighthearted comment as an affectionate overture to an evening of fine food with good friends. Hardly had I uttered those words when time, for me, would be wrenched into rapid fast-forward. In the microseconds that followed in real time, my brain registered everything in a kind of postproduction editing mode—one freeze-frame at a time.

As I replay it I see that I turn my head to look up and straight ahead. The *matatu* is veering crazily in front of us. Without warning, it swerves to the left. I pull to the right to pass it. Then, as *matatus* do, the bus drives wildly onto the left-hand verge. *Matatus* will stop in the wildest places to pick up and drop off passengers. But here it leaves the road to mount the raised soft shoulder. But I will never see that happen. Instead, my frozen gaze is transfixed ahead in a deepening horror. There, in front of us, is an oncoming truck—a horribly big truck travelling at alarming speed. Already it is impossibly close—and closing fast. I start mumbling something, "What does he think he is...."

There is a wonderful peace of never knowing in the silent night of unconsciousness. For me, there will be a lot of nothing to try to remember. In those next wild moments we collided—head-on—with a Kenyan Army military tank transporter. There was no contest—it won. Its extra-wide load trailer carried a forty-foot shipment container. It snaked around the bend in the middle of the road, riding the crest, its driver obeying the First Rule of African Driving: If you cannot see it, it does not exist. For him, we did not exist. Soon, I might not exist for my family—or anyone else. The truck occupied both lanes. There was a margin of only two or three feet of road on either side of it. There was time for the Second Rule, and so my hand was on the horn, pushing as if my life depended on it. But for the Third Rule we were out of time. No flashing of lights—instead we drove straight at each other. With nowhere else to go, I drove straight at the front bumper of the heavy military truck.

The full, head-on smash struck first on my side of the vehicle, demolishing the front quarter of the car that now lay concertinaed on top of me. As I fell back, I came to rest on top of Daniel behind me. The sudden impact broke his right femur, as the motion of the car caused him to be thrown forward under my seat. The boys were travelling without rear seat belts because none were fitted then in Kenyan cars. Like me, Daniel lay there unconscious and quite motionless.

Aaron says he remembers the windshield shattered into a spider's web of pieces that imploded towards him as if in slow motion. Lowering his head, his automatic response was to raise his arms, shielding his face and skull. His quick reflex action saved him from more serious facial injuries. He would nurse the superficial cuts to his forearms, neck, and head for the next week or two. Seven years later, glass would occasionally surface through his scalp, pushing upwards to break the surface, expelled and rejected by his body. The emotional trauma would take much longer to be expunged, and would haunt him for many years to come.

Out of control, with an unconscious man at the wheel, our small car hurtled forward, despite the abrupt and devastating impact. It had failed to stop us. Instead, we bounced off the truck's cab, and as the leading edge of the trailer tore into us, my side of the car caught its sharp edge at my eye level. Like a can opener, it sliced through the vertical supports lifting the roof at ninety degrees. It stood like an open door, hinged at Mary's shoulder level on her side of the car. Pointing into the air, no glass in the vehicle remained intact. A sharp shower of ground and broken glass sprayed over each of us. We would be removing it from skin for weeks and even months.

I am thankful—so very thankful—that my seat back collapsed. Had it not, or had we driven our van with its higher seating position above the road, my head would have been cleanly—or maybe not so cleanly—removed from my shoulders. My memory loss would then have been a permanent affair.

These microseconds stretch into an aching eternity of time. Reliving them, understanding them perhaps, will take longer than a lifetime.

So there we were, battered by the trailer's leading edge, bouncing and spinning over and over in a sickening roller coaster ride. Again and again, we slammed dizzily against the long sides of the trailer, shaken like a rag doll within the jaws of a demented steel terrier of outrageous proportions, our bodies limp and useless.

"I guess we may not make it for dinner after all, Mary," is what I might have said. But I could say nothing as I lay there unresponsive, lost in deep oblivion. Yet oddly, I reclined in a more comfortable space than either Mary or Aaron occupied in those chaotic moments. I should never have to live and relive the moments that followed—the events my eyes would never see.

Resilient hope is that peculiar virtue which stubbornly refuses to depend upon our circumstances; rather, it transcends them. It declines to be held hostage to fortune, imprisoned within the flimsy boundaries of one's state of affairs. Hope is a state of mind rather than a condition of our circumstances, as Václav Havel understands so well:

> I should probably say first that the kind of hope I think about (especially in situations that are particularly hopeless, such as prison), I understand above all as a state of mind, not a state of the world. Whether we have hope within us or we don't; it is a dimension of the soul and it is not particularly dependent upon some particular observation. Hope is not a prognostication. It is an orientation of the spirit, an orientation of the heart; it transcends the world that is immediately experienced, and is anchored somewhere beyond its horizons.[9]

Havel is right of course, but my mind was, during those moments, in no conscious orientation whatsoever. I was completely unaware. Unlike Job, I was unable to form the words to ask the question: *What strength do I have, that I should still hope? What prospects, that I should be patient?* (Job 6:11).

I was held fast in the silence of a coma, within the hands of God. Without strength, I did not yet need to learn patience. That tutorial would be conducted along the uneven path of recuperation. That dusty trail lay just ahead of me, and would stretch far into the remoteness of the doubt-filled days that haltingly led me forward.

In retrospect, the deep sleep of a coma is not such a bad place from which to awake to a hope that is firm; but meanwhile just a place to rest in it. Learning to trust in hope's future orientation as a promise that is true was about to test me to the core. To discover hope's promise to be secure would require more patience than I possessed, and demand yet more strength if I were to endure long months of recovery, stretching ahead into an uncertain future. This forced pilgrimage was about to take me into a dimension of fear I had never dreamed of, and drop me into a despair darker than my soul could ever imagine.

CHAPTER FIVE

The Golden Hour

> *"For I know the plans I have for*
> *you," declares the* LORD, *"plans to*
> *prosper you and not to harm you,*
> *plans to give you hope and a future"*
> (Jeremiah 29:11).

What kind of a madman chooses to park a car in a location so odd? Not me—not anyone—not on that dirt ridge beside the Limuru Road. But, in fact, that's exactly what I did, though "park" is perhaps an exaggeration. Rather, we skidded to a grinding stop, finally coming to an awkward resting place upon that soft shoulder. Beside the northbound lane, facing the wrong way, we had the distinct possibility of being struck again by the traffic that had been behind us.

Peculiar parking can be an inevitable conclusion following fast after a head-on collision with a military truck. Those large, intimidating means of transportation tend to win in any roadside altercation. They have the considerable advantage of size and weight. Greedily, they prefer to take the whole width of the road

71

for themselves. They leave you little choice but to end up at the roadside—wrecked and "parked" in a peculiar position.

We perched perilously close to a steep incline, falling sharply into chaos and only inches from us at the edge of the soft shoulder. Scenic views of East Africa, I am told, are not to be experienced while careening down some such incline that falls so radically into the Roslyn River Valley. That steep drop is not to be found in any standard off-road tourism guide, appears in no reputable travel itineraries, and is absent from the illustrated pages of guidebooks to favourite hikes and drives in Nairobi. There are simply no glossy pictures of that astonishing view adorning the double spreads of plush coffee table editions. It is, oddly, regularly skipped and dropped from the index of international places of outstanding beauty.

Thankfully, we neither clattered nor crashed our way down that unfortunate route to oblivion that day. Instead, we ground to a shuddering halt just a foot or two short of the precipice that drops the unwary to deep peril below. Soft banks of lush-leafed trees and verdant undergrowth climb the slope to mute it and camouflage its sudden drop. With little effort, however, a speeding vehicle might easily smash its way through to final demolition. That was certainly not a *normal* direction to take.

But that is entirely my point. Nothing is exactly *normal* in the horror of those moments after an impact like ours. "Normal" had quietly just excused itself, withdrawing from our lives. It would not return quickly—or, maybe, ever. In the days ahead, we would fight to forge a new "normal," but one shaped after our altered pattern of life that looked and felt so different. Each new day would reveal an odd "normal," redefined as we learned a different dance step for the odd rhythms that life's new lyrics held for each of us. Our challenge was to follow the demanding sequence of steps for this new and intricate ballet, but we had no musical score to assist us. It felt like the choreographer had worked out all the moves while she was dizzy or drunk. We fought to do our best to follow where these unsure footsteps might lead.

There would simply be no going back from here to life as we once knew it. Life would wear two labels: B.t.A. or A.t.A.—"Before the Accident" or "After the Accident."

A calamity, a loss, or an unexpected tragedy quickly becomes a watershed moment in life. It is hard to resist the *before* and *after* approach to understanding one's life. The problem is that the "after" snapshot is hugely disappointing. Consumer advertisers make us think that "after" is somehow always better. Not this time, though: "after" is simply a disaster. Everything that could go horribly wrong, just did. So now "normal" became for us what used to be in life Before the Accident—but on that day in Africa, we crossed our point of no return. In our lives After the Accident, nothing would ever quite seem normal, anymore.

In life After the Accident, you can discover some fascinating answers to trivia quiz questions. They are the questions I had never asked or thought much about before—questions about accidents. Doctors in North America tell me that the work of paramedics is critical to patient recovery. The doctors' success rate in treating these victims depends largely on what the paramedics first accomplish at the roadside scene. Paramedics claim that the first sixty minutes after impact is their "golden hour." It is their golden window of opportunity to rescue those who would otherwise die. Their actions and interventions in those moments immediately following injury determine outcomes for badly injured casualties. Bluntly put, they carry life and death in their hands for the casualties they treat.

In Kenya, there were no paramedics on the Limuru Road that day, or any other day—neither Jaws of Life nor any nationally operated ambulances, and no trained lifesavers. There was no roadside assistance system to kick into action at times like these.

Instead, my rescue team was composed of the passengers from the *matatu* that, a few moments earlier, had left the road for the safety of the soft shoulder. These were ordinary Kenyans—cheerful, industrious, make-do-and-mend, salt-of-the-earth types. They toiled freely for more than an hour trying to free my broken body from the car wreck. They worked with bare hands against the torn metal of the wreck—bending, pulling, and straining at twisted wreckage, stretching helping hands towards my trapped and twisted body. They worked with zeal. Zeal without knowledge is a dangerous asset.

Mary could no longer bear to watch as they pulled at my limp and lifeless shoulders. She found herself walking away from the car in numb horror. Slowly turning back towards me, she walked haltingly, and in pain, towards our vehicle. She knew she had to do something—anything—to help. But what—what could she do? She paced back and forth, over again, while shock rolled in like a sudden summer fog to cloud her judgement.

Shock misted the clear screen of Mary's mind; she could no longer think straight. Distress closed in on her like a vise-grip, compressing her thoughts into a tight knot of confusion. Endless ideas, like hope's wreckage, twisted themselves together wildly. They tied up her impulse for action within the tight bondage of inactivity. She glanced back at me, often. Helpless to stop them, she watched as our eager volunteers held my shoulders, vigorously shaking me backwards and forwards. They heave-ho-heaved, tugging desperately, trying to release the dead weight of my limp body bleeding from every visible orifice.

I lay firmly trapped below the waist, held tight in the grip of mangled metal and what, only seconds earlier, had been the fashionable plastic fascia that was now rendered less than attractive. If my injuries were spinal, Mary knew that I would be paralyzed from the efforts of our novice paramedic team. She could not imagine that I could still be alive. If I were just hanging on by a thread, she reasoned, it would not be for too much longer. If I arrived at the hospital alive, she felt certain I would be dead before this dark night was over.

And so the busy hands of Kenyans bustled the best way they knew how, to bring me their kindest and quickest assistance. Some hands that evening worked another agenda. They robbed me of my cash and my driving license. If I died I would not need them; if I lived, I was white and, therefore, rich enough to replace both items without much hardship. So why would they not relieve me of my excess baggage? This day would become a life or death fight for me; for them, every day unfolded into such a fight, so why not, they reasoned, take a little help when it came their way, as it had today?

Aaron clung to Mary: "Mommy, Mommy, Mommy," he cried, "I am so frightened. I just want to go home." A Kenyan *mama*, a mature lady wearing a beautiful hand-knit cardigan, stepped towards them. Seeing the shock and helplessness writ large on Mary's face, she drew Mary gently towards her with Aaron still clinging to his mother. She hugged Mary, holding her pain and nursing her emotional distress. Taking off her cardigan, she spread it out like a blanket and laid it in the damp red soil. She fully knew that the dye from the dirt was indelible—it would never wash out, and this fine-looking cardigan would be forever lost, given freely in an act of love to a stranger.

"Lie down, Mama, lie down. Easy, easy, Mama. Lie down here." The Mama's gentle words bathed Mary with love, and she did as she was asked. Now hugging Aaron to her, this mama began to pray aloud over Mary. Words poured forth from somewhere deep in the heart of this woman of faith. She prayed God's strong love into the dark disaster overwhelming us at the edge of madness on the Limuru Road. Though I would not know it for some weeks, this dear mama, her cardigan, and her love formed a tangible expression of God's assurance to us that He walked the Limuru Road alongside us, present to heal and to save.

My brother, Keith, is a Methodist pastor in England. On receiving the news of the accident he made a telephone call to Kenya the following day. Calling the Methodist headquarters in Nairobi, he asked to speak to the bishop, but was put through to the only official at work that day—the resident accountant.

"My brother has been involved in a terrible accident yesterday," Keith explained. "The only thing I know is that it happened on the

Limuru Road. Would anyone at your office be able to call all of the Nairobi hospitals to find out where he is? I need to know how he's doing—what his condition is. I have to find out some details of the accident. Can anybody help me, please?"

"Well, Bwana, I will tell you about this accident," the older Kenyan voice replied. "You see, sir, I was there. It's strange, because I hate the Limuru Road—it is so dangerous. But yesterday was Kenyatta Day and there were many military vehicles on the highway. We knew that there would be none on the Limuru Road because it is closed to military trucks, so we took that route instead. I am sorry to say that we saw your brother's accident. We were among the first cars on the scene. I need to tell you that I am not brave, Bwana, so I never halt at accidents. Those who stop to help often get robbed by others, but my wife insisted that we stop and offer help. My wife took off her cardigan and lay it down so your brother's wife could lie on it. I think I know the hospital where they were taken. I will find them for you and tell you their condition."

Strange things beyond our limited understanding may happen in our lives, more often than we notice. But at moments like this, I cannot help but hear echoes of divinity, certain and sure. They are intimations of love, the whispers of a God who cares and is attentive to all our needs. His promise is secure that He pursues us with a love that knows no limits. He will impart it upon each of us—if only we would let Him.

"Three vehicles were coming up the hill around the corner," wrote Farid Mohamed and Sue Carney in their eyewitness report, "a car, followed by a *matatu* and then Mr. Beckingham's car. The front car and *matatu* swerved into the left-hand grass while Mr. Beckingham proceeded on. As the trailer was right across the corner he met the front end of the side of the trailer almost completely head-on. Because of the bend, we doubt Mr. Beckingham ever saw the trailer from behind the *matatu* until he collided with the trailer, well on his side of the road. The front of the car crumpled, and the car spun up the side of the trailer and up the road to come to rest facing down the road on the right-hand verge. The trailer hurtled on, looking as if it was not going to stop, and then did stop a further few hundred metres down the road.

"We immediately pulled into the left-hand verge, which meant we stopped as the Beckingham's car came to a halt opposite. Mrs. Beckingham and her son were screaming and trying to get out. As the roof was gone, she climbed out and got her son out by the window and was standing behind the car. When I reached the car, Daniel, a young boy, was groaning in the back between the front and back seats. Mr. Beckingham was impaled upright between his seat and what was left of the engine, unconscious, with blood pouring from his face and nose onto what used to be the dashboard."

As I read those words again, they affect me strangely. I am moved to deep pity for this "Mr. Beckingham," as I would be for a dog crushed under the wheel of a truck, or for a stranger whose sudden demise I have sadly witnessed. I feel the response of a bystander: helpless to turn the clock back, for even a single nanosecond. I feel useless, unable to alter this awful outcome. Then—I know it is myself I am reading about, not a stranger.

Maybe I have become a stranger to myself. Without recall, lacking memory to put myself into the scene, I stand over it, watching in horror as if it is all happening to someone else. Yet I am there—I really am—after all, the report says so. I am central to all that has happened and yet I am blissfully and completely out of touch—cold and in a coma. My pain is waiting, lurking silently and wickedly offstage. It is about to explode in my face with devastating impact.

"The door was opened at the back and Daniel was taken out," the report continues. "Ten to twelve people had gathered. My husband and I decided the best thing to do was to run for help at the Village Market as a fair haired man with a mobile telephone, who worked for USAID, was not getting through. As I returned to our parked car on the opposite side of the road, a slim man, of medium height in light fatigues, was slowly walking up our side of the road. I shouted to ask if he was the driver of the truck. He said, "Yes." I asked what on earth he had been doing, driving so fast down the middle of the road. Why was he travelling so recklessly and why had he hit Mr. Beckingham's car? He replied that he was not, and that the car had hit him. He was strolling over to the Beckingham's car as we drove off hurriedly to Village Market. His co-driver, a rounder African gentleman, was also strolling up the road to our side of the road behind him. We did not see either of them again."

I never saw them then; I probably never will. Sometimes, I wonder if they understand what they did that day, and I wonder do they care? I pray for them that they will never have to live through this kind of event themselves as injured persons. I pray that never again will they cause others to suffer as I have, as my family has. *Haraka, haraka, haina baraka...*in hurry, hurry, there is no blessing. *Mwendo mbio siokufika...*run fast never to arrive. In a culture with a heritage opposed to hurry, the oddest things can happen.

Crushed and broken is a home that is real—but one that is only a temporary dwelling place. It is a brief stopping point along a larger journey. It is a place of brokenness, lies, and robbery. If you choose to stay there for too long or visit it too often you taste its dangers, for it is a hall of mirrors. At best, it reflects only distorted images of who you are. You see just the losses, the disfiguring changes, caused by your sudden loss. And you grieve and mourn the person you once were, the one you have lost. You are a wounded spirit and you are in pain.

As you read my account, you may recognize yourself somewhere in it all, if you have been injured and changed by uninvited calamity. Perhaps the mirror of suffering has persuaded you to believe the twisted images it parades, as the person you now are. But they are not all they seem to be. You face the danger of taking ownership of those bizarre, ugly, and warped shapes that now seem to describe you. Worse, you may start to treat them as real. You might start to cut the cloth of your self-image smaller, to design your outer garments of confidence, poise, and self-presentation meaner, and to match those diminished images.

You may end up styling your personality exactly to fit those hideous reflections of the person, that in truth, you are not. You might end up with a perfect fit—but a perfectly odd fit—for you are trying to fit all that God has made you to be into the narrow confines of your present loss. God in you is a more expansive truth, a gentler reality, than the diminishment of pain and suffering.

To believe such a limited view of who you are will cause you to lose yourself in dark places or surrender to defeat. The real you, the essential you, is enclosed and lost in the eccentric folds of crazy cloth that deform your inner personhood in an outward scaling down of your gift of self, and your identity as a human being created and formed in the image of God. This is the real person that others truly see when they look with the eyes of faith.

The garments of a broken spirit, on the other hand, are cut and shaped to mimic every oddity imaginable. Buying into the lie of your own diminishment, you will to go out into the world, thus badly dressed, presenting yourself to a gullible, believing audience. Unwise, unseeing people are too ready to accept an eccentric picture of who you are. Trusting the incomplete picture you present to them, they take you at face value, rejecting you or sidelining you because of it. They box you in and pigeonhole you. They do so with an all too convenient sticky tag: "Disabled," "Misfit," "Brain Injured," "Deserving Pity," "Not To Be Taken Seriously,"—or some other pejorative label. They quickly lose sight of you behind an unspoken, dismissive slogan.

It is always easier to label you than to love you—even if the label is given unconsciously. Those are the worst kind—the unspoken assumptions about you, the silent conclusions people draw from them. They are difficult—almost impossible—to argue against because they remain unacknowledged. You cannot defend yourself against eloquent silence, a subtle dismissal. Of course, no civilized human being would consciously label and dispose of another. But their knee-jerk reaction shows very clearly, that—without thinking it through—unthinking people first pigeonhole you, then reject you.

They have done it to me. They file you safely away to be forgotten, one day. But I confess that I have done it, too. In quiet moments as I think about what I have done, I am astonished, ashamed, and sorry for the ways I may have treated you and others.

I deeply repent the many times I have neatly, habitually—and absolutely wrongly—categorized you and others in belittling ways. I have squeezed you into a box that was smaller, meaner, and less significant than the valuable person God intends you to be.

So now, when others do it to me, I feel the same bitter sting that I have delivered to your spirit—it boomerangs back on me and pierces me with pain. Truly, I am sorry and ashamed, and so I ask you, can you find it in your heart to please forgive me? Without excuse, I have wronged you, for I have needed those labels to buoy up my inadequate self-understanding and bolster my own deep insecurities. Wanting to exaggerate my public persona I have parodied strength and competence. I have needed—so desperately needed—to project those strong personal qualities of power and control—until now. Today, I see the sham for what it is—injurious to others and to me.

Now I know myself to be weak—too weak, mostly, thank God—to crush others with brash bravado. My juvenile blusters, my shows of strength, impress some people but fool nobody except myself. These days, I am more comfortable, mostly, with my evident weakness. I am more prepared for honesty—to admit it, to myself, if not yet to you.

There, I said it: "I am weak. My strength is only an illusion." All I have to do now is live like I believe it. There is a big downside to God making His strength perfect in my weakness: it is the prerequisite of my "weakness." That is God's necessary and unavoidable preliminary condition. That is a course you will not find in the seminary catalogue: "Weakness 101."

All my life I have wanted to be "big and strong," like a toddler wanting to please his mom. Maybe, the accident is teaching me that weak is an okay, though uncomfortable, place to be, for it is the place where God shows up in strength. Weakness overtook me at the instant of a head-on impact. A truckload of weakness requires an extra-wide consignment of God's grace.

The normal orchestrations of my life suddenly disintegrated that day to become jarring and discordant. Like ripped sheet music, my elaborate and careful plans had been shredded—every one of them. On that day in Nairobi, my goals lay broken, as crushed as my body. My hopes, dreams, and plans lay crumpled in utter disarray, strewn in shredded pieces on the Limuru Road. Dreams are fragile commodities and, like a butterfly's wings, are easily fractured. They can be ground to powder by the swiftness of an oncoming military truck, and wafted away on the afterdraught.

As she rode to the hospital on that October evening, Mary's plans might have included designing a funeral service. Before she reached the hospital, she may have chosen hymns and considered the Order of Service—but the fog of shock prevented her from getting into any such details. But she had already started to strategize: her plans for her family would no longer include her now-absent husband—like a family photograph with a father and a husband carefully excised from it. Torn and jagged lines mark the place he once occupied.

Over the long months ahead, tactics that were neither of my own making nor Mary's would begin to unfold for me and for my family. These unfolding plans, in light of our losses, hinted at the renewal of a future, real hope for each of us.

How precious those life-giving qualities would become for us all. A Designer better and more able than any of us was at work on our behalf. His strategies come with an assurance that is no mere advertising hype, but is foundational to life itself. *"For I know the plans I have for you," declares the* LORD, *"plans to prosper you and not to harm you, plans to give you hope and a future"* (Jeremiah 29:11).

These plans became for us the architecture for a reconstructed hope. Our understanding of hope's profound meaning for life was about to be expanded, in the same way that Philip Yancey broadens hope's meaning to offer us a foundational definition to embrace our lived reality. He puts it like this:

> Hope means simply the belief that something good lies ahead. It is not the same as optimism or wishful thinking, for these imply a denial of reality. Often, I think, those of us who stand alongside suffering people tend to confuse hope and optimism.[10]

Our sense of futurity—that something more lies ahead for us—is not, by itself, a hope-producing certainty. It is the nature of that future—and its value to us—that becomes critically important. Nobody, after all, looks forward to a futile future that promises nothing. If, however, the future is linked to, and defined by, the bigger and brighter picture of an eternity planned for us in love, then hope becomes real. Hope is linked to a future that is identity affirming rather than a meaningless prospect of unplanned events colliding in a chaos of constant flux and random change. The German theologian, Wolfhart Pannenberg, puts it accurately and well when he says:

> A future without eternity amounts to meaningless change; and if people get exposed to that kind of essentially empty future, future shock results, because meaningless change endangers our personal identity. The continuous rise of transience, novelty and diversity in the social environment of men in the present and in the foreseeable future which Alvin Toffler so aptly described, will seriously aggravate the dangers of future shock and will render it more and more difficult to achieve personal identity.[11]

Over the long months that still lay ahead, a growing sense of a future began slowly—frustratingly little by little—to emerge through the unfolding of God's plans for us. His plans encompassed a dimension of personal future hope, for they are "the plans I *have for you*." It is in love that God reveals His personalized purposes for each of us. This other Architect of the future—our Master

Planner—was there for us throughout these apparently meaningless events, invisibly standing behind the scenes, ready to rescue us from beneath the thin ice on which we skated so dangerously. At work on the Limuru Road, God unfolded His plans for us in the face of hostile actions that might so easily have killed us all. The God of mercy, God of grace, tenderly supported the sinking weight of our lives, carrying us as we crashed through time to touch eternity briefly, and then come back.

God's blueprint was vastly different from my small ambitions. Slowly, His bigger purposes began to emerge. Mercifully, His plans for us included the restoration of two incalculable commodities for living—a hope and a future. Each of these vital signs of life had been erased for me. Disappearing from view so quickly, wiped from my own thoughts by the menacing skid marks of tires from a military truck, they would prove slow to reappear.

CHAPTER SIX

A Room Called Emergency

You will be secure, because there is hope; you will look about you and take your rest in safety (Job 11:18).

The brain is that part of the human anatomy which never ceases to function—until you are asked to stand up and speak in public! Then it completely shuts down.

When presenting talks in public, I would sometimes begin with that quip. As a humorous cliché, it proved to be an easy and amusing icebreaker. However, once you suffer a traumatic brain injury, it's astonishing how your sense of humour changes. You suddenly prefer to delete that particular witticism for some keener personal observations. In a personality-changing injury, you garner sharper and more painful insights that form some deeper wisdom learned from the less-than-humorous experience of pain.

A brain injury is significantly different from other physical injuries. If you break your leg, for example, it is hard for you to walk away without noticing that something is quite definitely wrong. Astonishing as it may be, it is deceptively easy to be completely unaware of your own brain injury.

It is quite impossible for you to reliably assess it. It is beyond a person's ability to accurately pinpoint personal losses. The reason for that is deceptively simple: the brain is that faculty by which you judge all other aspects of your experience. Therefore, if this function itself becomes faulty or damaged, you are completely unable to stand outside it to notice that it is broken. A faulty brain will give you false readings on everything—including yourself. No matter how smoothly and effortlessly your brain still seems to function, it gives you, nonetheless, a wrong interpretation of the world around you—and the world within you. You have no other point of reference from which to verify the information and data your brain delivers to you.

Having relied upon your brain—with good effect until now—to function reasonably and well over many years, it is preposterously difficult to accept that it might now be faulty—especially when it feels precisely the same as it always has. The present fogginess you are feeling is, you reason, probably due to your current medication, or is the lingering postoperative effect of a recent general anesthetic.

You simply do not equate your present confusion with a major system malfunction. You cannot comprehend that the head office of this company called "My Body Inc." might now be only working partially or with serious organizational errors. Various other departments—such as legs, vision, and appetite—are currently implementing their own self-imposed lightning strikes, without giving you any prior warning. They are not simply working to rule; they have abandoned the rulebook altogether, in favour of random acts of blindness. Though I was unaware of what was happening to me, others could see it clearly—and they were about to tell me.

I knew it was serious when the doctor arrived to talk to me at my bedside in the Vancouver General Hospital. She was a psychiatrist, either a senior student or a junior doctor in training, and she had already come to see me earlier in the day. During that visit we talked, but it seemed to me to be an odd and stilted conversation. Clearly, we had not understood each other very well. It felt like I was trying to solve the clues to *The Times* cryptic crossword puzzle. I understood all of the words she was saying—one at a time—without difficulty. Yet, listening to them in whole sentences defeated me. Now she was back at my bedside but this time with the big guns—the consultant psychiatrist.

Like a senior doctor in his position does—at least in all the old hospital movies that I watched as a kid—he looked oddly sombre and exceptionally serious—they both did. I wanted desperately to giggle. As they loitered with intent, I found it hard to take them as seriously as they clearly took themselves. With what seemed like an exaggerated carefulness, they sat down.

"Oh dear," I thought so loudly that I was sure they would hear me, "I think I am going to guffaw with laughter. I'm going to explode! I think I'm about to embarrass myself." Then I replied more sternly to my misbehaving self: "Get a grip on yourself, Paul! Look serious, now. No, don't! Just close your eyes instead. Pretend you are tired so that you won't have to watch their seriously funny faces."

I lectured myself in this way, in a futile attempt to put the clamps on an unstoppable tidal wave of laughter. I hid behind the fragile dam of my weak self-control waiting for it to burst, and for the uncontrollable giggles to pour forth like a waterfall from my mouth. Instead, I discovered that I had burst into tears. I was crying again, freely, like a baby.

The doctors sat with their chairs drawn up close to my bedside. By that time, I had been in treatment there for an agonizing seven weeks. The consultant leaned forward and then very deliberately—and painfully slowly—with a deep and clear voice, he said: "You have suffered a serious brain injury."

I stared back at him incredulously. He was looking directly at me. But was he really addressing his neat and sombre speech to *me*? Surely not. But indeed, it seemed that he directed his focus on me alone. His dark eyes stared me down. There was nobody else in that hospital bed with me. I felt certain of that much, at least, but I still looked around trying to identify the one whom his words described. Then, with equal seriousness, and all the authority I could muster, I pointed with my finger to the foot of my bed.

"You have the wrong patient, doctor," I announced with a breezy tone and with absolute certainty. "Just look at my chart at the bottom of my bed." I waved to it with an outstretched arm. They did not, however, seem to follow the direction of my hand. Now it was my turn to speak with an exaggerated clarity.

"My name," I announced with all the dignity that I could muster, "is Beckingham. That's B-e-c-k-i-n-g-h-a-m." I spelled it out with exaggerated slowness just for emphasis. "My first name is Paul. I'm the one with the multiple broken bones—the damaged foot. My brain, however, is okay."

I was genuinely puzzled, for they just sat there impassively, watching me quietly. In my head I heard myself screaming at them. "Can't you see for yourselves that you are wrong? Look at me, for goodness' sake! I'm talking. I'm lucid. I'm making sense—mostly."

My thoughts—anxious and uncomprehending—yelled out to them. Just then, the surgeon leaned forward, taking my hand cautiously, deliberately, and gently. I felt like some precious, rare, and fragile exhibit in a museum.

"There's no mistake," he said. "You have suffered a serious brain injury. You need to know that. We will, of course, be keeping a check on you—for seizures. You have not had one to date, and that's good news. If you do get a seizure at any time in the next twelve months I must be kept informed. You will need some ongoing help, so we'll make our recommendations to your care team at the GF Strong Rehab Center where you will soon be transferred. I want you to take these antidepressant pills for the next little while. I think that they will help you."

"Why?" I asked, desperately trying to take it all in at a glance, but still utterly convinced they had the wrong patient.

"You may be suffering from post-traumatic stress syndrome. It causes depression. We've noticed that you cry a lot. I would like you to take this medication. These pills will help you. Do have any questions you would like to ask?"

"Yes," I gasped emphatically, with tears spilling down my cheeks. I knew I had at least a million urgent questions. They pressed in on me, and I needed to ask him about so many things. Suddenly, however, every single question that had weighed so heavily on my mind unexpectedly now evaporated—gone without a trace. I racked my brain, searching for questions that were simply not there.

"No...no questions," I mumbled through my tears. I was as puzzled as the doctors at my sudden reversal. "Tell me, doctor, what did you say your name was?" I bumbled on.

Names and details seemed to escape me easily in those early days of recovery. They still do. I feel chagrined and embarrassed when it happens—to the point of avoiding people that I'm sure I know quite well. Some of them are close friends, yet I still struggle to recall their names even as I talk to them. I may have used their names repeatedly in a conversation, then, without warning, they fly away to Mombassa, never to return. Usually, I am stuck for answers without prompting from somebody else.

In a sympathetic way intended to relieve my evident discomfort, people sometimes say to me, "Oh, that even happens to me—but I don't have the excuse of having a brain injury. I'm just getting old." Then they give me a hail-fellow-well-met slap on the shoulder or add a chuckle of laughter of the genial variety.

But it really doesn't help me. It makes me feel so much worse, for it is not at all the same kind of issue. Before my accident, I was known for my good memory for names and details. Now, after just one blow, that once reliable facility is out of order. That is a grievous loss that deeply troubles me. Of course, I expect to slow down with age—but not in a brief period of twelve hours. That, I think, is how long it took for me to first awake after my initial emergency surgeries. They were slow and faltering hours of re-emergence into wakefulness—but it would take some years for me to tighten my grasp on a modified reality.

Mary was not there to prompt me as I struggled with those two doctors at my bedside. Sometimes—the worst of times for me—she is not always there to rescue me now.

"Dr. Anderson is my name," he said smiling gently in his kind and caring manner. "Goodbye, Mr. Beckingham. And may I wish you the very best for a good recovery."

In those early moments following the accident, time spun oddly out of control for me. It danced a jig in concentric circles. Each orbit moved at a different speed, and ran in opposite rotations. First, time spun slowly, winding down like a worn watch battery; then, it once more hurtled at the white-hot speed of light, frantically out of control. Both realities mixed awkwardly, like an emulsion of water and oil, now bonding together, then breaking violently apart. Past and present, the "now" and the "next," collided together, melding and moving, advancing and retreating, all at once in an agony of chaos, like a bizarre kaleidoscope of pictures traced onto time.

Whatever happened to linear time—those neat sequences of events that pass neatly in a good-mannered way from the present to the past as the future unfolds on the near horizon? The obedient future that once bowed to plans and appointments was now an unruly master delighting in victimizing the unwary. I was numbered among them in those days—and sometimes, these days, too. But I was not the only person to be victimized by our accident that day.

Daniel Kariuki was taken to Gertrude's Gardens Children's Hospital, a private care facility and the best children's hospital in the Republic of Kenya. He was carried there in the car of a passerby who had stopped to offer his assistance at the terrible scene of mangled wreckage. In a clean and comfortable ward, Daniel's broken femur was put into traction. For another five weeks, Daniel's bones would be held in traction to encourage them to mend, but at a different hospital. When it became obvious to the staff that he was just a poor village boy with no visible means of paying for his treatment—and the significant bills grew steadily, daily—they transferred him to Kenyatta Hospital, the government hospital.

Aaron, too, was in pain. Later, he would describe it to Mary saying, "Mom, when people see your hand in a sling they can tell you have been hurt. When Dad is in his wheelchair they can see he has been injured. But nobody can see my pain inside."

Some of those lingering feelings were to dog Aaron for many months, often appearing as survivor's guilt. He felt that he, not Daniel, should have suffered broken bones. He knew that his refusal to change seats with Daniel on entering the car had placed Daniel in harm's way, and now he blamed himself for Daniel's pain. Often, Aaron felt insecure and depressed, and on many occasions over the next two years he would slip into our bedroom while we slept. In the morning Mary would find him asleep on the floor beside our bed.

At the government hospital in Nairobi where Daniel was taken, drugs—if available at all—are in short supply. What they do have must be rationed in an attempt to meet the impossibly high demand. The hospital staff, according to some, has a reputation for selling the incoming shipments of drugs for their personal gain.

My missionary colleague, Paul Carline, visited Daniel later. He was naked in a bed that he shared with a grown man who, like most of the patients there, was also without clothes. Patients in this hospital frequently have to share three to a bed. The possibilities for cross-infection on these wards must be measured as certainties. Food is not supplied, and patients receive only the meals that family and friends are able to bring in for them.

When a patient dies, the body is not released to his family until all bills have first been settled. This often takes many months, and at that time the local morgue's air conditioning and cooling systems began to break down. With so many AIDS victims in storage awaiting release to their families, the organization was overstretched and bodies were corrupting.

Paul Carline insisted that Daniel be given his own bed, but it happened only after Paul gave his written assurance that our mission would cover all of Daniel's bills. He arranged for food, clothing, and other necessities to be supplied for Daniel. Without Paul's assistance, Daniel would likely not have survived.

Mary and Aaron were driven to the Aga Khan Hospital, the nearest medical facility to the scene of the wreckage and arguably the best in Kenya. When they first arrived, life whirred for them in a blur of medical activity. Treatment rooms—lights—questions. And glass. So much broken glass everywhere: in skin, clothing, shoes and, don't ask me how, even in underwear. Mary would puzzle over that phenomenon for many weeks to come. The only certainty she had on arrival at hospital was that I must be dead.

She tried to put it out of her mind, to busy herself instead with present realities that demanded her full attention. She comforted Aaron who, though calmer now, was nonetheless deeply traumatized. The attending medical staff inspected and cleaned his cuts and abrasions. *Nothing serious*, they reported. Mary's broken collarbone had fractured awkwardly. Surgery would soon reveal a complex break requiring a plate and several screws to hold it in place. They started preparing her for surgery.

I hate the smell of hospitals. That antiseptic, vaporized scent seems to assault my senses and upset my stomach. It makes me feel nervous and vulnerable. I have a terrible reputation for visiting people in hospital, whether friends or family, or on a pastoral call. I am arguably the world's worst hospital visitor. On many occasions during a visit, I steel myself in order to make even the briefest of stays without embarrassing myself. Sometimes, I even get to thinking that I am doing well, and then the challenge conquers me. I will catch sight of a drip line glug-glugging liquid or removing body fluids, and suddenly I become nauseous and faint. Soon, a heavy-eared deafness hits me, just before I pass out cold on the floor. Activity around me in those moments seems to proceed in slow motion. I rarely make it out of the ward standing. If I manage to arrive safely at the nurses' office, it is not long before unconsciousness turns out my lights for a few minutes. A concerned nurse passes me a glass of water—why is it always lukewarm?—and I offer my frustrated apologies for wasting her time. I see her saying to herself, "Men! So strong...so very weak!"

When I arrived at the Aga Khan hospital, it was a different kind of hospital visit for I was unconscious from the beginning—but not for long. The busy calm of the hospital was suddenly shattered by my piercing scream. I had appeared as large as life but near to death. Hearing my pained voice, Mary knew for the first time that I was alive. Her relief carried little confidence that I might continue to breathe much longer. How could a body so bloodied and broken return safely from this kind of punishment? Much later, my daughter Leah, then twelve years old, would tell me, "Dad, we waited five days for you to die and you didn't!"

Mary would add, "Yes...and there is a terrible sense of anticlimax when something you are expecting doesn't happen."

I have observed that when somebody you love faces certain death, one of the ways you can cope is by letting go—completely. And my family had begun to let go of me. They accepted—albeit reluctantly—the fact of impending death, and they released me from their lives. In their minds, they were already moving on to the future. They were considering the crisis of how they would cope, where they would live, and how they would get by—without me.

Mary did not come to see me when she heard my screams. She could not let herself look at me in those hours before my multiple surgeries took place. Starting just after midnight, the surgeons worked on me for more than four and a half hours. Meantime, Mary had already begun to release me to a foregone conclusion. At times like these, you must let go. You have to accept that what has gone has gone—never to return. So, you move on to other pressing urgencies, demands that occupy you, requiring your energy and urgent input. Busy pragmatism saves us from having to face unwelcome emotional realities, for a while at least.

These days, as I review the Gospel account of Jesus raising Lazarus, his dear friend, from the dead, I see it in the fresh light of experience. The story feels very different, now. I wonder if Mary and Martha, devoted sisters both, had already begun to let him go. Had they already released him from their lives when Jesus eventually arrived at their Bethany home? I am persuaded that they must have let him slip quietly out of their lives. After all, his body was already corrupting. The stench of death made the finality of it all an undeniable reality. They grieved—they were angry. Accusingly, Martha told Jesus that he was too late. Mary wept hot tears of grief somewhere offstage, holding her pain close to her heart, quietly nursing its sting.

If only—ah, all those terrible "if onlys." If only Jesus had not taken so long to get there, if only he had arrived sooner, it would all be so different. Different from what? From the reality of death. Death, that ancient thief, had robbed them of their beloved brother. Their loss was deep and real. Lazarus, the friend of Jesus, was dead—quite dead. He stunk. And everybody knew it.

These grieving sisters had surely released their dead brother from their lives—bitterly, painfully and completely. So completely that they were overwhelmed and unprepared to see him come forth. But forth he came, as large as life and smelling like a cadaver, his arms and legs still bound in soiled grave bandages. But they had let go of him by now; they had surrendered him to death. This was not altogether good news for them. They struggled to get their minds around it. He was alive. He was walking towards them and soon he would eat with them. The impulse to rejoice, therefore, was overwhelming. A moral imperative dictated that they should feel good, for he was home again.

Together once more—and yet what dissonance from so many conflicting feelings experienced in a day! What was the emotional roller coaster they clung to as it swooped and dived—up, down, and around at such alarming speed? Would they—could they—manage to let him back into their lives again? Would they believe him to be the same man they knew before? Would they trust him not to die all over again, right before their eyes?

They had already prepared his body for burial, washed him, bound him with burial perfumes, and laid him to rest. They had done it before and once was enough for these sisters—enough for anyone. Enough already, with all this grief!

The searing pain and the wailing of women in all parts of their house and the courtyard below had become too much to bear. Local friends now added their own wailing voices to the sisters' pitiable and anguished cries. The finality of death struck them as forcibly as an oncoming military truck. It was a done deed from which there would be no going back. There is no return from this final frontier. Except, astonishingly, there he is. Lazarus is walking straight towards them. He is calling them by name. He is trying to walk back into their lives, into their home, and into their hearts.

To grasp the impact of that biblical scene, in any adequate way, is difficult indeed. As Lazarus now appears, can you imagine the volatile mixture of feelings these women must be experiencing? Their raw emotions emerge all at once, in a turmoil of conflicting sensations churning together. Passionate thoughts bubble up to overwhelm those grieving-rejoicing sisters.

In another place, at another time, on a short journey along the Limuru Road to the Aga Khan Hospital, another family discovers those equivalent feelings. They spring up from a comparable place of confusion and pain. Would this contemporary family also let go of a husband and father? Will they allow him back into their lives? Would they—could they—manage to make the emotional reversal required to do that? This would be no easy or automatic transaction, and only time would tell the final outcome.

I am not the first person to face such uncertainties; neither will I be the last. It is part of the human predicament; it seems to me that, sooner or later, we will all face our cruel and painful realities. For many of us, critical issues will materialize that we would rather not deal with. Instead, we would prefer to wish them away if we possibly could—though we would not gift them to our worst ene-mies. A family so badly shaken witnesses its security falling apart. The old, familiar certainties it once knew become no longer recog-nizable—even in each other. Hopelessness carries within itself fea-tures that are deadly and harmful to human nature, to life itself, as Jürgen Moltmann, the theologian of hope details incisively:

> Totally without hope one cannot live. Without some goal and effort to reach it no man can live. When he has lost all hope and object in life, man often becomes a monster in his misery. To live without hope is to cease to live. Hell is hopelessness. It is no acci-dent that above the entrance to Dante's hell is the inscription: "Leave behind all hope, you who enter here." I have seen impris-oned men whose last hopes vanished. They lay down, became sick, and died. If there is today in our society a sickness of youth, though by no means limited to youth, it is this sickness of objec-tive and goal. The future becomes dark. It is the cold despair in which "nothing really matters" to a person and he or she suc-cumbs to the death wish.[12]

Some of us have landed on these bleak desert shores. We can-not wish that others should follow us on such a journey whose paths cross valleys of dry bones. Saints of old have gone before us and their suffering has exceeded our own. Job suffered more than his share of hopelessness that catastrophic personal loss imposes. Yet, he brings us comfort by carrying with him an assurance that resonates with our condition today. He declares with certainty: *You will be secure, because there is hope; you will look about you and take your rest in safety* (Job 11:18).

Security, hope, rest, and safety—these prove to be secure and pre-cious commodities in troubled times. Even the promise of them, if you dare to trust it, brings a deep measure of relief. To hear that there is hope, when you have lost all sense of it, is hugely health giving.

When, at last, you come through danger's darkness, deep joy emerges as you realize that you can take your rest in safety. The question for us then becomes will we dare allow ourselves to trust God's promise enough to do that?

I suppose we will only dare to do it if the One who makes the promise proves trustworthy. We will not be disappointed if we learn to put our trust in a promise that is secure. But you do not have to take my word for it. If you will allow yourself to do it, you might try this way of trusting for yourself. But as I was about to learn, trust is a flower that opens cautiously in the face of winter's chill.

CHAPTER SEVEN

What a Beautiful Hotel!

When times are good, be happy; but
when times are bad, consider: God
has made the one as well as the
other. Therefore, a man cannot
discover anything about his future
(Ecclesiastes 7:14).

I do not remember those first five days in Nairobi's Aga Khan Hospital. I have but a welter of half-remembered snippets, blurred extracts of conversations. I keep them like a collection of worn and torn old photographs—half glimpses and smudged images.

I was, according to the grapevine, very verbal. At times I almost made sense. My tone of voice was normal—even convincing to the unaware. But, to many of my visitors and friends, it appeared that I was trying too hard—much too hard—to show everyone that I was *just fine, quite normal,* and *much on the mend.* But my lapses were frequent and major. Attempting to appear normal—whatever that may be—and the feelings of my visitors and my medical team became my great concern. Like many a missionary I remained on duty far too long. It is hard for caregivers to be compliant care

99

receivers because their agenda to reach out to people around them constrains them still: they must help others.

"Where's my wife?" I asked a lady as she entered my room.

"I am your wife," she calmly replied, knowing that my reality was all my own.

"And where's your room?" I demanded.

"Not far away," she answered with deliberation.

"I have been involved in a terrible accident, you know," I said gravely. I did not notice, nor take on board, that Mary stood there before me pale, drawn, and in pain. Her arm rested in a sling and she gently guarded her collarbone.

"I know," she replied slowly and deliberately, "so have I."

"What a beautiful hotel!" I intoned that phrase with genuine delight. "Did you choose this hotel? I don't think I have ever seen such a beautiful hotel room. It's magnificent!"

I was overwhelmed with the beauty of my surroundings. And then, as if this brief interlude had never occurred, I started back to the beginning of the recording of this uninspired piece of dialogue.

Around we would go, again and again—interminably. I took it from the top all over again, as if for the first time, replaying it over and over until Mary tired of it completely. Then, exhausted, she quietly slipped back into her own room, uneasy and troubled at heart. Yet, she never revealed her distress to me. Or, perhaps, I was just too detached from reality to be able to read her anguish accurately.

Many months later, Mary told me, "Actually, that hospital room was not great. The paint was peeling off the walls in places, and the mosquitoes buzzed angrily around the room. Outside your window, a major hospital expansion was underway and the noise of construction was dreadful. Never in my right mind," Mary said, "would I ever choose a hotel room like that. It was barely adequate as a hospital room—though outstanding by Nairobi standards."

As hospital rooms go, I preferred it in the end to the larger, noisier wards where I would later receive my treatments in Vancouver. However, for me, in those early days, it remained the last word in hotel luxury. Nothing could persuade me otherwise—no matter how often I reran that soon-to-be-overworked and tired old script in my mind.

My remoteness from reality was not Mary's first experience of caring for a loved one with a brain injury. About a decade earlier, her sister, Jo, had been involved in a terrible accident. It was her accident that had brought us the awful telephone call that had spun me, years earlier, in tragedy's tailspin. Her accident caused me to want to turn back the clock. Those days of loss affected our family deeply.

Her husband, Mick, was attempting to change a propane tank in their motor home at a stop on their trip through Europe, travelling with their three-year-old daughter, Emma. Under the influence of some intoxicating substance, he was unable to make sound choices: wrong type of tank—secondary gas system left on—escape of propane—ignition.

Their world changed in a flash—with a sudden, horrendous bang. Jo received fifty percent burns and Mick, twenty-five. Emma, cruelly injured, died the next day. After seven days in a primitive hospital in Greece, they were air ambulanced back to Britain.

Bad as her condition had been on arrival at a military hospital in Britain that specialized in burns, Jo's injuries suddenly plunged deeper. Septicemia set in rapidly after only a week. Rapidly, all her body systems began to crash, one by one. Jo's extremities turned icy while her temperature soared to an impossibly dangerous 107 degrees Fahrenheit. A medical team worked on her with hairdryers on her feet and hands, and ice on her head. Their goal was both to heat and to cool her extreme and opposing conditions.

Kidney failure led to months of dialysis. An emergency tracheotomy kept her breathing. Her body, edema prone and puffy, slipped into a deep coma. They stitched her eyes closed to minimize the risk of infection entering her body by that route. Eleven horrible months of treatment—and family tension—ensued.

Her father suffered the first of several heart attacks due to the strain of it all. The damage to his heart would hasten his early death. And through it all, because of a lack of oxygen, she suffered her brain injury. It would rob her of her eyesight, the hearing in one ear, her ability to walk without assistance, and she would lose her motor coordination. Her speech became slurred and her thinking, at first, lacked lucidity. But slowly, over many years, Jo made small but significant gains. Today, living on her own, she is able to care for herself.

By the time our accident caused me to mumble inanities, Mary had seen it all before—and worse. She trusted that what she saw and heard in those early days would not be the final end state for us both. Mary's persevering faith began, at once, to coax me back to a truer reality. But it would be a long haul—and the final destination would not be back to "normal"—to where and what I had once been.

There is no going back from events like this; there is only going forward into an unknown future. The path of recovery leads towards a new and uncharted pilgrimage where everything looks and feels approximately the same, yet all is now so utterly different.

Arriving at a new "normal" would entail a journey of recovery and a voyage of discovery. Each began from a place of sorrow and damage but might lead, at last, to new possibilities. Such journeys are not quick or simple; they are measured in years. The new normal, as descriptive of my personality, would feel as strange as if first seeing my face in a mirror after radical cosmetic surgery. I could not fully recognize the familiar stranger before me. So much is still the same and yet nothing is quite the same any more. The game of getting-to-know-you-now would be forced upon every member of the family. But only one member would have to learn the unwritten rules of this game. And I guess that would be me.

My family would not altogether like the new me; nor would I. They kept mistaking him for the old Paul—me, too. We planned our lives as we used to, as if the new Paul could cope with the old challenges, stresses, and schedules. That path led directly to frustration, anger, and disappointment.

Have you ever felt sidelined—chewed up and spat out—passed over and made to appear like a nonevent? It is like you have exceeded your "best before" date. Or worse, you never made it up and onto the display shelf in the first place. People can make you feel this way in the simplest of ways. Colleagues, friends, and family will sometimes say or do things that wound, but mostly it is your own performance that dents your confidence and hope.

In the end, you want to simply give up on this imposter-self who, like some alien, has entered by force and occupied your old familiar body. This creature works to prevent it from reaching its peak—or even average—performance. The body looks somehow the same, but reacts so very differently, now. I quickly realized that I had become a massive disappointment to the ones I love, and to my friends. I fear I am a disappointment to myself.

At the age of forty-five, I ploughed into that oncoming military truck as a young man—at least in my own imagination. Likely, nobody else on earth thought of me as young, but *I* did. I regarded myself as still quite youthful. It is one's self-assessment that feels so vital, so important.

Two and a half years postaccident, I knew myself to be old. I somehow managed to escape my middle years, and middle age got lost along my leapfrog journey in time. Life felt suddenly over, and rather than planning for an active future, I thought and planned, instead, for retirement—the one that had hastily arrived.

My planning is plainly overdue and painfully too late. So just how did I get here from there? I am really not sure. Maybe I took a significant bump along the way. But this is really not how I had imagined life to be in my forties—not one bit of it! Instead of rising to the pinnacle of my performance, I simply fell off the peak—and that really hurts.

I consciously try so hard to resist feeling cheated. Actually, not true. I indulge those feelings from time to time. Then I am overwhelmed by the most repulsive of emotions: self-pity. It makes me doubly angry: angry, first, for all this crazy stuff that makes me pity myself. Then I am angry all over again for allowing myself to indulge those nauseating feelings, even if only briefly.

Yuck! How I hate myself for it, because I am a *man,* damn it! Real men don't cry, do they? Except if they are Russian: "You are not a man until you have learned to cry!" say my Russian friends. You cannot pretend to be strong any longer—not even to yourself—when you have suffered a loss so complete. At such times, stinging tears may freely flow.

Oh, how hard you try: to be in control, to be normal, to be capable, to become the self you so much wish to be—the person you think everyone expects you to be—your imposter-self. The more you strive, the stronger becomes your denial. You rapidly appear to be exactly what you are—overcompensating and incompetent. Yet, it is hard to break the habit, to halt the driven-ness, and perhaps you never will. Old habits cling and, like a strong undertow, they suck you out to sea, abandoning you in their choppy surf. Farther out they sweep you into rough waters of immeasurable depth.

"Where is God in all of this?" the haunting question rings. Ah, yes—God. Possibly, just maybe, He is to be found right there, in the certainty of a tough reality. Maybe all truth is, after all, God's truth. God is more truly present in the honest telling of the difficulties of my story than He is in the thin veneer of victory that I prefer to place over them.

It is the testimonies of triumph that people want to hear, rather than the journey of pain. For many people of faith, the struggle feels too threatening. "You are far out, Paul. Come back in; come home again," I hear them tell me, saying it without words. Better they first address their own discomfort before they lecture others about honesty. Hasty conclusions prefabricate an appearance of truth that quickly crumbles when forced to face adversity.

Our faith, if firm, is made of stronger stuff. It looks upon disaster without disintegrating. It emerges again, without depending on well-rehearsed, orthodox, or knee-jerk responses. It shuns them as suspicious. I do not deny the truth of old answers we learned by rote as children, but I cannot run there in haste before I have first weighed the pain. Quietly, faith absorbs it, balances it, and holds it.

The horror of pain's tutorial is surprisingly simple: real pain really hurts real people—even people of faith. Recipients of God's love may themselves experience a dreadful sense of abandonment in times of loss. Even when our theology—stoutly orthodox—protests that He never leaves us nor forsakes us, we can feel lost and alone. To deny this reality is merely to lie in the service of the God of Truth. To do so becomes an ironic and uncomfortable denial of God who is everywhere present—even in our experience of aloneness. It is not sufficient to reject the struggle to understand, in favour of an unthinking theology that is content to parrot religious clichés.

The journey of faith, through loss, uncertainty, and failure, becomes a path that leads to a God who is truly able to carry our pain. Such faith goes on believing when easy answers falter and finally fail, as inevitably they must. Only those answers that have paid the price—that have emerged from life, not merely lips—can ultimately satisfy. Answers in our heads must be also grounded in our hearts.

That has become, perhaps, an unorthodox belief for this generation. But saints of bygone days knew it to be the "way of the cross." While unfashionable these days, perhaps, the cross is a truth that stands; more attractive ways to salvation are merely temporary trends that fail us, in the end.

Everything about the cross of Christ is unfashionably orthodox. To carry one's cross is bloody and sweaty work, painful and unpleasant, and will take us towards a sense of abandonment, leading us to the very gates of hell. Yet, heaven awaits us there, for death is not the end but the beginning of a promised hope and a future. This is a reality more real then anything to be touched or tasted today. For the person of faith, there is no easy end run around suffering and pain. It comes to us all in the end. Its shadow falls across our path of faith.

In those early days of life-or-death recovery at the Aga Khan, I was not a perfect patient or, indeed, perfect at anything—either then or now. Like a self-made plaster saint I crashed from every pedestal. Yet God began gluing me back together again—with evident imperfections—as evidence of His grace in a time of brokenness.

"Dad, you were so embarrassing!" Leah said, with a twelve-year-old's indignant voice.

"You should have heard what you said, Dad!" she protested.

"Well," I asked, "what did I say?"

"You spoke in a South London accent and you told everyone you were twenty-two years old—and then you started hitting on the nurses—*all* the nurses!"

Well, how are you supposed to answer such an accusation—especially knowing that anesthesia can cause you to indulge in all kinds of odd conversations? What could I tell her?—*I don't remember anything!?* No excuse. But genuinely, I didn't. Maybe it would just be easier to believe her implausible story and to plead, *Guilty as charged!*

Although I would never admit it, especially to a stranger, I am quite capable of such caddish behaviour. How does my refrain go? *I'm a man, damn it!* Red blood courses through my veins—and my injured brain. With St. Augustine, I know that the habits of the flesh emerge from just below the surface of a life that God has not yet finished sanctifying. Unlike Augustine, I am no saint! The cracks show plainly, despite my vain attempts to paper over them. Worse, the people I try to impress—onlookers, friends, or ghosts from my past—all see them unmistakably. With clarity they are able to map those scars and fissures accurately.

In Kenya—in hospital—in denial. Trying to be good—so very good—yet being quite bad. Oh, the ironies of life. I've become verbal—so verbal that the doctors confidently tell Mary: "Look, he's doing fine. He's normal."

"No!" she says, alarm bells shrilling in her voice. "He's not *normal*. He needs help! He's making little sense to those who know him."

Quizzically, the doctors look over to me, then back to her. They are taken in by my performance; a wife knows better. Mary understands that I am far from anything she recognizes to be normal. She finds herself talking to a recognizable alien in the bed where I now lie. In the coming days, I regain some familiarity, but as she tries to get to know me I will become even more of a stranger.

A silent negotiation has begun before either of us can figure it out: Can Mary come to love her new husband while grieving the one she has lost? In some ways the new arrival seems better than the previous one; in others he is not so good. Better or worse—who is to say? Only time will tell. Different? Ah, yes, most definitely. Different is as different does—and all that he does now is very different. Not to mention all that he can no longer do.

Reality can be very cruel. It hit me like a heart-stopping body punch. Around day five or six in my Nairobi hospital bed, Mary entered my room accompanied by Dr. Paul Wangai, the Kikuyu doctor who saved my life. He had hand-picked a team of surgeons to work on me under his watchful eye. A man of faith, he combines grace, compassion, and complete professionalism. How I thank God for that man whom I count as my African brother. Long before saving my life, as my family doctor, he became one I call "friend."

Mary sat close to me. She pierced my heart with her eyes. She held my gaze within her own. I could not look away.

"I have made a decision," she said firmly. "We are going back to Canada. You are badly hurt. You need the specialist care that is available there."

I felt the haze lifting suddenly, blown back by truth intruding like an icy wind. Slowly, reluctantly, I emerged into harsh reality, and it hurt—a lot.

From somewhere deep inside, wrenching sobs arose that shook me to my core. I sobbed as only a man can. As any woman will explain, uncontrollable bawling comes from a pain too deep for words, a hurt too real to hide. So I moaned and wept in overwhelming spasms against all the training received since childhood to check, stifle, and deny it. Such sobbing may not have reached you, yet—or it may be your dark companion in these days. If not now, then in a time to come it may visit with you for a season.

When such pain comes, it serves you poorly to smother it in clichés—even clichés of faith. I will not call them "Christian" clichés, for they are neither redeemed nor yet set free. Victorian, maybe. Stouthearted, probably. Dishonest, ultimately. Standard answers, unconsidered stop-gap replies, offer only a place of counterfeit refuge. Hope does not dwell there. A faith that moves forward into fear discovers, beyond the reach of fear's muscular grip, a stronger hope by far. Courageous hope ascends the terror of outrageous circumstance to shine its peaceful light into the darkness of despair.

There was pain aplenty for us as a family in those early days. But there is a pain that goes deeper than skin deep. It is a profound inner pain that presents us with our greatest human challenges. Emotional pain distorts our affections; spiritual pain twists us out of shape. No longer are we able to recognize God or see ourselves with clarity or accuracy. This becomes a disconcerting myopia when firm parameters of our lives begin to crumble and we lose sight of the shape of who we are. Like dust, our identity and self-understandings are wafted away on the chill breeze of adversity. So the questing journey begins; it is a search to find the truth of our selfhood once again. Like a child's first experience of being lost in the mall, finding who we are can be a fearful search.

"So I met a Somali woman the other day," I am telling my colleague and friend, Paul Carline, as he visits at my hospital bedside in Nairobi. With Kelly, his wife, he works among displaced Somali people in the Eastleigh district of Nairobi.

"I gave her a lift to her home in Eastleigh," I tell him, "and when we got there she invited me in. She introduced me to her extended family, her aunt and her cousins. And then she told me she would like to marry me. So, Paul," I continue with a note of serious consideration in my voice, "I'm thinking of marrying her."

Paul looks at me, open mouthed and dumbfounded.

"Yes," I say after a moment's consideration, "I think I will marry her. What do you think?"

I do not remember this conversation for myself, but Paul Carline does—vividly and in detail. He recited it to me, blow by blow, more than two years later on our first reunion after my departure from Nairobi. He was rather worried as he told me the story. He was nervous that it may offend me—or, worse, upset Mary. I laughed out loud and, thankfully, so did Mary.

"That," he said, "was when I knew you were not your normal self."

So verbal—so lucid—so completely out of kilter! Brain injury is like that.

The first weeks of recovery were not the best of days for our family. We had known happier times—much happier times. The writer of Ecclesiastes urges: *When times are good, be happy; but when times are bad, consider: God has made the one as well as the other* (Ecclesiastes 7:14).

This was now my time to be troubled, confused, and challenged in so many ways. Yet the author of all my days had not abandoned me. He knew these days were bad for me—for all of us. Living in the ever-present moment of illness means having little or no regard for what lies ahead. There is a link between being a person of faith, and the fact of having to face human suffering. Eugene Peterson notes it well when he says: "A Christian is a person who decides to face and live through suffering. If we do not make that decision, we are endangered on every side."[13]

Collectively, our generation feels the withdrawal of God from our lives and we are puzzled by God's silence. We feel ourselves to be living in an age of abandonment. The French theologian, Jacques Ellul, asks where hope finds its centre in such times. He observes:

Man is capable of great things, positive as well as negative. That is obvious. But he cannot fill the void left by the withdrawal of God. In the midst of this silence no other response than hope is possible...The only honest and courageous attitude is to see things

109

as they are, then to respond to God's decision with hope...But if we are firmly convinced that hope has nothing to do with falling back on man's capabilities, on his greatness...then we have to understand that not only is hope the only response to the abandonment, but in addition to that it can take place only in an age without hope.[14]

My sense of abandonment, however, became intense and deadening. It was not based in fact, for God had not gone away. Looking back, the lines are drawn more clearly than I could see them then. I could discern no future beyond my next meal, but God was quietly, imperceptibly near me. He held me in His strong and gentle hands, knowing all my days. *Therefore, a man cannot discover anything about his future* (Ecclesiastes 7:14); but he can, with more grace than I exhibited, begin to rest in God's love and relax in His care. His careful love becomes the basis for hope and the future He has planned for us—however much our painful circumstances cause us to feel totally abandoned and utterly isolated.

But before I could move forward into God's future and mine, I had to deal with present moment issues that delivered one overwhelming challenge: recovery. I would be held captive to the entrapment of injuries for longer than I could anticipate, struggling to make sense of events that appeared utterly meaningless. Surprising lessons in faith lay just ahead of me; but would God now give me insight to apprehend them and a heart to receive them willingly? Would I even want to? If I had thought that quick and easy answers would come to me soon, I was about to receive some uncomfortable instruction in how to grow a crop of patience.

Chapter Eight

Reality Bites

*Know also that wisdom is sweet to
your soul; if you find it, there is a
future hope for you...*
(Proverbs 24:14).

When I opened my eyes, I'd lost five days of my life. It sounds rather clumsy, but that's what happened. It is not my habit to throw away whole days like nickels and dimes. But there they were—gone. They fell from my life the way small change slips through holes in a coin purse. Easy come, easy go I suppose—but these were not easy days.

This was the time right after the accident. Like a rowboat in an ocean fog, they bob back and forth in memory's waves. They have lost their sharp focus, though I guess it is untrue to say I don't remember anything. What I recall is rather like the proverbial Curate's egg—only good in parts. Memory stores a mixture of fact and fantasy, reality and random thoughts.

"Do you realize what you just did?" Mary asks the question

indignantly one evening, after our guests had gone. "You just told that story with *you* as the central character. But that event never happened to you—it happened to me! It is not your story—it's *mine!*"

I search my memory. No, I cannot find her in this story. My stored imprint records that it happened to me, and my wife tells me it didn't. Do I believe my wife or my memory? Mary may have the edge over my shaky powers of recall but the picture in my mind is so vivid. It feels to me to be as much a fact as in reality it is a fiction.

From time to time, I glimpse unformed, unfocused images. They emerge slowly and silently to appear on the screen of my memory. Gradually, they come into focus as vapours, thin and clear. Slowly, they rise above the miasma of patchy recall. Blurred images—past events, people in my life—pass fleetingly before my conscious recollection. Sometimes, they arrive through the prompting of those who were there; then just as silently, they leave again. It is as if these half-remembered events are too shy to trouble me by leaving their permanent thumbprint on my thoughts. Astonishingly, the imagined memory of the unreal is as vivid, or even more intense, than the real.

A day or two after my emergency surgeries in Nairobi, I lay in my bed, hardly able to move. Yet, I doubted the reality of this hospital experience, utterly convinced that it was no more than a sophisticated charade. I felt it to be some incredible spoof that "they" were playing on me. This accident—the one for which I had, and have, no recollection whatsoever—was an elaborate hoax. It did not matter to me then that I did not know who the pranksters were. Nor did I know why they would wish to play this trick on me. But a trick it was, and with a deep certainty I knew it in my heart. Despite bandages, cuts and bruises, and the multiple tubes that were attached to my body—despite it all, I knew that medically I was just fine—really.

My confidence flew directly in the face of the intense pain of intravenous injections many times a day. The inexpert nurses administered them hastily and in a matter of seconds. They should, instead, have been given slowly, over the course of several minutes. Nurses with more fervour than knowledge pushed their needles into veins.

Despite all of this evidence to the contrary, I knew the truth. "This is a game," I reasoned. "They are kidding me. I know it. I am sure. I am convinced of it. But I will get to the bottom of it all," I determined. "I will discover the facts."

My reality was vivid and complete. But I was vividly wrong— and completely driven by the need to prove that I was right. I was on my personal quest for the Holy Grail of Reality.

In the darkness one night, I started to unwind my bandages carefully. Around my right leg they covered the skin from hip to toes. I bared the flesh of my thigh from my hip to my knee. Making this job a tad easier, I stood at my bedside, my fingers exploring the exposed skin, feeling out the long incision for half a metre along the muscle line. A deep cut sliced the length of my thigh. As my fingers plunged down into the open wound, I gasped in sharp pain. Suddenly, the truth dawned and the sheer horror of it overwhelmed me.

They were not lying to me after all; they spoke truly. "I am as badly injured as they tell me." It was odd to hear myself saying that. I felt suddenly faint and I pulled my hand back, sharply recoiling with pain. Horrified, I saw my fingers, red and moist with warm blood stains rising to my second knuckles. Chagrined and dismayed, I allowed my tired body to fall back on the bed. I felt enfeebled, utterly tired. Shaky fingers tried to cover up the exposed surgical wound, as I lay there exhausted with eyes squeezed tight against the intrusion of truth.

Mercifully, sleep overtook me. Silently and heavily, I sank into the enfolding, dark embrace of unconsciousness. I fought no more. The sheer horror of those moments fell away from that tired body under sleep's gentle caress.

The next morning, Mary nodded her head sombrely as I told her the grizzly details of my night's escapade. Sensing something needed to be done, she promptly called in some nurses. They, in turn, rapidly called the duty doctor. Clearly, they were concerned. They looked at me with serious faces and worried expressions. Anxiously, they repeated my story several times to one another, standing a few steps away, just out of earshot, conferring in a huddle. From time to time in their busy conversation they shot me worried glances before hurriedly speaking together some more. Then carefully, slowly and meticulously, they checked all my bandages. They shook their heads and looked somewhat relieved. Untouched. Undisturbed. The bandages were perfectly intact. What they saw in those moments did not match my story.

Only a few hours—or perhaps a few days—before this, a microsurgeon had reattached my right foot. In emergency surgeries, my right femur, fractured at the midpoint, had been set in place by a long steel plate and many screws. To do this, the surgeons made a major incision along the length of my thigh. They had attended to my broken facial bones—my jaw, nose, and the orbis around my eye. Inserting a metal plate to replace my crushed and missing cheekbone, they worked long hours and fought to stem the massive internal bleeding. The neurosurgeon worried over a fracture to my skull at my right temple that refused to stop bleeding for the longest time, until eventually he succeeded in stemming the flow. They picked small bone fragments out of torn socks in an attempt to piece them back together—jig-saw fashion—as they laboured to reconstruct my all but severed right foot.

A steel plate and screws now held my broken femur together, bridging the fracture to my thigh, keeping it in one piece. Despite the reinforcement that this strengthening and supportive metalwork gave me, there was simply no way I could stand up. I could not support my body on a fractured femur, a crushed foot, and the other boasting three dislocated toes.

With or without assistance from another person in those early days, it was clearly impossible for me to stand for the briefest moment. Had I been able to lower the cot sides of my bed—a ridiculous impossibility—I could not support my body weight on shattered bones. Had I attempted to get out of bed, I would have collapsed with a bump, wrapped in several metres of drip lines plugged into my body. I might even have strangled myself in their tangled web.

Even now, sitting here recounting my story, those vivid nonrealities breathe a life of their own so fresh that I can smell them. They are warm and soft to my touch, as if they happened only last night. I still feel the warm blood oozing through my fingers, exploring deep inside my surgical wound. The sickening horror of it rises in my throat.

But it was simply not real; it was a dream's distortion. Was all of this an elaborate ego defense mechanism, some self-protective device played out in my subconscious? I ponder it at length. Was it an internal defense system responding to the alarm of my own feelings of denial? Was I projecting truth visually onto the movie screen of my mind, delivering the message that I still struggled to accept? I was fighting to grasp the objective reality of my woundedness. It was a fact that I could neither accept nor comprehend. I was in denial, and had you then told me that I was, I would have denied your assertion.

By the end of my dream, all doubts disappeared; truth stared me starkly in the face. When forced to face veracity, could I accept its candid vibrancy? Could I receive the truth, acknowledging the requirement to own the facts as my own? I had to believe the certainty of my injuries, though their validation was delivered in Technicolor. The falsehood of my dream conveyed the hard data in a compelling way; I now knew—and admitted—the certainty of all that others had tried to advise me.

More than we commonly admit, fiction may be the vehicle of fact—a dream, a revelation, and the reception of truth. No longer would I refute the authenticity of my condition. To accept that this night's adventure never happened as I dreamed it, would take longer. Through events that never were, I could accept what really was. From a dream's darkness, the sharp light of raw reality illuminated my interior uncertainty. Nighttime revelations became sunshine for my daytime world. At last, I could admit to myself the depth of my injuries: I was totally beaten up. Rehabilitation only begins when you have something to recover from. Now, it could start in earnest. Suddenly, a place called "well again" could be seen faintly on my far horizon, though I would travel some distance to reach it.

Reality, however, was a relative term for me in those early days—and sometimes today. Perception is reliable in patches only. Mary came one day to see me and left tired from visiting with me. At that time I operated only in the ever-present "now." Being totally present to the now moment is overrated. I did not have any extra capacity to juggle the past and the future while coping with the overpowering challenges of the present. When I tried to cope with memories and plans, odd things seemed to happen. I could not connect the past with the present. In this, I sometimes still struggle.

My colleague, Paul Carline, was my next visitor, hot on the heels of Mary.

"Hi Paul! How are you today?" he enquired with a caring smile.

"Just fine!" I claimed, preposterously. Even as I said it I struggled to adjust the pillows around me. I wanted to prop myself up between the driplines and the bed's cot sides. He leaned over, supporting my weight, and together we wriggled my uncooperative body into place among the pillows.

"Where's Mary?" Paul asked me.

"Oh," I replied with instant focus, "she's had to go to the store. She will probably be back soon. Why don't you have a seat until she comes?"

I spoke sincerely in such a convincing tone that even I believed the words I voiced. It all made perfect sense—unless, like Paul, you had recently seen Mary. He plainly knew her to be an in-patient, unfit to travel beyond the hospital's walls.

"OK..." Paul said slowly. "I'll take a seat and we'll chat until she gets back." Like an expert character actor, he didn't skip a beat while playing to the gallery. It was a masterful performance. Maybe Paul thought I was planning to marry my Somali girl—even while

Mary was at the store. Or, maybe by now he had clued in to the fact that I was rather clued out.

I lacked the facility to remain in a shared objective reality. I was in an *out to graze* mode even if I was not yet completely *out to lunch*. I was missing something fundamental, despite my plausible-at-first-hearing kinds of responses.

The missing piece was a vital connective thread called memory. Like silken strands that hold our lives together, memory forms a meaningful flow that links action, planning, and recollection. The ability to savour and reflect upon those highlights in one's journey is part of what it means to celebrate our lives. We do it in stories, and we do it in songs that lend meaning to experience. Commemoration prevents the happenings of our lives from falling like dead autumn leaves into a wintry vacuum of lost days and forgotten memories. The connective threads of memory recall apparently random events from the personal histories that shape us.

My interior struggle reflected devastating external challenges: the loss of memory, a changed personality, physical pain, and social inappropriateness, to name a few. Some serious challenges were medical and presented significant risks to my survival.

Two significant people had warned us about the dangers of complying with the hospital's physiotherapist. Sean, our recent friend and a senior member of a foreign High Commission in Nairobi, was the first. He told us that one of their embassy people had been in an East African hospital, recovering well from an accident. Wanting to speed his recovery, he had complied with the advice from his hospital physiotherapist. Tragically, he paid for it with his life. The second person to warn us was my family doctor, Paul Wangai. He instructed us carefully and repeatedly in this regard. Mary repeatedly told me to heed his stern warnings, but despite this, she came into my room one day to find me sitting up, puffing hard, and staring at my foot.

"What are you doing, Paul?" she asked. A rapidly growing note of alarm became a crescendo of concern.

"Oh," I said, "I'm trying to wriggle my foot, to keep it active inside my cast—like the physio told me to."

"Stop!" she yelled. "When did you see him?"

"Just now—he just left."

"Don't do it!" she insisted. "Do nothing he says. I've told you before."

"When?" I asked, without a glimmer of recollection. My short-term memory was, and continues to be, a challenge.

Moving my foot inside my cast would bring the prognosis from five Canadian surgeons over the next two years that I would lose my foot. They warned me that they would need to amputate my leg six inches below my knee. In an effort to do that physiotherapy, by moving my foot in my cast, I created a critical misalignment of the neck of the talus bone. It caused avascular necrosis—bone death through a compromised blood supply. The large dome of the talus bone suffered death in the top third of the bone's crown. Dead bone is bound to collapse, they told me. I would have to lose that foot.

I found the prospect to be more than a little intimidating. To be honest with you, it was downright depressing. But I was not aware of that gloomy outcome when I wriggled my foot with all my energy inside my cast that day. I had never been warned, you see—except by Mary dozens of times, and Sean, and Dr. Wangai.

"Mary, I'm hearing this for the first time. Why haven't I been told?" That would become my constant plea.

"No, Paul, you're not," was her consistent, firm reply. "You've heard it many times." It is depressing to hear that so many times each day—or, to have to say it.

"She's wrong!" I angrily told myself. "She can forget, too. Her memory is not infallible." Thus I reasoned with myself. Self-justifying arguments inevitably led me to erupt in defensive anger. *I have a good memory—exceptional—and my college transcripts prove it! I completed a three-year MDiv program in only two years, as well as being joint valedictorian of my graduating class.* In this kind of angry internal dialogue, I continued to fight it out.

The truth is I was struggling in no man's land—the space between present and past realities. Eventually, I would have to start using my claims of having a "good memory" in a past-tense-only context, and admit they referred to whom I once was, but not to the person that I am today. That awful admission—even to myself—could not happen for some time to come.

The emotional baggage I carried while journeying clumsily from one reality to the other, from present to past and back to a modified understanding of the present, was perfectly crushing. My disappointment with the person I'd become proved to be bigger than my emotional shoulders were designed to carry. Coming to terms with a diminishment so great is a lonely soul safari into a barren landscape emptied of life. It hurts to think that you may already have peaked at forty-five. You feel robbed of fifteen good years—no, your fifteen *best* years.

"So, I have made a decision," Mary said with shocking seriousness. It was around day five, at the Aga Khan hospital. "We leave for Canada in four days' time." The news hit me with crushing force.

"But…" I sobbed, "I have utterly failed as a missionary. I have let down those people I came to serve. We *can't* go home." I was broken, devastated.

"No, Paul. You haven't failed!" The warm voice of Dr. Paul Wangai comforted me, his hand resting lightly on my shoulder. Had he really been there, standing beside me, all this time? I was only then aware for the first time of his proximity.

"You haven't failed," he insisted. "It's time for you to go home to Canada. God knows that this is best for you."

His warmth and kindness caused me to bawl again, my shoulders heaving and shuddering. His was the permission I needed in order to let go of my responsibility. As an African brother, he spoke for all of his people, releasing me from missionary service, to become whole again. Reluctantly, I would return to Canada—but not before praying with each of my nurses and all of my visitors. Before any of them could leave my room I would take their hand and begin to pray out loud. My prayers were heartfelt and spoken with the deep emotion of a man who knows that he is leaving never to return.

Though I had no inkling of it then—or during the next two years—one day, I would return. For now, however, I would leave my heart in Africa—and six pints of my blood on the Limuru Road. They say that eventually Africa gets into your blood—but my blood got into Africa one Kenyatta Day, on the Limuru Road, heading north out of Nairobi.

In Kenya, an older man is given a term of honour; he is called *Mzee*. Age alone cannot confer that title, only the wisdom that accompanies it. If he is found to be wise, even a younger man will be called *Mzee*. I once greeted an older man with a courteous *Shikamoo Mzee*. He looked at me quizzically, then with an accent from the American Deep South, he said: "Ah dunno what yer just said to me, boy—but ah do know yer called me an *old* man!"

Blushing deeply, I made my hasty apology to this African-American visitor to Kenya. It would take too long to explain this term of endearment as a title of honour for a wise man. Wisdom teaches that in an age that has lost its ability to anticipate the best, hope is real and vital, even if it is sometimes conspicuous by its absence.

Hope, it seems, has the ability to easily evaporate, causing Walter Holden Capps to wonder where hope went in our generation. He observes:

> There was a time, not long ago—some of us remember it well— when people were excited about hope.... There were people who hoped, and there was widespread advocacy of hope. Each nurtured the other. It was in music (usually to guitar accompaniment). So to speak, hope was in sermons. People discussed hope. They talked about it. Hope even inserted itself into deliberations regarding man's future. Often the concern about "the year 2000" was influenced by hope. But all that was some time ago. Not so long ago. Some of us remember it. And then something happened.

What happened? Perhaps we'll never know. But something did happen. It happened to persons who hoped. It happened to persons who talked, sang, and wrote about hope. It happened in books, no longer about hope. It happened to sermons, to music, to concern about the future, to "the year 2000." It happened! What happened? What ever happened to hope?[15]

The collective experience of a whole generation is a distressing loss of hope. But it is far more devastating when personal tragedy robs an individual of hope. However, the reflective person of wisdom knows that hope is a gift from One greater than us— and greater than our circumstances. Wisdom, therefore, brings its own assurance of a hope and a future, as Solomon, the wisest ancient Near Eastern ruler once said: *Know also that wisdom is sweet to your soul; if you find it, there is a future hope for you...*(Proverbs 24:14).

I began to find that kind of wisdom in Africa. Wisdom is fashioned and built on an immovable foundation: God's secure promises. It cannot stand on shifting sands, precarious personal circumstances. Towering above the transience of our affairs and our temporal condition, hope's wisdom lends them perspective. The Limuru Road almost succeeded in robbing me of a hope and a future. Steadily and with certainty God was about to return new hope to my family; it would be a life-sustaining gift to us—and one that would lead us into some surprising twists and turns.

CHAPTER NINE

The Long
Journey Home

"So there is hope for your future,"
declares the LORD. *"Your children*
will return to their own land"
(Jeremiah 31:17).

The stretcher moved forward precariously. In a comical attempt to synchronize their clumsy movements, its ineffective bearers staggered. They risked rolling their precious load headlong from the canvas before they reached the St. John's ambulance waiting nearby.

"Ambulance" is a rough approximation of the vehicle lurking in the shadowed driveway of the Aga Khan hospital. What appeared to be a vintage model "VW magic bus" had, like a broken wand, lost its power to cast good spells. Generous patches of rust bled through primeval white paintwork, forming images that resembled pictures in the clouds, the kind I loved as a child.

The antique ambulance had arrived to pick us up at the hospital more than an hour late. It clearly operated on African time. So did I, for I was in no position to rush, though our flight to Canada was about to take off desperately soon. Jomo Kenyatta Airport lay a half-hour's drive away, and Mary's stage-whispered voice mouthed her anxiety to the driver and his assistant, "Come on, come on! What if we lose our flight? You should have been here ages ago."

The ambulance crew smiled disarmingly, full of deferential apologies. How can you be cross with such charming and amenable people? Hastily, clumsily, they manhandled my stretcher aboard their creaky vehicle. It appeared they may never have done this before.

My boss's wife, Cathy Loden, was there too. As a nurse, she was ready to take my vital signs every two hours throughout our lengthy flight to Vancouver via London Heathrow. She clutched a large haversack containing medical supplies and her carry-on belongings. As an experienced, qualified nurse, she volunteered to stay with us. Dr. Wangai had been frank with Mary and with Cathy: their patient was in critical condition, the risks were high, and he would need constant attention. She would continue to take care of our family with a watchful eye over the next thirty-six hours.

The look on her face formed a perfect blend of great concern and deep care for our whole family. To nurse people who are close to you is far from easy, because they keep treading heavily on invisible boundaries that divide professional care and friendship. Cathy, however, combined both qualities in perfect balance. In my dependent condition I was prepared to do exactly as she told me—no more and certainly no less. I knew, intuitively, that a lot was at stake, and Mary constantly reminded me that my nurse was deeply worried about me.

Cathy travelled with us to the airport inside the small ambulance, riding up front with the driver. Mary climbed into the back beside me, followed by a paramedic. The ambulance was not big on space, and we were jammed in close and cramped. My stretcher seemed too long for the short space available and my feet hung over the open back door. Not aware of the problem, the paramedic reached up an arm to secure the vertically closing back door. With sudden strength he heaved it down, bringing it to an abrupt close right on my injured foot. It connected with a solid crunch on my plaster cast. As my foot was forced down my body sat up. Despite the terrible sound, I felt no pain through my jolted body. The shock of it frightened us all.

"Watch out, Bwana!" Mary called out anxiously.

"Sorry-sorry, Mama," the paramedic said sheepishly, laughing nervously as many people in his culture do when they come under pressure. Clearly, I was too long in the body or his vehicle was too short. Try as he might to shove my stretcher up towards the driver, it just wouldn't budge. He pushed while the driver and Cathy leaned over to pull on the stretcher's handles. No go—it wouldn't budge another inch. So he held the door down with his hand to prevent it from rising up and opening again on the bumpy drive to the airport.

The ambulance team almost ditched me in those early moments as the driver gassed down, revved the engine, and shifted into gear with a loud crunch to take off like a rally driver. Suddenly, my stretcher slid back alarmingly as the ambulance lurched forward. Mary clamped a strong hand on the side rail of my stretcher beside her to anchor me securely. And all the while the ambulance continued to weave drunkenly and at speed through the streets of Nairobi. Now it was the paramedic's turn to fight to stay inside the van. With one hand, he attempted to grab the back door shut while clinging firmly to the edge of his seat with the other, while the driver hit the gas.

While we lurched like a roller coaster, black and noxious diesel fumes spewed thickly from the tail pipe and seeped into the ambulance, filling it with an ominous cloud. Steady, black swirls filtered up through the gap in the door where my feet protruded, rapidly enveloping us. Coughing loudly, we began to feel decidedly travel sick in the van as up and down we bounced, and the thickening murkiness of fumes gathered round us. Mary opened her side window to its full extent. Cathy did the same, and instantly a fresh breeze began to blow from front to back through the length of the van, thinning the dark fog.

I did not have enough energy to be anxious. I sat back and enjoyed the journey with the same alarm and glee as I might have on a ride on the wild mouse at the fun fair. Mary has always hated those fast and furious rides, and today was no exception. Cathy, her eyebrows raised, shot us backward glances in a protective gesture of goodwill.

The ambulance slowed to a halt, drawing alongside another vehicle at some traffic lights. When the lights turned green both vehicles jerked speedily forward. Each driver now competed to be first to the point in the road where their two lanes merged. The newly formed single lane headed straight towards a nearby round-about—a large traffic circle—left behind by the British road builders. Incredibly, our ambulance driver had decided to race flat-out against the other driver. From my cramped vantage point I thankfully saw nothing to alarm me, but Mary gave me a breath-less running commentary. It was like a day at the races except that we were the ones bolting out of the starting gates. The race was on. Both men leaned hard on their horns. Neither was willing to give in to the other. Incredibly, even in an ambulance, Kenyan driving imperatives rule supreme. Mary closed her eyes, offering up a quick but intense prayer for safety, but held on tight to me in any case.

Arriving at last at the airport, we sighed in audible joy; our relief was palpable. The British Airways crew was, however, less impressed than we were by our safe and hasty arrival. We were late. The airplane was long past its scheduled departure time. The crew anxiously awaited our arrival while someone dealt with our lug-gage in double-quick time. It had arrived in the two other vehicles together with our children.

The children were ushered into their seats in tourist class. They moved down the aisles, struggling to carry their awkward multi-plicity of hand luggage, and it was obvious to everyone that they were way over their personal limit for carry-on bags. Meanwhile, the ambulance drove me, with Mary and Cathy, right up to the nose of the Boeing 747 jumbo jet, as it waited fully prepared and ready for takeoff.

An extendable hydraulic platform had been positioned there to receive us. No less than seven Kenyan men struggled as each tried to get a hand on my stretcher. Both it and I swayed alarmingly, first one way and then another. Nervous laughter was mixed with their intense babble of conversation to each other in Swahili. Each of them attempted to give instructions to the others. Their energy and efforts created a great deal of busy noise as they hauled me up on my stretcher aboard the platform.

Mary and Cathy stood beside me, bemused and caught up in the adventure of climbing aboard the jumbo jet. We boarded it as if we were cargo. Eager stretcher-bearers placed me squarely on the huge contraption, ready to begin our ascent up the side of the large Boeing. They eased Mary and Cathy to one side of the overcrowded platform. Glistening brows on Kenyan men shone hot and wet from the flurry of their labour and from the heat of their nervous tension. The rich smell of honest African toil rose as their sweat flowed freely and evaporated into the still, warm air.

Smoothly—slowly—the hydraulics pulled the platform up, and it rose silently beside the nose of the aircraft until we drew level with the first class cabin. We seemed to be climbing forever, but I did not look down to the runway below. It lay horribly far away—straight down as the stone drops—to solid ground.

The door of the aircraft was open and ready to receive us. The first class purser spoke sharply to the Kenyans, and then turning to another crew member he delivered a sour comment about their inept performance. Clearly, he wanted to protect the passengers in his care from unnecessary intrusions.

Those passengers could not believe their eyes. Glancing up, they were in time to see a body on a stretcher being inexpertly carried in a faltering motion above their heads. I peered gingerly over the side of my exceedingly wobbly stretcher to catch their astonished gazes.

Feeling rather precarious, I knew that at any moment I could make their sudden and intimate acquaintance falling spread-eagled onto their laps. That danger was real and they sensed it acutely as they slunk lower in their seats. Smiling a friendly greeting, I passed overhead at an uncomfortably low altitude like a scene from a black comedy. But nobody laughed at my comic role as the angel of death waiting to fall from the ceiling upon their well-manicured luxury.

Reaching the seat allocated to me, our efficient steward smiled benignly at us. Looking towards Cathy who was just ahead of us, he said in a clear and friendly voice:

"Welcome aboard! Perhaps Madam is looking for the button located here." Mary and Cathy quickly found the correct button just at the end of his pointing finger. One push and the seat quickly converted into a bed. Humming steadily, it smoothly transformed itself into a flat kidney shaped alcove. It looked inviting as they eased me gently down so that I could nestle exhausted into it. The drama of our journey had taken all of my energy.

"If there is anything at all that I can get you, do let me know," our steward continued.

"How do you manage to smile at all times," I half wondered and half muttered to myself, "especially on these long flights?"

"I will return in a moment with your aperitif order card," he beamed, and then he was gone—off to assist another passenger. Already the rich smells of first class food wafted through the comfortable cabin. An anticipation of luxury seemed to fill the air. I thought to myself how flying can feel so humdrum to some people—as ordinary as taking a bus, unless they guide the controls of a microlight aircraft or hang-glider to solo the Atlantic. But for our little family, this flight—one that had Cathy concerned I would actually survive—was no simple bus ride.

I busied myself by snuggling into the extra pillows we had brought to pad out my cot. On medical advice we chose to fly first class British Airways for one reason: this fully reclining bed-seat. Neither before nor since have I travelled in such opulence, but this long flight would be possible only because of the bed option on these seats. Safely lowered onto my bed, wrapped around with blankets, I nodded at the retreating team of stretcher-bearers. Tripping along between bewildered passengers, they beat a noisy path towards the door and the waiting platform. It lowered them silently to firm soil below, and in an instant they disappeared into the enveloping darkness of the African night.

I feel very warm towards these Kenyan men whose antics had all the essentials of a British pantomime or an old Ealing comedy. They went the extra mile in helpfulness to be caring to me, and their cheerful qualities endear me to these lovable people. Lacking the social sophistication of the West, they are deficient in the guile that accompanies it. When they are cheerful they just draw you into their fun, and when they are upset there can be no mistaking it. What you see is genuine, and it appears childlike to our cloaked and guarded manner of self-expression. In Africa life is simpler, more direct. They had helped me and I was grateful, and now I felt sad to leave their world behind as we circled somewhere over Mount Kenya, a mountain I have still to conquer.

I never was a mountain climber but I shall forever be in the debt of one—Hamish McIness, to be precise. A Scot of great renown in the world of mountain climbing, on one of his trips he set his mind to overcoming a pressing problem. When you climb Everest or K2, as he has done, you will at some point need to attend to nature's call. If you are a man, you face a tricky problem when needing to pay what my Kenyan friends describe as "a short call."

Gently explained, you face the question of how to accomplish it without suffering intense personal frostbite. Hamish will forever be a legend among grateful mountaineers for developing the "Hamish McIness Pee Bottle." Like all good ideas, it is deceptively simple. Instead of disengaging your personal equipment into the open air you simply place Hamish's equipment—the Pee Bottle— into position inside your clothing. When you are done, the bottle is removed and emptied with a gloved hand against the subzero temperatures, and all is well. At this point I want to say to Hamish—whom I have never met—thank you for your foresight and for your wisdom. You helped me out of quite a fix on that long flight home, my friend.

An essential condition of British Airways allowing me on their flight was that I had to be able to use the washroom facilities on board. Someone had told them, *Of course—no problem!* They lied. But Cathy, like Hamish, came prepared. Inside her duffel bag was a Hamish McIness Pee Bottle or, at least, its hospital equivalent. For me, this would test the absolute limits of my friendship with Cathy. But for Cathy, it appeared to be no chore at all. Each time I needed it—frequently due to the medication—she pulled out a crisply laundered and pressed pillowcase containing Hamish's brainchild.

As quietly and discretely as I could, I lowered it under my blanket and prayed desperately that everything was in perfect alignment as brief moments of deep relief began. Horror—to me—the tell tale sound resonated to fill the first class cabin. It began as a low drumming sound, turning to midtones of an alto saxophone, reaching the unmistakable ascending soprano notes of a bottle filling up. Alarmed, I looked up nervously to see who might have noticed. Thankfully, the cabin crew were busying themselves some way off with orders for food and drinks, while the passengers around me had their headphones on, gazing fixedly into their personal video screens.

So far, so good. Now came the tricky part of the procedure. Safe disengagement—done! Carefully, slowly, and under cover of my blanket, I replaced the bottle inside the pillowcase, trying to steady it to avoid a tidal wave inside the bottle. Taking a quick peek, everything looked as it should. Catching Cathy's eye, I passed the bottle wrapped in the pillowcase over to her. Standing, she stood to receive it and moved deftly towards the washroom all in one easy move, as if everything was just as normal as could be. Less than a minute later I sensed her presence again as she returned. I had not so much heard her, as I had smelled her sweet re-entry. She had washed the bottle thoroughly, and with the complimentary first class body spray, had generously saturated it with perfume. It filled the cabin with a delicious floral top note like a mountain-meadow breeze.

Hamish, did you ever imagine that innovation upon your good idea? How could any self-respecting Everest team get to the top of their climb without the heady whiff of BA's first class, complimentary body spray? Surely, a splash or two might add a *joie de vivre* to restore a spring to their step as they wearily climbed to the same high altitude as our current flight path.

Our steward served us the finest selection of world cuisine. While other passengers scanned the menu, tucked in eagerly to the finest fare, and sipped their wines of note, I ate nothing. Even the legendary Hamish has not yet found a way of helping me around the rather more intense challenge of eating—and its natural consequences. Any business more serious than a "short call" to the washroom was to be avoided at all costs. I watched the food passing me by and appreciated the artistry of the nouveau cuisine. Presented on fine china, it formed a work of culinary art. Swirls of legumes, balanced against the well-placed and carefully reckless splashes of sauce, exquisitely graced plates now passing me at nose level—but I could not eat.

Just recently, on a flight from Heathrow to Glasgow, I sat next to an older Scottish gentleman. Telling him this part of my story, he smiled broadly and recounted how he had spent the previous weekend hill walking with Hamish McIness. As I write, that veteran walker is still hail and hearty and is to be seen most weekends walking along the Pap of Glencoe. Does he, I wonder, carry a bottle in a pillow case—or floral body spray—on his travels? I suppose not.

Mary tells me that I became an embarrassment on that flight home. Apparently I could not stop talking—loudly—and she had to shut me down repeatedly throughout the long journey to London. My chattering bothered other passengers who huffed accusingly in my direction, but I remained unaware of the disturbance I caused. Mary handled me calmly and firmly, lifting her finger to my lips each time I tried to launch into another long, loud story. Eventually, the dulling drone of the engines lulled me gently into a deep and dreamless slumber.

I do not remember our arrival in London, as if someone clumsily cut and edited my version of the journey, leaving significant gaps in the flow of events. Cut to hotel room: we took three rooms at the Airport Hilton. Cathy retired to her own room, worn out by her constant attentiveness to Mary and me, and now ready to catch some sleep. Mary's sister, Ruth, was waiting for us as we entered our room, and she—an experienced nurse—helped the ambulance men to transfer me to a large, comfortable hotel bed. Ruth was on hand to take over from Cathy and swiftly and professionally gave me a bed bath and a welcome change of pajamas. It felt so good to freshen up, but the small effort involved on my part exhausted me nonetheless. I nuzzled down and promptly slept for seven hours straight.

In the third hotel room, members of our extended family gathered in an impromptu family reunion. Chatting animatedly, they quickly caught up on news as they waited for me to awake and greet them. My children preferred to explore the hotel and its shops together with their cousins. I don't remember the complete register of who gathered there at the Hilton that day. But I do remember the light carnival atmosphere that filled my room as visitors came in to see me. It was Mardi Gras combined with a genuine concern shown by my visitors, and I drank my fill of their deep love.

At that time—and for a couple of years or more—I suffered from disinhibitionism and a new, if inappropriate, social freedom that it gave me. The inability to hold back will often indicate that a particular location in the brain has been impaired. So, I pulled back my covers in the Hilton again and again to show my visitors my scars. But at this stage I had not yet received my clean pajamas, or, indeed, any pajamas. They saw me as they had never seen me before—or would ever wish to see me again. I hauled those covers off me with careless disregard—and Mary tugged them rapidly back again, apologizing red-faced to those who gathered.

I could not work out what was wrong, but it did not stop me from repeating the ritual to all my visitors in the months ahead. It was a challenge for company to move from this inappropriate display of scars towards a more meditative mood of praying for me, but usually they did it smoothly, without revealing their discomfort.

Our transfer from the hotel back to Heathrow airport signalled the beginning of the final leg of our journey to Vancouver. We travelled in a spacious, American-built ambulance that had every imaginable piece of equipment on board—in striking contrast to its Kenyan counterpart. The totally professional crew was trained to the highest standard of excellence and added their own brand of Londoners' wit and humour. Nothing was a problem to them, and in no time at all, we were on the aircraft and in the air.

I remember nothing of that flight. But I do remember arriving in Vancouver on Halloween night, 1997. Unseasonably cold after Africa, it rained steadily in a West Coast drenching downpour. Unknown to me, my stellar hopes were unrealistically high. I had come home to Canada where I knew my healing would be guaranteed, my recovery automatic and rapid—if not instantaneous—at least in my unreasonable estimation. My goal was simple—I was to make a 120 percent recovery.

Part of any recovery process is the restoration of a fractured hope, and with it a renewed new sense of a future. But that future is sure only when it is rooted firmly in God. More than any medical system, country of promise, or material provision, He alone is our future. Gerhard Ebeling makes that observation strongly when he says:

> Faith confesses that God is the future.... If you confess God as the future, then the future becomes quite different, even though and just because you have the same future before you as everyone else of your time. Faith creates a new and true future, in that while enduring this human, all too human, future, it praises God as the future, and so transforms the face of this human future.[16]

My family's future involved a return, with our children, to Canada where they had grown up and where we had discovered a home. God was profoundly involved in this process of piecing our fragmented lives back together. *"So there is hope for your future,"* declares the LORD. *"Your children will return to their own land"* (Jeremiah 31:17). That is how it was for us—a hope, a future, and a return to our own land. Yet such hope promises us no more certainty of any particular outcome or guarantee of our anticipated results than does an experiment whose outcome is unknown.

Trust is about letting go of desperation, releasing the overwhelming desire for the small details and anticipated particulars of our lives to be fulfilled. It is letting go of what we want so much to control, and trust is required for hope to thrive. Trust knows that whatever transpires we rest in a place of ultimate security. Peace is being able to say from a deep place in your spirit *it is well with my soul*—and meaning it while enormous challenges confront you. Trusting in hope is to be acquainted with risk. It is, after all, within the nature of an experiment to fail. Hope is that kind of experiment; it will not guarantee predicted outcomes. Hope, however, does not disappoint us. It sustains us through the shocks we experience along our journey of faith. Jürgen Moltmann understands this well when he writes:

Hope is an experiment with God, with oneself, and with history. If one begins with experiences, one arrives with some degree of maturity at wisdom. But the proverbs, which express the everyday wisdom of experience, tend to emphasize resignation more than hope: "He who lives on hope dies of hunger." But if we look more closely at beginnings, we shall see that every beginning contains a surplus of hope. Otherwise one would begin nothing new but remain as one is and hold on to what one has. Whoever begins in hope is aiming to create new experiences. Hope does not guarantee that one will have only the wished-for experiences. Life in hope entails risk and leads one into danger and confirmation, disappointment and surprise. We must therefore speak of the experiment of hope.[17]

Our family's return to Canada was such an experiment in hope. It began with unrealistically high hopes that were soon to be dashed. Like trading in a bull market, our expectations took a major "correction," coming down to a more balanced, reality-based equilibrium. The ground of our hope was cleared of debris from our initial, disappointed anticipation. Those hopes illustrate the kind of expectations that are brittle and easily fractured, controlling and quickly broken.

Clearing away those wrecked pieces created the space for a real and deeper hope to emerge. Such hope is larger than our circumstances and focuses on ultimate, long-term prospects rather than short-term provisional ambitions. We received a deeper hope as God's gift to us. It involved then, as it involves today, learning to bloom where we are planted—even in the face of pain—with the sure promise that the bruised reed He will not break. To bloom in a desert is an unwelcome challenge—and our old home city of Vancouver suddenly felt like a Sahara of impossibilities. How could such a familiar place suddenly feel so strange and hostile? How does the familiar place become an isolating desert shore? Until hope slowly re-emerged nothing could—or would—seem right any more. How could it?

CHAPTER TEN

A Hope and a Future

There is surely a future hope for you,
and your hope will not be cut off
(Proverbs 23:18).

It was a sellout. Nearly all of the 2,800 seats were occupied. One member of the management team was overheard saying, "The Vancouver Orpheum never gets this full, even for visiting musicians and special concerts!" One thing was clear, however, they had not come to hear me—even though I was due to speak for two minutes in this two-hour program.

Each year on Easter Sunday, First Baptist Church takes over the large concert hall, home to the Vancouver Symphony Orchestra, for a colourful extravaganza of celebration in music, song, and the spoken word. Choirs, soloists, and ensembles fill this large auditorium with a rich variety of blended sounds. A superb selection of traditional and contemporary praise music pulls everyone along in joyful worship fit to raise the roof. In 1999, almost two years after my accident—walking with a cane and still experiencing low-grade chronic pain—I was delighted to be able to play a small part.

A highlight of this event is the presentation of a special annual award given for service to the community. In past years, the award has honoured the Vancouver Police, the Palliative Care Unit of St. Paul's Hospital, and others who have given value to the wider city neighbourhood. It is given to organizations making a significant difference in the lives of the people of Vancouver.

In a bygone age, when church adherents were the majority of the population, the community would take note of the church and all that its members did. Now a visible minority, church people have begun to take note of the community, applauding and affirming what is praiseworthy within it, wherever they find it. Dr. Bruce Milne, the minister at First Baptist, stands before a capacity audience at these events to do just that. He builds—with characteristic, casual brilliance—significant bridges into the lives of the people of that city. This is never clearer than when he publicly recognizes acts of heroic kindness or consistent care within his community.

"One year," he told me, "two burly policemen stood to receive the award on behalf of their colleagues in the force. They looked streetwise and work hardened. They'd seen it all in the course of their work. The streets of downtown Vancouver can be tough. But there was still one thing they hadn't seen." Bruce's tone became very warm. "Two little girls from Sunday School, carrying huge floral bouquets as big as themselves, climbed the steps up onto the stage. Everyone watched in hushed anticipation as they stepped forward. They looked up into the eyes of the two muscle-bound policemen and presented their bouquets to each of them. Choking back their moist-eyed emotion, these men said to me, 'Nobody has ever said "thank you" to us before for being policemen.'"

On this occasion, the award was about to be presented to another group serving the community in outstanding ways—the GF Strong Rehabilitation Centre. I have many personal reasons to call their work outstanding. I had, by then, spent eighteen months—with still more to come—in their Acquired Brain Injury programme. On that day, Bruce Milne allowed me the honour of bringing some carefully chosen words of thanks. With a full heart I addressed my expressions of gratitude to the therapists and care team that had become like my other family—so central to my recovery and to my life. I would introduce the presentation of the award and I was as delighted as I was anxious to do a good job—for Bruce and for these outstanding professionals who had poured themselves into my life. They had done it generously and well over long months of rehab, and as best I could, I wanted to return the compliment.

I cleared my throat and walked unsteadily to the podium at centre stage, leaning heavily on my cane. Like a Dickensian novel, this was the best of times and the worst of times for me. My foot raged in pain, swollen and hot as I limped forward making every step a study in agony. As soon as I left the building, I was to be taken to the emergency department at Vancouver General to be checked over, fearing this to be the day I would lose my foot to amputation, so intense was the pain.

I swallowed hard as I looked out at hundreds of people silently gathered there. Scanning the eyes of the audience, I recognized many faces—family, friends, and acquaintances. Like a sprinkling of pepper they lightly seasoned the crowd that day. How special to be among so many good friends. I smiled warmly, delighted to see nearly two dozen of my therapists coming to witness the presentation of this community award. It was to them that I addressed my remarks.

I paused briefly—not for dramatic effect but simply to collect my thoughts. I focused hard, fighting to concentrate on this moment and upon my present task. I deliberately put out of my mind the internal babble of conversation buzzing loudly through my head: *Do I look okay? Will I make it through without blubbering? How can I see this script clearly under the glare of such bright stage lights? How will I hold the paper straight and steady at an angle where my double vision will not bother me?* So many worries; so many distractions to overcome.

I breathed several deep breaths and slowly let them out between clenched teeth. I needed to compose myself, to gather my thoughts. I wanted to sharpen my focus on the job at hand and block out all diversions, and that meant a lot of blocking out for me to practice in that large theatre. But there was so much more going on in the smaller auditorium inside my head. Then, with my voice bursting with deep feelings of gratitude, I made my start.

"Today," I began strongly—and at once was startled by the sound of my booming, amplified voice filling every corner and crevice of the huge concert hall. Recovering quickly, and hoping the timbre of my voice would not break shakily, I continued. "Today, we honour many highly skilled and deeply gifted specialists who are the driving force that is the GF Strong Rehabilitation Centre. Their dedication makes it a leading North American rehab centre and Vancouver is privileged to own them."

"Specialists at GF Strong give their co-ordinated care to people suffering spinal cord injuries, crippling arthritis, paraplegia and quadriplegia, strokes and aneurysms, traumatic brain injuries, Lou Gehrig's disease and much, much more."

I felt the tears welling up from somewhere deep inside me. I knew I had to fight them, or I would be awash in an emotional flood, quite unable to finish. It all began to feel very personal. I had wanted it that way, knowing that I needed desperately to keep it personal. It was the only way I could pull it off. Injuries of this kind are, after all, personally devastating. They do not happen neatly at arm's length; they are ugly and embarrassingly messy. They invade our private and personal space, violating our self-understanding. Every patient I know, each one I have spoken with at rehab, would affirm that this is so. I continued with a personal reference.

"I arrived at GF Strong sixteen months ago using a wheelchair and crutches. Today, thanks to their care, I am slowly progressing along a challenging and uncharted course called 'recovery.'"

Now, I fully confess that I've fallen in love with just about every one of my therapists. I am not talking about romance or inappropriate behaviour. I mean a real relationship of trust and an intentional and warm openness. When you are so debilitated and someone shows you genuine concern, kindness can break your heart; concern and care steal a chunk of your affections. In return for their professional attention and personal concern, you gladly give them a small piece of your fragmented heart.

"My deep, personal thanks," I continued, "go to my particular team in the Acquired Brain Injury programme.

"To Laurena in Physiotherapy—you believed in me and taught me to walk again.

"To Marnie and Bill in Pool Therapy—with your help I took my first baby steps after four months of not being able to walk.

"To Dorothy and Radha in Occupational Therapy—you showed me I can be useful again—whatever!

"To Agnes-Mac, Susan, Cathy, Linda and Teresa—your smiles and kind words mean more than I can say.

"To Catherine in Music Therapy—you returned to me the courage I needed to pick up my trumpet and to play it once more before a musically astute audience.

"To the two Jennifers—your Skills group gave me practical strategies to cope with my challenges and the courage to speak in public once again.

"To Dr. Verna and Anita—your Emotional Support group gave us a path from despair to hope with space for tears along the way.

"To Dorothy, my nutritionist—you helped me shed some weight and protect my joints and my damaged foot.

"To Alison—your patience, care, and wisdom restore my hope of someday working once again.

"To Dr. Gabriel—your keen eye noted injuries that others had overlooked.

"To Dr. Maribeth—you held my pain, you understood who I am, you taught me to name my fears, to face them, and then to dare to go beyond them.

"To Chaplain Laura, at my hospital bedside—you listened so well, and you prayed for me when I could not pray for myself."

What a team! And what commitment to making me functional again. But not for me alone was their effort given. This is what they do, day in and day out, through the four seasons of each year. Every client receives their personal and complete attention, and many of us feel them to be our friends.

"Allow me now," I said, "to be the voice of every resident and every outpatient like myself. Words are simply not sufficient to tell you how deep our gratitude is to you all. To every ancillary worker, secretary, receptionist, administrator, therapist, specialist and doctor—thank you for your care, your skill, and your compassionate professionalism. To each of you from each of us, we bring warm thanks. Today, we thank God for you, we honour you, and we say from every deep place within us 'thank you.'"

I would like to tell you that I made it to the end of my short monologue without the sting of hot tears blurring my vision—but I didn't. My voice began to crack somewhere towards the end. I took deep and steady breaths to fight my way through to the finish. But my wet eyes were not the only tears that glistened moist and warm during that presentation. The giving and receiving of thanks, deep thanks, is profoundly moving and deeply healing. I do not think that I do enough of that kind of thanking—enough of any kind of thanking—in my life.

Patti Flaherty, an educator within the Rehab Centre came forward to receive the award on behalf of her colleagues. The warm hug she gave me became a fitting symbol for the way this organization and its team of outstanding caregivers embraces the lives of its clients—every one of them. Arriving in all kinds of conditions their clients share one key characteristic. Each is *in extremis,* in some way pushed to their limits and beyond. Regardless of a therapist's particular specialty, there is one commodity that each handles daily, dishing it out in huge quantities. It is hope—and hope's gift is to endow us with a future that goes beyond our present infirmities, our overwhelming challenges.

My experience echoes that of so many other patients. We arrive at rehab having been robbed of hope somewhere along the way—deprived completely, beaten and stripped naked. We have little concern for what we have and for what we can do. Instead, we are focused on all that we have lost, all that we cannot do any longer—and maybe, will never manage to do again. We are traumatized by a profound sense of personal diminution, and private violation.

Each therapist then takes us into his or her care, one on one, an hour at a time. They never talk about what we cannot do. Instead, they begin to re-orient us, to turn us right around. They focus on just two or three small things that we are able do with their help—things we can do today. And they show us how. They watch our first attempts, correcting us, and encouraging us to try another way to accomplish something, and to do it right.

Then we go away to our homes or to our wardrooms and we practise, practise, and practise again. Quite soon—in fact, astonishingly quickly—we realize that we can do these specific things and do them quite well. Returning to our therapists, they show us two or three more—small but hugely significant—things that we can do. Almost before we realize it, we suddenly have a whole repertoire of learned skills. It is small but growing daily, and we are learning that there might be hope, even for us. We are able to put into practice more and more as we rehearse the skills of living again, and trying to live well.

Suddenly—and almost despite ourselves—hope begins to re-emerge. The small green shoots of recovery break through the frosty soil of adversity. The apostle Paul understood this synergy: sharing in suffering can give birth to hope. He realized that hope is a shared experience lived in community together. We hope for one another; we comfort each other with hope, especially when another is suffering. He puts it this way: *And our hope for you is firm, because we know that just as you share in our sufferings, so also you share in our comfort* (2 Corinthians 1:7).

It is real, this hope, and the comfort it brings is enormous. It is tangible and it makes a measurable difference to our lives. Hope is there, right before our eyes. It is the evidence that winter will someday soon be gone and spring will come—despite the lingering winter's darkness. Arriving with colour and freshness, hope is warm sunshine and blue skies after ice and fog. It bursts with the promise that summer is coming soon. It fills our gray lives with a power that can utterly transform, for that is the nature of hope. And already we almost hear those sounds of spring as birds again begin to sing. If not today, then the waiting will not be long, for hope will not disappoint us.

Beyond the straining, the tears, and the grunting of physiotherapy—and every other kind of therapy on offer—rehab is simply defined as the giving back of hope, a reason to go on living. In the long hiatus of waiting that recovery imposes, hope becomes essential for finding meaning for life. Henri Nouwen puts it well when he says: "To weep, to keep vigil, to wait for the dawn, perhaps that's what it means to be human."

In this waiting time it becomes profoundly comforting to receive the company of others who will wait with you. Waiting is essentially a spiritual activity. Simone Weil accurately pinpoints this insight when she says: "Waiting patiently in expectation is the essence of the spiritual life." Therapists have caught something of the deep spirituality of what they do, though few of them would describe it in those terms or in the conventional coded language of church. However, each therapist who worked with me was more than ready to talk openly and with self-disclosure. I would say to them, "You know, it's none of my darn business but if someone like me were to ask someone like you 'Where are you on your journey of faith?' what would you say?" Astonishingly, they gave me their ready answers. Each of them had plenty to tell me—regardless of where they might be along this path. Their candid openness became a bridge over which many rich insights were traded back and forth.

Faith is a journey of discovering ultimate values—and we are all on it. Some choose to ground their experience under the umbrella of truth that is God's story, outlined in His dealings with His biblical people. When I read my own narrative, and weigh the text of my life, I deliberately place it within that meta-narrative, the overarching story of the nature of God—His acts of love in dealing with His people. The writings of those biblical authors record His tender involvement with His world. Hope grows as we read our own story in that light, and against the backdrop of this bigger story in which we find ourselves. Our story is caught up within it as it becomes part of the ultimate resolution of our pain, and healing for our brokenness. This is the hope towards which God is moving us, if we will let Him.

Someone recently commented, "Paul, the problem with you is that you sometimes come across to me as sounding very sanctimonious." I raised an eyebrow waiting for the humorous punch line. But it never came. I realized she was serious. It stung, of course, but then I started to feel almost grateful.

"Call me on it, please. Hold me to account," I said to her, "every time you hear me speaking in that way." I guess my challenge, and maybe yours too, if you are a believer, is to be sanctified without becoming sanctimonious. I hesitate somewhat as I write, for I want to express those things I have discovered to be dependable and true, without descending into dead religiosity. It is the relational dimension of faith that interests me. That is a dimension that includes my relationship with others and with God, the God from whom I discover my faith and receive my hope.

Faith's journey is about ultimate values—the things that matter most as we face the deep issues of our own mortality. Faith is about the things that we, one day, might be prepared to die for—the values that will remain long after we have gone. Faith is a long and irregular journey, and each of us is already on it—wherever we may be in our lives. The pathway of faith is a trail marked by milestones along the way. They memorialize the significant moments we encounter, instances of growth and sometimes of defeat.

For me, a primary and major milestone came early in my journey, when I encountered the undeniable reality of Christ. I experienced His profound and amazing love for me and received for myself His deep forgiveness. It did not make me perfect or fault free, just forgiven and free of the dreadful weight of guilt that I had shouldered for far too long. This was my defining moment.

It is the event that continues to shape my life and out of it grows my self-understanding. All that has come after it is interpreted in the light of it. Everything acquires its measure of significance and becomes meaningful only as it is measured against it.

This encounter is a benchmark and a measuring rod. It does not shift, even at times when everything else in life seems to move or fall apart in the chaos of an earthquake-sized event's undulating turmoil. This encounter with Christ becomes the anchor to steady my life, to stabilize my rocking and otherwise rudderless boat. It is firm and steady even—especially—in times when nothing, for now, seems any longer to make sense.

Faith and hope are intimately connected. One speaks of the other. Faith believes and, therefore, hopes as it looks forward to the fulfillment of faith. Yet hope stands taller than mere wishful thinking. Hope trusts for the thing in which it is invested—it trusts that it will come about and, therefore, it speaks of faith. Hope and faith are thus intertwined. Like Siamese twins, they cannot easily be separated. To do so risks damaging either one or the other. Jürgen Moltmann, the German theologian, puts it this way:

> Without faith's knowledge of Christ, hope becomes a utopia and remains hanging in the air. But without hope, faith falls to pieces, becomes a faint-hearted and ultimately a dead faith. It is through faith that man finds the path of true life, but it is only hope that keeps him on the path. Thus it is that faith in Christ gives hope its assurance. Thus it is that hope gives faith in Christ its breadth and leads to life."[18]

Old King Solomon, that wise ruler, understood this intimate faith-hope connection. He traveled the faith-hope corridor on his journey of faith. He achieved astonishing successes and garnered deep wisdom as he did so. Yet, in his advancing years towards the end of his life, he began to turn cynical and sour. It seems he had begun to focus more on national success than on remaining motivated by faith and hope.

As your faith grows it is as if a voice speaks to you. As you hear it, a deep excitement grips you and your hope begins once more to be stimulated. But you cannot "unsee" what you have once seen. Solomon had seen the hope that springs from faith. He knew that as his faith deepened, his certainty grew. He felt the deep assurance expressed in his proverb. I wonder if he gave this proverb as a gift to a friend, or perhaps he simply rehearsed the truth of it to himself, reminding himself again of what he knew. He put it this way: *There is surely a future hope for you, and your hope will not be cut off* (Proverbs 23:18).

Such certainty is precious beyond the scope of national policy, military strategy, or economic planning. It is more valuable than personal monetary gain. It feels even more priceless when hope returns after it has been shaken loose, bruised, or has fallen from view. Solomon invites us to join him in a risk-taking venture, to walk with him along the faith-hope corridor as we journey together in faith.

Hope is not hurried nor hasty in its grasp upon answers that are too easy, preferring quietly to wait until its time is fully come. When false hopes have everywhere faltered and failed it springs up undaunted. Unnoticed, at first, hope drives down into faith's rich soil with roots that seek depth. As it grows steady and strong, hope is not troubled by clouds of darkness, fickle breezes, or petulant storms. Between the most heartless of rocks on the journey of faith, hope appears undaunted.

One rock is able to make the pilgrim stumble along the personal journey of faith—it is deep personal pain—the kind that wounds the spirit. Into each traveller's path may fall some pain of that kind as I would soon discover. Some unwelcome surprises still lay in store.

Pain is the gift that nobody wants, and woe unto the one who holds it when the music stops. It would soon be my turn again to unwrap pain's parcel. How does hope endure such pain? My questions sought answers, but the answers are worth hearing.

Would the conclusions I mumbled persuade me more than the questions that dogged me? Time alone would tell—but the clock began to tick interminably slowly as the early weeks of recovery stretched into years of yawning questions. Would hope be strong enough to lighten their load? Could hope recover days held captive to injury? Would hope teach me how to reach out for tomorrow while releasing yesterday's regrets?

I longed to believe it would, as much as I feared imminent disappointment. Cheap answers were readily available. What of my availability to God? Would I receive His timely answers? Is that why He waits, keeping me waiting on Him? Answers lingered yet.

CHAPTER ELEVEN

Oh Canada!

And as if this were not enough in your sight, O God, you have spoken about the future of the house of your servant. You have looked on me as though I were the most exalted of men, O LORD God (1 Chronicles 17:17).

Stories with sad endings bother me; they leave me unsettled. Either the story has finished too soon, leaving me hanging over the tragic edge of a precipice, or the storyteller deliberately intends me to feel rotten. If that were the author's intent then I feel it to be an unworthy goal—maybe even a little underhanded. Moreover, the thought that a writer may intentionally wish to cause me a sense of unease is a sting that wounds.

Tragedies happen, of course, and they are deeply disturbing. They can be painted with a sunny disposition at risk of doing violence to the truth of their pain. I do not dispute the tragic. However, I look for redemptive features that emerge through even the bleakest of circumstances. Partly, I like a story to have a happy ending—but a credible one. Also, however, I cherish a core belief that, in the end, good wins over evil.

I like the way a story with a happy ending wrestles painful, torrid and twisted issues, and somehow straightens them out in the end. When I read a book, I like to wait and puzzle out the happy ending ahead of time. In my daily life, I prefer to hasten to a happy ending and avoid the pain, because pain hurts too much.

Yet, in lived experience happy endings frequently arrive only after ugly scenes, or at the end of extended narratives of anguish, or dramatically nail-biting episodes, if that happy ending comes at all. Sometimes the cheery conclusion remains on hold or is deleted.

The words of thanks I offered on that Easter Sunday at the Orpheum Theatre for my rehab care team were deep and sincere. I was in a contented space then, though not yet at a happy ending. Many painful moments were to follow—moments I would entirely wish to avoid. Instead, I wanted to move right along, directly towards the triumphant finale that I felt surely must one day come. Looking back to earlier days, I see that the path leading to the Orpheum Theater first had to traverse—as you doubtless have guessed—some complicated and intimidating territory. Two moments of challenge stand out clearly in my mind.

Challenges have an odd way of creeping up on you. The first challenge moved stealthily upon me in that Nairobi hospital and was all about how unexpected or tricky transitions impact our self-understanding. Some psychologists observe what happens when we experience sudden shifts in our lives. They refer to the losses we are unprepared for, the ones about which we have not negotiated with others before those changes happen. We certainly never gave our consent or permission for them to explode in our face. They note that this kind of dramatic alteration to our circumstances sparks a significant emotional chain reaction within each of us. All change, they say, is registered as loss somewhere deep within us, acknowledged or not. All loss creates, they argue, a cycle of grief response within us. All grief, they conclude, leads in the end to some form of reciprocating anger.

So the big question that begins to worry each of us is, what will we do with our anger? Usually, we don't handle anger well—more often we handle it quite badly. As we deal with the energy of anger ineptly, we can do it in at least a couple of less helpful ways. The first is that we can respond in outbursts of rage and unfortunate displays of public anger. Our explosive eruptions, with their loss of control, inevitably frighten all of us. They especially disturb the people who witness them, putting them on edge in our presence. So, through experience, we learn to fear and to avoid extravagant anger responses whenever we possibly can. This may often lead, however, to a second unsatisfactory way to handle our anger. In becoming fearful of these outbursts, we simply swallow our anger, determined that it will not get the better of us. Our feelings slowly turn from a hot and destructive energy to a chronic low-grade depression stalking us wherever we go.

Festering repression is a toxic, destructive response to anger, no less harmful than an uncontrolled outburst. Anger when ignored or denied is first subverted and then diverted. It reappears in the form of chronic anxiety, and in its turn, anxiety disables us through subjecting its victims to debilitating terrorist attacks. Anxiety will suddenly paralyze its captive in both public and private settings. Subverted anger will self-morph into a neurosis of one kind or another—a functional nervous or emotional disorder often marked by depression or anxiety or both. Clearly, the way we deal with—or deny—our anger has a major impact upon both our own lives, and those of the people who know and love us most.

Should we, then, simply capitulate as the helpless victims of our own outbursts in an attempt not to subvert our anger? That is both misguided and wounding, for we remain personally responsible for how we choose to express surging feelings of anger. Are there, then, any better ways to handle anger? We might, for example, choose to take that extra response time that creates emotional space by stepping back at the first onset of anger. Does this buy some important emotional time? Can it allow us to choose an appropriate expression of our feelings? Yes, but only if the deliberate choice is made to resist the outburst and to elect more creative forms of response that spring from nonvengeful motivations.

Later, the need to return to deal with the underlying issues, when we are calmer, must be addressed. Counting to ten, or a hundred, or waiting an hour or three may be an appropriate delay mechanism to positively redirect those initial reactive feelings. A delay may allow the necessary emotional space to return later to address the issue. It buys the opportunity for reflection and evaluation of other possible options. Calmer discussion and reasoning may then have a fair chance to surface more clearly. The extra thinking time allows one to establish and use some principles for fair fighting in a personal conflict.

All these strategies—pause, ponder, postpone, plan, revisit—will help us. Yet, I have observed over many years that people of faith experience besetting problems when handling their anger. Often, they experience great difficulty admitting to themselves that their anger is real. Instead, they prefer to flat out deny it. Avoidance and denial may be as true for you as for others. Small wonder then that sometimes you will find yourself trounced at dealing effectively with the anger you refuse to admit exists.

For persons whose anger eventually erupts as rage against God, these difficulties are especially at work. How can people of faith find themselves so at odds with a loving heavenly Father? When they do, they feel understandably distressed, dislocated from a vital spiritual connection. They will often ask: *Am I allowed to be angry against a holy and a just God who does all things well?* They wonder: *Won't God, after all, just ditch me and abandon me to my anger? How can I get out of this lonely rebellion against Him? I feel sinful and sullied through it all.* They worry that their hostile feelings will put them beyond God's loving reach; they are certain that such feelings disqualify them from His care.

The time has come for them to read again—to absorb and to meditate upon—the book of Psalms. Throughout the history of the

Church the Psalms have been the prayer book/songbook for people of faith. Their dismissive critique by some biblical scholars caused the once widely held habit of reading them as personal devotional prayers to cease as a common practice among believers.

In recent years, however, the work of Eugene Peterson[19] and Walter Breuggeman[20] among others has helped to renew popular interest in the Psalms. They are the cry of the human heart, matching the heights and depths of life experience. King David, the best-known psalmist, remains a truly remarkable person for all generations. He is the one of whom God says: *"I have found David son of Jesse a man after my own heart; he will do everything I want him to do'"* (Acts 13:22).

Yet, this man in whom God's heartbeat finds an echo is able to shake his fist at the sky and rail against God in a number of his psalms. His anger is real and he does not deny it—instead, he gives voice to it. As he looks back on those times the psalmist says: *When my heart was grieved and my spirit embittered, I was senseless and ignorant; I was a brute beast before you* (Psalm 73:21–22). David pounds on the gates of heaven or even throws emotional rocks at God in primitive outbursts, petulant eruptions, or bad-tempered emotional upsurges. Amazingly, he continues to do so until God hears and answers his cry, or until he arrives at a new-found assurance for his praise to God: *I call on you, O God, for you will answer me; give ear to me and hear my prayer. Show the wonder of your great love, you who save by your right hand those who take refuge in you from their foes* (Psalm 17:6–7).

The Anglican Book of Common Prayer reminds us that the anger of man cannot work the righteousness of God. One Collect for the day asks God to turn the anger of man to the praise of our God. This seems to be a wonderfully healthy way for us to deal with our anger, allowing God to transform anger into praise. It is healthier than denying it—or exploding with anger at others—and using it as a lethal weapon of self-defense or brute attack.

In his angry explosions at God, David lost not one iota of his faith. He simply declined glib and easy answers, refusing to receive spiritual fakery like placebos from unthinking and religious well-wishers. Instead, he required authentic spiritual answers for his healing and genuine spiritual medicine for his well-being. He would rather wait to receive God's prescription for his situations in life where he is weighed down. He insists that God be God to him—doing for him the things he cannot do for himself. God is—after all—able. David discovers that God will hold both our honest questions and the deep anger in which they are frequently gift-wrapped.

David's anger—and ours, too—may surface in a condition the Bible describes as "poor," or "poor in spirit." Such poverty is not concerned with riches, for David is a wealthy national leader, a war hero, a popular writer of worship songs, and Israel's future king. But in Bible terms, he is undeniably "poor."

Poor because he lacks the resources to get himself out of the mess which entangles him. Putting it bluntly, if God does not show up for him—and pretty soon—it is "game over" for this man of God. He calls out: *O Lord, do not forsake me; be not far from me, O my God. Come quickly to help me, O Lord my Savior* (Psalm 38: 21–22). David is stressed and anxious.

At this point, it is important to observe how David turns *to* God and not *away* from Him, in his anger and despair. And in the end, God does not disappoint David. David's anger towards God becomes praise of God, as he worships the God with whom he wrestles. This is a transformative process in which David discovers God's majesty and power to rescue him when all other supports fail.

Astonishingly, in our pain we will frequently turn away from God towards more immediate kinds of support. Looking instead to our hoarded resources, our habit of self-reliance, we attempt to get by, yet quickly grow disillusioned upon discovering the bankruptcy of our moral and spiritual capital. It rapidly fails, turning out to be less than they promised. We are promptly shocked on receiving an "insufficient funds" notification from the bank of our own resources. Our means and our methods, skills and gifting, are simply unable—in the end—to match the overwhelming demands put upon us by life's complex and painful surprises, with their resulting stress and anger.

David demonstrates one manifestation of his annoyance on those occasions when his anger turns to urgency—his pressing need to ask the question: *Why?* He asks: *Why does the wicked man revile God? Why does he say to himself, "He won't call me to account"?* (Psalm 10:13). Or again: *My God, my God, why have you forsaken me? Why are you so far from saving me, so far from the words of my groaning?* (Psalm 22:1).

He enters a questioning dialogue with God: *I say to God my Rock, "Why have you forgotten me? Why must I go about mourning, oppressed by the enemy?"* (Psalm 42:9). David even questions himself, his thoughts and his feelings, and affirms his faith in God: *Why are you downcast, O my soul? Why so disturbed within me? Put your hope in God, for I will yet praise him, my Savior and my God* (Psalm 42:5).

Frequently, the *why* question bubbles to our minds' surface, too. It arrives in a variety of forms, such as "Why me—why this—why now?" In those early days after my accident, these were not my own particular questions. I do not claim any credit for that. They just did not happen to be the uncertainties that teased or occupied my mind. However, I did have a burning question that bothered me greatly and troubled me much. My urgent and compelling question was "Why am I alive?"

One day, as I lay in my bed at the Aga Khan Hospital, I finally addressed this question to God. I was surprised and taken aback, however, when—as he did with David—God answered me. I was not expecting that at all. I could hardly form a prayer as I lay in that hospital room. Never had I imagined that I might one day find myself in a place on my journey of faith where I could no longer pray. I am, after all, a professional pray-er—I even get paid for it. So why would I *not* be able to pray? Simply put, disaster can rob us of our words, especially words that might begin to build a prayer.

Finally, I heard myself quietly say: "Lord, why am I alive?" Immediately having voiced my nagging question I rolled over, psychologically at least, to rest awhile. It was as if God himself was sitting there on my pillow with me and I heard him speaking up close and personal in my left ear. Before the men in white coats come to carry me off to a place of quiet safety, let me explain. I did not hear that voice in a way that could be tape-recorded as an "audible other" in the room, but as a voice within. I had the profound conviction that this voice was God's voice speaking directly to me. I recognized the One whom angels worship, the One to whom all believing prayer is addressed.

I asked him: "Lord, why am I alive?"

"Well, it's not because you're white!" he said, and I was shocked. *Where did that come from?* I wondered. I felt chagrined by the bald announcement of my own deep-seated and carefully hidden superior tendencies—my working assumption that I am, after all, better than the people I came to serve.

"It's not because you are a minister or a missionary," God continued. This was getting decidedly uncomfortable but He had my full attention.

"It's not because you are a Baptist. It's not even because you are a Christian." This last statement would give me pause for thought for many months to come. One day, however, I understood its truth. God's love for me did not begin the day I committed all I am to Christ. Nor did His love for me commence when I submitted willingly to His Lordship over my life. His love predates my coming to Him. He first came to me, taking the initiative, not waiting for me to come to Him. He has known me and loved me before time began until now.

"It's not because I have 'some important work for you to do,'" He said emphatically.

"So why am I alive, Lord?"

"Because I love you, because I love you, because I love you," He concluded gently and strongly. I felt bathed in His peace, cherished in His love, and held close in His presence.

On reflection, it seems that God's reply addressed none of my intellectual questions, but totally satisfied my heart. The reality of His love and presence to me in those moments replaced my need—and stemmed my desire—to ask elementary questions of the sort that are logical, mechanical, or theological. There was no longer any need to voice such questions. God's presence was all. That answer, that assurance of His deep love for me, grew to be foundationally important. God only required that I receive it—no, that I receive Him—as a gift. This gift must be appropriated with more than a finite mind; also with an open heart with which He fully wants to engage.

That moment of initial challenge turned out to be one half of a twin event. The next moment of challenge—the second of the twin events—occurred a week or two later. I arrived in Vancouver to undergo my first round of surgeries. In the twenty-four hours following surgery, the doctors discovered that they could not control my pain. The discomfort was intense as the pain proved to be unresponsive to even the maximum safe doses of morphine. A few days later came a second round of surgeries. This time, I woke up unable to move, paralyzed, and in extreme pain. When they tried to lift my arm to take my pulse, I screamed out in agony. My joints puffed up, swollen and tender. I could not move. When I tried to operate the self-administered morphine pump with my thumb the effort produced extreme tenderness too sharp for me to bear.

Upon moving me to the intensive care unit, the duty nurse called Mary to let her know where I was in the hospital, and reminded her that she could visit me twenty-four hours a day. Ominously, she suggested that Mary should do that. When the care team nursing you thinks you are dying, they do not have to say a word to you about death. There is something in their manner, their huddled conversations and glances back to you over their shoulders, their nods and grave gestures that eloquently and loudly announce: *You are dying.*

With hands folded over my chest I felt and looked like a corpse. Somehow, I gathered enough words together to make a prayer: "Lord," I said, "I think I'm dying. Why am I dying?" As I spoke the word "dying" I suddenly knew that this could be tough for Mary and for our children. I trusted God to care for them—I had no other option. With no fight left, I had no steely will to continue to live, no positive mental attitude strong enough to lengthen my life. I was utterly empty; fully spent. Facing a death that I could do nothing to avoid, I had become one of the "poor in spirit" that the Gospels describe so accurately. I lacked all of the necessary resources to help myself. If God did not show up for me now it was "game over" for my life on earth.

Predictably, when God spoke to me a second time, I was as surprised then as I had been on that first occasion. Again, He sat on my pillow, right next to me, and spoke into my left ear. When I asked him, *Why am I dying, Lord?* he answered me, gently, simply and strongly, *Because I love you, because I love you, because I love you.*

In the moments that followed, I knew that it mattered not whether I lived or died. What really counted was whether I would live, or die, in the love of Christ. Could I do that? Would I set my heart towards that goal for whatever time remained for me? I had no energy of my own sufficient for this great task of living with my face towards God. And I was ready to slip away, to fly home to a God who deeply loves me. My intellectual questions remained unanswered, but it did not matter at all, for once more He had satisfied my heart, fully and completely. I knew no fear—only His love for me. Safe in the arms of Jesus, I experienced His strong and gentle embrace, holding me close. That was enough; there could be nothing more.

Like the biblical chronicler of old, I was amazed that God had spoken, and had spoken personally to me. His words were a good fit for my experience when He said: *And as if this were not enough in your sight, O God, you have spoken about the future of the house of your servant* (1 Chronicles 17:17). Together with the psalmist I, too, felt special. I had heard the voice of a loving Father and I, too, wanted to say: *You have looked on me as though I were the most exalted of men, O LORD God* (1 Chronicles 17:17). I am loved, truly loved, and how very good—so deeply healing—that feels. Such assurance takes you beyond the here and now towards an ultimate future—the hope of heaven itself.

An earlier generation of believers had discovered this to be true for their generation too, as J. I. Packer comments:

> One noticeable strength of the Puritans, setting them far apart from Western Christians today, was the firmness of their grip on the biblical teaching about the hope of heaven. Basic to their pastoral care was their understanding of the Christian's present life as a journey home, and they made much of encouraging God's people to look ahead and feast their hearts on what is to come. [21]

Such hope is firmly rooted in an anticipation of a future that is better than the present. People of faith—followers of Jesus—are, by definition, people who look forward to something better while working hard to make today the best it can be.

The intrusion of a catastrophic loss into the ordinariness of our days becomes a setback on our spiritual journey. It can knock us off course, for a season. Robbing us of our hope, we may lose sight of our destination. The recovery of hope is essentially a spiritual journey. Leading us far beyond the brutal boundaries of our present pain, hope moves us forward towards a promised future for Christian believers. Its guarantee is found in the biblical promise of a personal restoration patterned after the resurrection of Christ. It is given freely to all who follow Jesus as their resurrected, living Lord.

Between now and then, however, comes the practical challenge of living well enough to make a good death. That test still stretched before me, if I could live a little longer to face it.

CHAPTER TWELVE

The Home Run

But now, Lord, what do I look for?
My hope is in you (Psalm 39:7).

"What are you facing today, Paul?" I looked surprised at this question from one of my doctors. She gently explained what she meant. "Life is all about facing challenges, one after another. What is the challenge you are facing today?"

My first thought was to reply "Why, nothing, of course. Everything is just fine." However, no sooner had the words left my mouth than they were seen to be as thin and fragile as in reality they were. Almost in self-defense, I recited a litany of things that were going well. Pretty soon, however, we were into the things that were not going as well as I would have liked. Now we were dealing with a bundle of issues categorized under "the challenges I face today."

As I consider today's challenges, many are journey-of-faith issues. We face such spiritual challenges day by day. With each dawn new trials arise with tests and challenges in tow, and a natural inclination is to fear them. From their onset, overwhelming trials prove to be large enough to daunt and defeat the person of faith.

The voyage of recovery involves learning to face those fears head on—and even going forward to meet them. Sometimes, that same doctor would ask me, "So Paul, what are you avoiding today?" And I hated being confronted so starkly with my issues. But then she would help me understand how I might begin to confront them. To become intentional about facing the fearful helps a person to gain the strength to face them—mostly. Sometimes, I was simply unable to do that on my own.

On the journey of faith we are never alone. Though hidden frequently from our view, assistance is ever at hand. Help comes to prayer-folded hands; it is given by nail-printed hands, splintered by a cross. Hands that once curled in grief still bear great pain for others. This I see because they take hold of my deep anguish. They touch the tenderness of the challenges that face me today, the distress that suffering brings me. If I will let them, those nail-wounded hands will hold me close and bear me up.

This truth emerges when I am feeling low or drifting far from shore—distanced from the safety of friends or family. Does suffering still feel sore? Yes, for that is what pain does—it hurts deeply. I find it hard to understand the ache I must accept. Many of my friends cannot understand my hurt, and so it becomes an isolating experience. I begin to fear telling them, lest I burn out another friendship. But there is one Friend who understands my pain, and He does not grow weary of me.

In our journey of faith—no less than in our journey of recovery—we each must face our Goliath challenge, appearing as an armed giant. At those times, courage will sometimes falter as the temptation arises to retreat to an avoidance position. Avoidance, however, is a temporary shelter that will fail us should we attempt to stay there. We are pilgrims and the pathway towards our spiritual home will face us with moments of significant challenge.

Sometimes, just getting to the physical place we call home, the address where our mail arrives, has its own peculiar difficulties for us to face and overcome. That was to become the practical puzzle I was about to face, presenting its own faith challenges. My urgent need to find a place called home arrived as I faced imminent discharge from my Vancouver hospital.

The thought of leaving the hospital filled me with sheer terror. After seven long weeks in hospital, two chilling realities gripped me. The first, I suppose, was the simple realization that I had become institutionalized. I knew it—but could not fight it. I was simply terrified of leaving my hospital bed. This bed was at once both deeply uncomfortable and yet hugely secure. All of the help I needed—which was, in those early days, quite considerable—was right around me. But beyond that, I had lost a great deal of body mass. I felt weak and terrified of falling off the crutches that I had just begun learning to use. Once my full weight rested on them, I could barely control them. Like a circus clown, I teetered with ungainly forward progress on my stilts and imagined my audience to be laughing at my expense.

The doctors and nurses worked tirelessly, bowing beneath the pressure of a creaking health-care system. Like caregivers everywhere, the burden of high demand for medical care outstripping any adequate supply weighed them down. The doctors decided that they now needed my bed for another patient needier than I. Ready or not—and I was not—I'd have to be out and on my way. A minor drawback to their plan, however, was that I had nowhere to go, no place to call my home.

Mary and the children were staying in short-term, temporary accommodation, a small but comfortable missionary apartment too tiny to house everyone adequately. Our daughter, Naomi, then sixteen, slept on the floor in the lounge. Every nook or cranny was more than crammed with clothes, possessions (mere bric-a-brac!), and travel bags filled every corner. Still tightly packed and bulging, they awaited a place for Mary to empty them.

In her long, tiring days Mary made regular searches for an affordable rental property, between her twice daily visits to see me. Tired and stretched to her limits, she also had to keep house and look after our family. She could secure nothing big enough at a small enough price. So many houses presented stairs aplenty for climbing up to the front door—a huge challenge for me for many months to come. Wheelchairs and crutches dislike stairs—it seems they were not made for each other's company.

Our crisis became acute—I had nowhere suitable to go home to. Mary requested a visit from the hospital social worker who listened to me with concern about our plight. However, the physiotherapist saw me later that day and promptly came to our rescue. She watched me wobble drunkenly on my crutches for just five paces down the corridor before collapsing, exhausted, into the strong arms of a male nurse.

"No!" She said emphatically. "You just aren't ready to leave yet—I'll talk to the surgeons. They should've spoken to me before suggesting you be discharged." Her tone was adamant—she was gloriously unmovable. I sighed deeply in great relief as the surgeons responded to her scolding report by granting me a stay of execution, a short reprieve. Instead of leaving today, Thursday, they would hold over my discharge until next Monday.

The weekend was all the time Mary needed to secure exactly the right accommodation for us. A phone call later that day brought her news of it. The property had recently housed a local Anglican priest who had returned with his family to Australia. Mary viewed the house that night and our family moved in on Saturday morning, just thirty-six hours later.

They spent two busy days unpacking and sorting our few belongings. With no furnishings of our own, it should have taken just a few hours but Mary was receiving a constant stream of visitors. Amazingly, many of them were delivering every piece of furniture we needed—and some that we didn't. Some were on loan but most was ours for the keeping. The generosity of kind people from many local churches was overwhelming. They heard about our situation and freely opened their resources to us. They included delicious hot suppers each day, delivered to our door. People kept arriving with an array of culinary delights for more than two weeks. Their practical outpouring—love and care coming from so many good-hearted people—overwhelmed us.

Upon moving into our home, those early days of recovery dragged by in a dull slowness for me—nothing significant seemed to be happening in my long healing process. In truth, all recovery is filled with slow yet significant days, and every day my body fought hard—invisibly—to repair itself. My mind scrambled to understand things clearly, to remember names and events, to connect them together accurately and in ways that gave them meaning.

Many months of slow progress were to follow. To track your own progress you sometimes have to jump ahead in order to look back from a future vantage point. From there you can see more clearly that even an apparent plateau can be a springboard towards more progress. After a significant time lapse you can look back and compare how you once were with how you are now. This "then-and-now" approach is massively encouraging—especially when a friend meets you after a long absence and starts to enthuse with you about the real progress they can see. It is like an adult saying to a child: *My, how you have grown!* Unlike the child who winces at those comments, I was desperate to hear positive words of encouraging comparison. They sustained me wonderfully.

At the new home I slept in a borrowed hospital-style bed. With cot sides raised, I would not topple out during my frequent but short-lived moments of deep sleep. Mary slept on a foam mattress beside me on the floor in order to be near at hand, around the clock, to help me. She claimed that she was comfortable sleeping on the floor, but friends suspected she made too light of her own needs. Unable to walk safely on my healing fractures, I needed her assistance to get in and out of bed, to use the washroom, or just to move from room to room. I slept with fourteen pillows to prop me up and to elevate my massively swollen foot as I slept.

I suffered fatigue and needed to sleep a lot, maybe four or five times a day for a couple of hours at a time. During the day I spent long hours in our fireside room on a reclining chair that I operated with an electric switch. Adjusting it into a bed position, I would lay there quite still.

December in Vancouver is not particularly cold. It rarely drops below freezing, but I shivered uncontrollably. I had arrived from a hot country to a hot hospital then directly to a cool home—I had not acclimatized. Mary covered me with a couple of duvets as I lay motionless on that La-Z-Boy chair. I was terrified to move—I felt sure another bone or limb would break, or fall off completely.

Hope comes in many forms and in different shapes—often it walks on two legs and wears a warm smile. It sometimes knocks on your door before walking right into your life. It happened one day like that for me. At the end of my first week at home, the community physiotherapist visited me for the first time. I must have been on her duty list. She was in the late stages of pregnancy and looked wonderfully motherly. Her caring manner suited her to her role as a mom.

I said almost nothing to her as I lay there trapped in a cold, lonely space. I answered her questions with single, low syllables—more grunts than words. I knew the doctors had sent me home to die. In November, a month earlier, I was given an AIDS test; until the end of February I received no results. Even my family doctor had to fight to finally be given the all-clear for me. In those four months, I was convinced that I had been given bad blood in Nairobi and that I must have tested positive, so that I was now at home to die. Keeping my icy fear to myself, I could not bring myself to share those dark forebodings with my wife. Instead, I kept her at arm's length physically and emotionally. I was utterly isolated by fear; I couldn't see beyond it. Somebody had turned out the light and my world had become darker than I imagined was ever possible.

As I look back, my reactions don't seem to add up. They make little sense to me now, except to mirror my despair in those early days, struggling to feel well again. In poor shape emotionally, I handled sinister thoughts and unfathomable misgivings with little grace. Bursting into tears easily for no reason, I risked no further injury by simply not moving, thinking that I might last just a little longer that way. I had lost all confidence in my ability to last another day; I fully expected to die anytime soon. Catastrophic loss robs you of every shred of self-confidence—even self-belief in your ability to go on breathing.

After only the longest pause could I look up to meet the gentle eyes, the caring gaze, of the recently arrived physiotherapist. She spoke quietly and slowly: "I have been following your case with some interest for the last seven weeks."

"Why?" I asked in a tone of surprise that sounded like a scandalous accusation.

"We have been praying for you at our church," she replied with a profound depth of tender attention. Suddenly, I knew that someone had pulled back the curtain in heaven to let God's warm sunshine spotlight me there on that reclining chair where I lay. Instantly, I knew that someone was on my side; I was not, after all, alone. In those brief moments, the seeds of hope were planted for me.

Patiently, she showed me three simple exercises that I could do safely on my own, asking me to do them once daily. The moment she left I started those movements and did them again twice more before bed. At last, I knew three things that I could do without killing myself, opening wound sutures, or breaking more bones. It was a small but hugely important beginning for me. This was a critical first step along the bumpy road of recovery. Stepping out gladly, I knew then that a person beyond my family really understood and cared about me.

By June 30, 1998, the time lapse was complete—the one I needed to give me some perspective on my progress. By then, I was well enough to travel with my wheelchair to Calgary. Mary and I were invited to speak at a triennial gathering of Baptists, and felt excited but daunted at the thought of presenting at a major public event.

I felt completely overwhelmed at the prospect. It would be the first occasion for me to speak in public since our accident, and I was only too aware of the challenge of it all. I knew I had to speak about the pain I had suffered—that we all had suffered—in the nine months since the accident. Mary would also speak, and I knew she would tell it just the way it was. We would share in this event together—just as we had shared in the pain of the accident and in the challenges of the recovery process. I knew that I could not do this on my own. It felt very good to know that Mary would be there, right beside me.

Intuitively, we knew we had to address and connect with the pain of others in that large auditorium. For many months I had been learning with Mary's help to stay on topic when I spoke informally with visitors to our home. Frequently I would go off on a tangent, losing the plot of the conversation, unable to focus, forgetting the thread of discussion. I would embarrass myself and others. Mary could not trust me in normal social interactions, let alone in some attempt to communicate convincingly in public. For her own part, she was deeply troubled by the unwritten rule she felt that would compel her to give a Christian testimony to God's grace as if she once had a challenge, survived it, and was now gloriously over it all. This was a lie she could not tell, for life still felt hellish for Mary. She was trying to get to know her new husband, the new father of her children. He looked and sounded a lot like her old life partner, but he now was significantly changed, and not for the better.

Another speaker at the conference addressed the problem of the loss of transparency in our communities of faith. Encouraged by what she heard, Mary felt the courage to begin to speak movingly as a mother, with disarming honesty about her own struggles since our accident. She had tasted the agony of seeing her children in deep distress. She felt their emotional pain, walking with them through their spiritual struggles since landing back in Canada. She revealed her heart and her tears flowed freely.

Some months earlier, I awoke in the wee hours feeling God's prompting to write something to share at this event. Pulling out some scrap paper I sat in bed and wrote freely as I was prompted. At that time, we had not been invited to attend and had no way of getting there as paying guests. Yet, I had the profound assurance that we would be there and so, with only a few weeks left before the scheduled date of the meetings, we received our invitation, and I knew what I must say.

As I took my turn to speak, I catalogued the many symptoms that had painfully challenged me, and we both spoke with the authority that only experience bestows. Looking into the many faces before us, we reached into their pain, yet we spoke out of the experience of God's loving presence through it all. Wanting to build a bridge of hope from my grief into their pain, I began.

"I'd like to be personal with you for a moment, if I may." I prayed I would get through this without breaking down in a flood of tears that would wash away my words completely.

"I want to talk to *you* today," I continued, "if you are someone who suffers aches and pains in your limbs—aches that maybe never bothered you in earlier years; if you suffer with stiff and painful toes, or a limited mobility in your feet; if you get pain or swelling in your ankles, heels, knees or hip joints, or twinges in your back; if the scars of old injuries now pull tightly and awkwardly against your bones or muscles; if you have difficulty bending your knees or limitations in the movement of your arms; if you get tingling pins and needles or loss of blood supply to your fingers or toes; if your vision is blurred, your peripheral vision is limited, or you suffer from double vision and the nausea it causes; if metal plates in your face or body cause unusual sensations or pain; if your features are altered through injury and now you are embarrassed by the way you think others may perceive you; if a brain injury through trauma, stroke, or aneurysm has robbed you of your self-confidence or self-esteem; if you have suffered personality changes, subtle or very evident to your family and friends, making you feel like a stranger among those you love; if you have to take daily medication against pain or depression in order to normalize your condition and get through a day; if you have ever, even fleetingly, lost your hold on the sense of a hope and a future; if you walk now supported by crutches or canes or are confined to a wheelchair; if you cannot sleep at night and cannot stay alert and awake through the day; if you have ever wondered if the ones you love might not, after all, be better off without you; if you've known your pain to be too intense to bear and to last longer than anything should; if you have suffered the privation of having to depend totally on others to wash you, bathe you, dress you, feed you, and attend to your most personal needs; (or maybe you are the one who sacrificially gives your time to attend to these needs for someone you love); if you have lost the ability to drive your car, enjoy watching TV, or keep your interest while reading a book; if you have felt the walls of home to be a prison or public places put you into a panic; if you have lost the ability to concentrate or to remember, or the confidence to make sound decisions or appropriate social responses; if, despite the kind words of friends, you feel you have become a burden to others, especially those you love the most; if the sports you once played, the work you once loved, and the places you once cherished are closed to you now; then it is to *you* I am speaking today.

"To you I say: I think I understand a little, in some small way, something of your struggle. But, more than that, and much more importantly for you, even when my head can find no answers that make sense any more, my heart is comforted by the certainty that the Man of Calvary, Jesus of Nazareth, the Living Saviour, has borne my pain and loves me still, with a love that reaches beneath my tears, beyond the grave, and behind the disappointments of this life. Today, He draws alongside me, and tomorrow I know He will carry me home and wipe away every tear, ease every pain, and fill every sigh. Why? Because He loves me, because He loves me, because He loves me. And more than that, I am persuaded He also loves *you*! His love lasts from eternity to eternity. It is rich and real and deeper than your deepest need.

"And you can know and receive it for yourself as we pray this simple prayer together: The bruised reed you will not break and the smoking flax you will not quench. Almighty God, Master, Saviour, Loving Lord, speak your peace into our pain. Great Physician, bring your healing touch to our bodies, minds and spirits, we pray. And where you have chosen to keep us weak, teach us to depend on you, Mighty Lord, and to trust your promise that you will perfect your strength in our weakness.

"Father, we pray for those we know and love who are in pain today, physically, mentally or emotionally. We commend them to your unfailing love, dear Lord. Afresh today, we commit ourselves to bearing one another's burdens, not with cold orthodox answers or glib formulas, but with open hearts, ears to hear, and arms to embrace in Jesus' name.

"And Father, where our minds struggle for answers to difficult questions, comfort our hearts with the sure knowledge of your presence by your Holy Spirit. You promise never to leave us, never to abandon us. We trust you, Father; we take you at your Word, Lord Jesus; we depend on you, Holy Spirit. Draw near to us Spirit Divine. Do for us those things we cannot do for ourselves. Be our Lord and our God, our master and king. And we shall be careful to give you all the praise, the honour, and the worship that is due your holy name.

"Father, Son and Holy Spirit, we yield ourselves afresh to you this day. Reveal yourself to us now in these quiet moments together, even as we pray. In the strong, strong name of Jesus Christ our Lord. Amen."

As we spoke, first one person in the audience, then another began to break down in tears. One person started to sob loudly, and then everyone heard the haunting sounds of someone wailing noisily into his or her cupped hands. Two long lines of people formed at the close of that meeting along the aisles leading to the stage. One lineup was for me and one for Mary. People, mostly in tears, wanted to talk, pray, or deal with the pain they'd carried for too long. The first man in line said to me, "Thank you for your talk. It was so good."

"What about you?" I heard myself ask him. "Where's your pain?" Immediately his eyes filled with tears and he began to sob.

Sometimes, it takes only a gentle question from someone who is personally concerned about you to cause your emotional flood-gates to burst wide open. *But now, Lord, what do I look for?* asks the psalmist in Psalm 39:7. We all seek something more, especially for hope to be re-ignited after it has been doused. We look for hope in all the wrong places. The psalmist did, too. He finally found it in the One whose love is neither flippant, nor whimsical, nor partial. Coming to his own conclusion, he says: *My hope is in you.* That, too, is the place where so many look for hope, as Philip Yancey reminds us when he writes:

> I take hope in Jesus' scars. From the perspective of heaven, they represent the most horrible event that has ever happened in the history of the universe. Even that event, though—the crucifix-ion—Easter turned into a memory. Because of Easter, I can hope that the tears we shed, the blows we receive, the emotional pain, the heartache over lost friends and loved ones, all these will become memories, like Jesus' scars. Scars never completely go away, but neither do they hurt any longer. We will have re-created bodies, a recreated heaven and earth. We will have a new start, an Easter start. [22]

I think that might be a good place for us to start, you and I, if we both have tasted the grief of a wounded spirit. We could begin there to look for hope to flower once more. It is the right place to look for some assurance that there is a future stretching out for us beyond our present pain.

CHAPTER THIRTEEN

Family Matters

*We wait in hope for the LORD; he is
our help and our shield. In him our
hearts rejoice, for we trust in his
holy name* (Psalm 33:20–21).

"How's your family?" people ask me. But where can I start to answer that dangerously innocent question?

"They are all teenagers," I offer enigmatically with a smile. "Hey, what can I tell you? We have a house full of hormones!" I reply with guarded humour. I hope to avoid the painful details of the current minor crisis. With a large family a crisis is ever brewing. By the time I finish recounting it, the crisis will have passed already—and the next one started.

As I write, we have five teenagers living at home with their parents. Since the car wreck, our lives have felt at times like seven roller coasters—emotional and spiritual—but with no reliable brakes as we speed along a wet-and-wild adventure. Holding our breath, we pray that they will not be derailed or completely jump the wobbly tracks. Thankfully our individual emotional roller coasters are neither all up, nor all down, at any one time. There is usually some emotional surplus strength around so we can pull each other through those tough times. But one thing has become very clear—my accident has truly become *our* accident. Moreover, the research seems to validate our personal experience.

Within the medical profession these days, there is a growing body of research data that focuses on traumatic brain injury (TBI) and its effects upon entire families. This research focuses upon more than simply the brain injury survivor—it incorporates the whole family. The data shows that each family member becomes "the victim" of the brain injury in significant ways. Researchers stress that the injured person is not the only damaged person in a family. The family unit suffers injury, and so do close colleagues, peers, and the injured person's significant other. Friends and caregivers do not directly suffer the plight of the physically injured one. However, they witness and therefore share in the debilitating effects of loss or injury. The hurt will impact their lives—sometimes profoundly—as they continue to interact with the TBI survivor. Frequently, they will find they need to deal with important and linked issues, ranging from their own sense of shock and ongoing caregiver challenges, to the need to re-orient their relationship with this injured and changed person.

In one support group in which I participated, a social worker reported that when a child is injured or disabled, therapists and friends must deal with a disabled family. My own therapists not only agree with that statement, but are at pains to stress its validity over a wide range of injuries. One scholarly article begins:

> Brain injury is not an isolated incident in one person's life. It's a life-transforming event that affects not only the injured person but that person's family, friends and work mates.[23]

Health-care professionals dealing with traumatic brain injury resonate positively with those findings. So do support groups and associations working to help the families of acquired brain injury victims. One group says:

> The brain is the main control center for everything we do, think and feel. When someone's brain has been injured, that individual may no longer be able to do the things most of us take for granted—walk, talk, think, laugh, play, love. The individual's life and the lives of loved ones and friends will have changed forever.[24]

So what does that feel like? As an injured person it felt like I was on a steep, and often cruel, learning curve—and so were the significant people in my life. As a father and a husband, I watched their pain, helpless to ease it. Worse, I knew that my condition became the cause of their discomfort. John Goldingay, a British pastor-scholar, accurately describes the pain that he experiences as the life partner of a wounded person.

As a husband, he writes about his wife's multiple sclerosis. This illness prompted her to cease working as a psychologist. He struggles with the issue in terms of his understanding of God, and specifically in relation to the image of God within each of us, whether abled or disabled. Like many of us in a serious situation of challenge, he wrestles with the issues of identity—his own and God's, and God's identity within him. He wonders about how each of us—injured, wounded, or free from disability—bears God's image, and he wrestles with the implications that those realities hold for us. With honesty and insight, he writes:

> The presence of the disabled among those who are in God's image implies that the abled need to learn from the disabled how to go about creativity, world-making, control, and authority, just as the disabled need to learn from the abled.[25]

Disability faces us with many questions of faith. Some questions seem to have no easy or credible answers—even when we take the long-term view. The first days and months of recovery demand massive and radical readjustment for the family and for the victim of a traumatic injury. They often speed by in a blur of activity.

In the hurry and busyness that accompany the onset of an illness or loss, there is seldom time enough to reflect upon such new and disturbing experiences. Pragmatic demands press in. They squeeze the energy out of us, and the time we need to process our situation adequately—or at all. The family is overwhelmed by the need to bring practical and corrective solutions to the immediate series of challenges that face them. There is high involvement as everyone tries to ease the situation at hand. Activity predominates in these early days of recovery. The injured person may or may not even be conscious or *compus mentis*. He or she may not operate from the same shared understanding of what is real or important. She may be unable to engage in the lived realities of the moment. Even to communicate effectively or to relate normally in any way to those around her may be too much to expect. Frequently, this will cause deep distress for the noninjured family and bystanders.

The emotional effect of the accident or injury may be emotionally most devastating on the family and close friends, especially in the early moments following the accident or traumatic event. The injured one may not, after all, be fully aware of her own condition or the gravity of its impact upon others in her life. They, on the other hand, may experience all kinds of adverse reactions to the situation. Their responses might be anything from survivor's guilt to shock-induced emotional paralysis; from an immobilized helplessness to an unfocused flurry of frantic action; from a panic attack response to a total emotional withdrawal or uncontrolled hysteria. The negative possibilities are endless. In the midst of it all, the injured person may be mercifully unaware of either his own condition or the real upheaval that the family is suffering.

Looking back to those early days and months of recovery, I recognize that much of this applies to my own situation. I had no real awareness of how my condition caused such distress to my family. I had no accurate perception of how I looked physically, how I sounded to others, or the frequent departures from reality that I took in favour of inner-world excursions, full of distorted images and lines of meaning that made all the wrong connections.

Mary had to deal with my confusion as well as caring for our family, without even being able to explain to me—I wouldn't understand or remember, anyway—exactly what my condition was doing to our children or to her. When one person is in crisis, a family unit—and a circle of personal influence—is thrown out of kilter.

I use *family unit* in a loose and broader sense to include all the important people in the life of the injured party. The initial event that triggers the crisis is the same for the family as it is for the injured person. It is *de facto* a measurable and defined event that has happened and all can broadly agree on what that was. However, the nature of the crisis it generates for individual family members can be oceans apart from the kind of impact the event has on the injured person. Moreover, the positive responses of family members may, over time—or even right from the beginning—lapse into toxic forms of caregiving that in the end damage all concerned. The injured party is, too often, invested with all that ails the family as a system: *If only she were well again we would be alright, once more.*

How do we begin to understand and analyze some of those dynamics at work in this kind of family challenge? Experts who have studied the family as a system have come up with some interesting findings that serve as a helpful guide. They suggest that we need to widen our angle of vision, and focus on more than simply the individual victim of disability, loss, or pain. When we look more broadly, we notice that the family is like a complex web of causal relationships. It is a collection of friendship groups in a variety of different combinations in which the injured person is but one of many key players.

The Jewish rabbi and family therapist, Edwin H. Friedman, digs deeper.[26] He defines, enlarges, and applies some basic concepts of systemic family therapy. As I read him—and read my accident in the light of his insights—I begin to see our family dynamics at play. He moves us away from viewing the individual as the only victim, towards an understanding that the family, viewed as a system, is itself the victim demanding our attention. Cause and effect when viewed through the lens of this model become complex, nonlinear, and dynamic. Friedman sums it up this way:

> The most outstanding characteristic of systems thinking is its departure from traditional notions of linear cause and effect.... Each part of the system is connected to, or can have its own effect upon every other part. Each component, therefore, rather than having its own discrete identity or input, operates as a part of a larger whole. *The components do not function according to their "nature" but according to their position in the network.*[27]

My brain injury dramatically altered my position in my family's "web" of relationships. In so doing, it displaced us all. All our positions relative to each of the other family members changed in that moment. They still have not returned to the equilibrium that we knew before the accident. That may never return.

There likely will be a new kind of symmetry established that looks and feels quite different from the old one. To understand this, I sometimes imagine that all of us in our family have multiple invisible threads connecting each of us to all the others in the web, and in every conceivable combination. If one person is suddenly pushed out of balance, we all tumble and fall. If that person has not returned to her place in the group when we stand up again, then all of the dynamics within this complex web of connectivity remain changed. When one person is displaced, everyone is displaced.

Clearly, this way of viewing the family has enormous implications for all of us as we deal with the effects of a traumatic injury or illness. Instead of focusing upon the injured party—as in the standard medical model that treats only the patient—the focus becomes holistic: the family as a system. It is within this web of relationships where the injured person finds his position and place. Now, however, his position has been dramatically displaced with a resultant displacement of all the others within the system.

Interestingly, the question then becomes: *Can the family system itself correct this kind of imbalance—and how?* Friedman puts it clearly when he says:

> Instead of trying to analyze the infinite variety of A-Z connections in a system, it [*i.e., family systems theory*] once again treats the structure as a whole and tries to correct problems not by eliminating or fixing the "bad part," but by inserting new input designed to cancel out what has gone wrong.[28]

In other words, if we were to focus only on my getting better, that would not be sufficient to help my family. Ultimately, it is insufficient for them and for me.

As I drive my car, I sometimes take a local mountain road called the Coquihalla Highway. It heads over a long steep mountain incline, putting a huge strain on any vehicle. Alongside the highway there are cars and trucks that have broken down or are taking a break before continuing. My injury is like that highway. It, too, puts a huge strain on the vehicle of my family.

Like any other system—the engines of these vehicles, for example—a family system starts to blow at its weakest point. My illness or injury did not create the weak points in my family. Those weaknesses already existed in my family system before that time. My injuries simply produced some critical additional pressure on the system. That pressure will then cause the weak points, through failing, to identify themselves.

So in an odd kind of way, my injuries did us all the favour of pointing out some real, underlying issues we should now be working on. Or, we could just ignore them and continue to blame my condition as being "the problem" that needs to be solved. However, should we choose to go that route, we are being dishonest—or we are in denial. Then we risk allowing hidden, underlying problems to continue to re-emerge, and grow worse each time another pressure attacks our family system. In car terms, if the ride up the Coquihalla Highway shows my radiator is weak and the engine is overheating, either I fix the leak or I risk, on the next occasion, causing my engine to blow up. Either I can blame the highway or deal with the leaky radiator. But dealing with it is hard work and may mean getting my hands dirty or bruised.

If we take the family systems approach to defining and handling the problem, we begin to shape and change the focus of our attention. The point of focus for our activities in supporting the injured person shifts from a single person to a larger complex unit of people—our whole family—in a shared process of recovery.

Friedman suggests four important insights. First, he says, we would do well to focus on the emotional process, rather than simply concentrating on the symptoms of the injury. Instead of just getting practical and fixing things, putting out bushfires, we might begin to reflect on where each person is in a process of emotional recovery. My observation is that for this we may need the outside help of a counsellor or trusted friend who is able to offer an unbiased third-party opinion and some wise and insightful observations. For my own family, it has meant many rounds of family counselling at various times to help get us through the next small part of the family recovery journey.

Second, Friedman suggests that when problems or challenges surface within the family unit we'd best examine our family structure. It is too easy to blame one family member and to label her as *the problem*—and we usually do. Instead, he suggests we should begin by seeing difficult issues as integral parts of a structure rather than an end point in a linear causal chain. In other words, challenging concerns involve more than the relationship with one other demanding person. The conflict points to our relative position in the family web—that system of linked interrelationships—and is shaped by all the interactions within the family unit.

Third, he asks us to stop directly trying to change the dysfunctional part—the identified problem person. Instead, he recommends that we eliminate the problem symptoms through modifying our dysfunctional structure. The web of relationships needs fixing by making some positive readjustments to the whole—and that will rebalance the person who is out of kilter. Gaps need to be filled and excesses trimmed if we are to re-establish harmony and equilibrium.

Finally, Friedman believes we can predict how a given part—a person—is likely to function. But we don't do this by analyzing her nature; instead, we observe her position in the system. This has enormous implications for approaches to, say, premarital counselling. One implication is to focus on the position of the bride and groom in their respective families of origin, rather than just concentrating on achieving a good fit with one another according to their individual personalities.[29]

After my accident I was definitely "the patient"—the problem person in my family. They thought I was broken and needed to be fixed. You might ask: *What's new about that, given your injuries?* Just this. There may be a problem with my family members seeing me that way. Friedman talks about the whole notion of the "identified patient." However, he points to some important insights and distinctions:

> The concept of the identified patient is...that the family member with the obvious symptom is to be seen not as the "sick one" but as the one in whom the family's stress or pathology has surfaced.... The purpose of using the phrase identified patient is to avoid isolating the "problemed" family member from the overall relationship system of the family.[30]

Interestingly, Friedman insists that the *identified patient* concept is a convenient excuse. It becomes an easy path of escapism from some deeper and pre-existing family realities. They were there all along and troubling the family just below the surface. He maintains that:

> The creation of an identified patient is often as mindless as the body's rejection of one of its own parts. A more important reason

for not calling this labeling process scapegoating is that the pathology can also surface as a "superpositive" symptom of a strikingly high achiever, for example an overly responsible sister. Such family members are just as likely to be overly stressed, particularly at times of crisis because their position in the system allows them little freedom to function differently. As with the human body, severe overfunctioning, as well as severe dysfunctioning, is itself evidence of a problem in a system and will, in turn, promote problems elsewhere, whether the system is a family or congregation.[31]

Clearly and carefully, Friedman suggests that a toxic response to an injured person can even appear as an apparently positive reaction as well as having clearly negative manifestations.

On a personal level, I see this to be true. One of my daughters, for example, tends to respond to my own traumatic brain injury in a variety of overfunctioning ways. These include the well-intentioned and protective actions she takes to save me from everything she perceives as threatening—to me or to the family. This shows in the ways she protects me from stumbling as I walk on crutches or with a cane. She intervenes out of fear that I might embarrass myself in a public setting through misunderstanding a social cue or direct question. She is uncertain whether I am able to make any clear decisions (e.g., shopping choices or lunch arrangements). She is not convinced it is within my ability to get them right.

Her interventions can become, at times, rather anxious and preemptive. When I drive a car, she gets tense, irascible, and even bluntly unhelpful. She insists that she alone be allowed to drive. If I try to speak in public, she feels it necessary to try to shut me down before I blurt out something inappropriate or embarrassing to her or to myself.

All of this is very understandable and her interventions are desperately well intentioned. But it is difficult for both parties to live for very long with the high anxiety that her interventions provoke in each of us. They have the effect of further disabling me from risking the merest attempt at some activities. There seems to be too high a cost: the possibility of public failure.

Yet, it is precisely these new ventures and activities that may assist my forward progress. They lead to further recovery, a re-orientation to this new, post-trauma life of mine. In order to reach a successful outcome you must first be given the opportunity to fail.

As the oldest of her siblings, my daughter takes on the role automatically, and without negotiation, of mothering, protecting, and doing everything necessary to make life happen "normally." In so doing, however, she sometimes puts unbearable stress upon herself and others. In Friedman's terms, this is toxic behaviour through overfunctioning. It is toxic because it poisons the trust relationship of father and daughter. It also causes inordinate amounts of stress between two people, and within the wider web of family relationships.

They watch tense situations developing and spilling over into frustration, anger, and outbursts. Her interventions—and my responses—become a cause of tension for the family and other onlookers. They are one of the weaknesses in the system that emerge under pressure from trying circumstances. They form part of the web of issues that we can either choose to deal with or to deny.

The issues at play here relate to the relative positions in the family of a daughter and a father. My displacement as a father has also displaced my daughter. It has pushed her into an overprotective and overfunctioning position. This creates some challenges for the whole family. We need to re-orient family relationships to accommodate both a father's desire to be self-directing, and to reduce the personal stress levels in an overprotective daughter.

By contrast, a younger child has chosen the opposite strategy of almost total disengagement from me as a father. He ignores me when I call him. He ignores and refuses requests for practical help. He feels unduly put upon by the demands of his father's condition. In those early recovery days, Dad occasionally—and too frequently for him—required assistance in fetching and carrying things. This child was used to being cared for. He chose to underfunction in the absence of the levels of care he was used to in the past from his father. This, too, is a form of toxic dysfunction. It is a toxic reaction in the face of what he perceives to be the unreasonable demands of his father. He has lost the functioning father he once had. Understandably, grief and anger dominate his responses—and often, mine too.

At such times, what are we to do? How can we cope? On occasions like these, a time out is required—a safety period for waiting, a brief season for cooling your heels. This is neither purposeless nor time wasting; it is not a pointless delay to indulge avoidance. The psalmist describes this purposeful pause well when he declares: *We wait in hope for the* LORD; *he is our help and our shield* (Psalm 33:20).

Hope focuses on a point beyond present difficulties; Christ's cross anticipates promised resurrection. Hope looks towards security, a future rooted in the Lord. *In him our hearts rejoice,* the psalmist continues, *for we trust in his holy name* (Psalm 33:20).

In the face of puzzling, painful circumstances, trust requires us to be intentional in laying down anxiety. We do this as we relax in God's love and rest in His care. There we find that trust gives us reasons for joy. When you trust in the Lord—and His name declares that He is all we need Him to be to us—surrendering to Him turns angst towards new praise of God's faithfulness. Praise takes us by surprise; we find it welling up from deep, hidden places within. And praise feeds and fortifies our hope.

If the journey of faith is made along the prickly pathway from self-pity to praise, I was still playing in the thorns, a long way from the sunshine of God's grace. But even the heaviest thunderclouds must, at last, give way to hope's ray.

CHAPTER FOURTEEN

Families in Pain

There is surely a future hope for you,
and your hope will not be cut off
(Proverbs 23:18).

"It almost never snows in Vancouver—but you can expect rain of all kinds in abundance..." so the catalogue of a local college advises its prospective students. It was Christmastime in Vancouver as, wet and cool, the drizzle softly soaked the Pacific coast, dripping along the leafy edge of the rain forest. No snow—no soft-lined, crisp-underfoot whiteness—not even a light dusting to cleanse and charm bare branches of dark, leafless trees lining city streets.

Riding with Mary in the car, we set off to visit friends when something ordinary caught my eye. A teenager danced her way forward in the rain to deliver newspapers to the houses along the street. She was walking fast, trying to miss the heavy raindrops.

"Mary, look! That's what I want to do," I said with a sudden rush of deep emotion, tears burning my eyes.

"What? Deliver newspapers?" Mary asked her puzzled question in a surprised tone.

"No," I said, choking back hot tears, "I really want to walk again."

Desperate to do this, I felt useless when in my wheelchair or hobbling on crutches. But it was to take five months before I could take my first steps as I stood in a hydrotherapy pool. The hot water, over ninety degrees Fahrenheit, lapped around my neck. Steaming like a hot bath at home, it looked inviting as Marnie—my therapist—rolled me in my wheelchair down the ramp. Hot, buoyant water supported almost all of my body weight, encouraging good circulation to flow to my damaged joints. There in the rehab pool I learned how to distribute my weight. Repeatedly and patiently, Marnie showed me just how to move my legs in the cushioned safety of that enchanted water.

At home months later, I would still need to practice daily walking. My first outing was to be in my wheelchair. It came unexpectedly, a few days after my hospital discharge, at the suggestion of my friend Colin, who sensed my desperate negativity as he pushed me along. It would have been hard to miss it at that time. He attempted to cheer me up, sharing his conviction that I would one day write my story. It would, he claimed extravagantly, be published as one of those miracle stories in the Reader's Digest. At that time, it all sounded pretty far-fetched to my dulled ears—but Colin spoke like he really believed it. His confidence in me gave great hope. As a professor of Dentistry, Colin is not given to easy exaggeration. I trusted his word, even when I could hardly imagine it.

By the time I had progressed to crutches, another friend started to call each evening after work to walk with me. He knew that he needed to guard me carefully because falling came astonishingly easy to me. He walked unwearyingly beside me at a snail's pace, concentrating on slowly increasing the length of our walks by just a few paces each time. From starting out with the short walk from our house to the sidewalk, he built it up gradually to take in the whole block. Progress appeared to be painfully slow as I kicked my legs forward in an uneven gait, much of my weight resting on my crutches. My swollen and painful right leg moved bit by bit with a will of its own. Gradually, I learned to get around slowly-slowly, though the crutches pushing against me felt like I was walking on my rib cage and shoulders rather than my feet.

Patience is not a limitless commodity in this world, or in my family, which I would soon discover. My daughter, Leah, was thirteen years old and she struggled to accept my injuries and the limitations they imposed. She adjusted—reluctantly—to the new and diminished dad that she had now. Slower, and easily fatigued, he was emotionally unavailable to her when she needed him most.

Leah was not altogether happy with her new imposter dad. He looked almost like the original but so much about him now was different. Every day she felt like she was meeting a familiar stranger. She tried hard to re-orient herself to a long-time relationship that now appeared to have acquired some new and disconcerting character traits. Important old characteristics of her dad were now missing; odd new traits served to make a bizarre mix. She was disconcerted; me, too.

One noon hour, Leah offered to walk with me around some quiet roads near our home. Leaning hard on my crutches, I put as much weight on my legs as I safely dared. Pausing to breathe deeply and steadying myself often, we moved slowly across the street in front of our home, proceeding forward gingerly. A warm and sunny day, it was perfect for walking together.

Glancing back towards our front garden, I noticed a workman's white van parked in front of my neighbour's home. Two workers sat inside the cab taking their bag-lunch break and staring across at me with a frozen look of fascination. As I looked closer, I noticed that their gaze was focused on the space just behind me—the place Leah chose to walk. I glanced back, catching sight of her. Walking two paces behind me, she fell into perfect step with the movements of my ungainly slow march and mimicked them precisely. Exaggerating and amplifying my goose-step movements—the sway of my body—she mirrored my unsteady gait by her awkward, jerky locomotion. Her larger-than-life performance was a powerful parody, a sort of comic relief, or a pantomime version of my inelegance. Leah was not laughing; deep anger was etched on her face as the laughing workmen looked on. Leah was hurting. So was I.

In moments like these, I catch a glimpse of the impact my injury has upon us as a family unit—upon the whole system of our relationships. If the noted psychologist Edwin Friedman's analysis of family systems is as true as his arguments are convincing, then there is a tragically wide margin for them to be applied.[32]

Within traumatic brain injury—my particular wound and my family's special challenge—the North American statistics are sobering:

> Traumatic brain injury, caused by motor vehicle accidents, falls, assaults, or sports injuries affects approximately seven million people each year. Early and rapid management of the initial brain injury and reduction in secondary insults can lead to improved outcomes.[33]

Some reports indicate that about half of these victims do not survive their trauma, suggesting that as many as three million families each year struggle while attempting to re-establish some healthy family equilibrium, while 100,000 will require lifetime support.

Family systems will face the challenges that ride on the heels of any individual's injury, pain and loss. In its own way, each family experiences the loss of hope and the evaporation of a sense of a future. Patience will be in short supply for them over this extended period. They, too, will see that friendships are quickly worn thin by the demands that their new situation places upon old friends and family members. "How did we get to this place?" Mary would often ask me. We both needed to take stock, to remember again the reasons for all that we faced.

A recent Consensus Conference report has taken a finer focus on the problems of traumatic brain injury in its concluding remarks. It notes:

> Traumatic brain injury results principally from vehicular incidents, falls, acts of violence, and sports injuries and is more than twice as likely to occur in men as in women. The estimated incidence rate is 100 per 100,000 persons, with 52,000 annual deaths. The highest incidence is among young persons aged 15 to 24 years and 75 years or older, with a less striking peak in incidence in children aged 5 years or younger. Since TBI may result in lifelong impairment of physical, cognitive, and psychosocial functioning and prevalence is estimated at 2.5 million to 6.5 million individuals, TBI is a disorder of major public health significance. Mild TBI is significantly under-diagnosed and the likely societal burden is therefore even greater. Given the large toll of TBI and absence of a cure, prevention is of paramount importance.[34]

The report stresses the long-term or permanent implications of a traumatic brain injury for the family of the injured person. The majority of injuries occur in the very young and moderately young sectors of the population. These victims face the possibility that for many years they will need strong and healthy family support. In some cases, families face a long-term or permanent need to deal with the challenges presented to both the survivor and to the family members.

Such challenges provoke deep questions and raise serious issues of personal spirituality. All manner of questions—and anger and pain—arise insistently, demanding answers. They bubble up as survivors try to understand and accept both God and themselves. They frequently question their worth and value to Him and His love for them, in the light of the pain of their present experience.

An understanding of systemic issues can help others to give those victims and their families the kinds of pastoral care they need—and to do it in more appropriate ways. Family-based spiritual caregiving suggests helpful adjustments that the entire family can make as a whole. Meanwhile, the injured person is usually being treated by doctors and therapists under protocols that employ a purely medical—and therefore individualized—model.

Minuchin and Fishman stress the need to move away from that kind of approach when dealing with family challenges. They say:

> Families coming to therapy after a prolonged struggle have usually identified one family member as the problem. They pour out to the therapist their struggle, the solutions they have tried, and the failure of every attempt. The therapist, however, enters the therapeutic situation with the assumption that the family is wrong. The problem is not the identified patient, but certain family interactional patterns. The solutions the family has tried are stereotyped repetitions of ineffective transactions, which can only generate heightened affect without producing change.[35]

In other words, they create more heat than light. Clearly, the real problem lies elsewhere than in the injury survivor alone. It is hidden in the complex web of interactions that we call *family*. Moreover, it involves more than simply the presenting problems of the injured person.

One thing remains very clear: the family is hurting at a time like this. It wrestles with conundrums, puzzles, and challenges in attempting to care for an injured member. That observation gives us pause to consider some of the personal struggles that individuals face in recovery from a traumatic brain injury. One victim writes:

> I used to have a close friend, but then he had a nasty accident. He was not always my best friend; he did not always act in my best interest, but it was not humanly possible for two friends to be closer. He was better than me in almost everything. He was faster, smarter, stronger, and more popular. I always wanted to be just like him and I was always angry and frustrated when I came up short.
>
> Then one day I decided I could never be like him because he and I were two different people. We looked a lot alike. We even

had the same name. Everyone would encourage me to be just like him because they didn't want to acknowledge that he was gone. Finally, I decided enough was enough. I wasn't him. Trying to be him meant not being true to myself and it was cutting myself short. I had different roads to travel. I had seen things he had never got to, things that made me a better person.

That's when I started thinking about him/me before my/his accident.... He stopped being in that accident and I came to be. I needed to do this to separate my two identities, who I was and who I am. People rarely change that dramatically in an instant so this is a rare measure to take, but [it's] one I need for my sanity. I don't even tell anyone I do this. It is my secret. When people tell me I'm just like my friend I just smile to myself and thank them for the compliment. I would like to meet him/me again now that I have experienced and learned so much. I know that he/I would like whom I've become.[36]

I resonate with those feelings and the self-observation of this TBI survivor. He records them with accuracy—movingly and honestly—reflecting my experience. His account is packed with issues of identity, self-recognition and significance—and the responses of others to an injured person. The writer struggles to come to terms with the unwelcome changes thrust upon him. Another victim struggling with the unchangeable alterations he now faces, writes:

On the date of March 8, 1988, my life changed totally, completely and irrevocably...(I kind of knew what that meant, but I looked it up anyway. The definition is "incapable of being brought back.") And that pretty much sums up traumatic brain injury! You can't be brought back to your "old life" because everything is now different. You are not always the same person you were before and never will be again. But that does not mean your "new life" cannot be as rewarding and maybe even more satisfying!...After relearning everything from walking to speaking, I know how lucky and blessed I am to have come this far in my "new life."[37]

The "new life," however, is not without its considerable challenges—even for those who score highly on neuropsychological tests. Simpson comments:

> Over the years, I have become more and more aware from those living with the effects of brain injury, how much distractibility affects them. The vast majority of testing is done in a very quiet area but life is not a quiet, peaceful room. So many, in fact, that a survey of a support group showed that 100% of those at the group, and there were in fact 37 in that particular group, said that distractibility was one very serious problem for them. Listening to a lecture, they find themselves sucked into, as it were, an air conditioner, hearing a hammer somewhere, the hum of machinery and so on. Teenage students have told me that before they were hurt they could do homework and have the radio on and sometimes the TV and still they were honor students. Afterwards, they have to sit quietly in a room to do their homework and even that takes longer than before. When considering on-going education and/or vocational programs or, indeed, any rehabilitation, distractibility must be taken into consideration.[38]

The issues affecting families are complex and unique to each family. However, they share many common features. These shared experiences form the stuff of family discussion, and, if it is done with a deep care and patience, a mutuality of benefit emerges for family members caring for injured relatives. Support groups often provide a useful and appropriate self-help opportunity. Groups provide for the injured person and his family through facilitating a meeting with others facing similar circumstances. Some support groups focus on the injured person; others include family members. Some groups are designed specifically for family caregivers as their principal focus while inviting an injured person to attend, from time to time.

A wide variety of support groups meet for all kinds of target audiences. For a spiritual support group for cancer patients I helped lead in Vancouver, we met one evening per week. It welcomed both cancer patients and their significant friends or family, including a spouse, child or close friend.

The meeting would begin with a short talk by a speaker, often a medical expert or practitioner, who was also a person of faith. Open discussion and questions followed the talk. Family and personal issues about treatment protocols and questions about family reactions and responses were freely aired. A circle of prayer brought these issues before God in faith-affirming and hope-empowering ways.

Some attendees had a church background; many did not. Some described themselves as Christians, others as Muslims, but most were simply people in pain seeking definitive answers to some of life's ultimate questions. As followers of Jesus, my co-leader and I shared our personal journey of faith and life experience. We read from the Christian Scriptures and promised to hold each person in our prayers. From time to time we visited them individually between our meetings. We would go for a walk or for coffee, and talk together. They were free at any time to call us for support or help or just a friendly chat.

Some faced the big issue of how to bring healthy closure to ragged situations in their lives. Others struggled with physical pain or were caught in the vise-grip of fear. Many worried for their families and loved ones. Nearly all found support and encouragement among their peers as together they placed deep issues and real concerns into the hands of a God who cares.

Those who attend support groups freely share their experiences, challenges, and insights while voicing their questions. Doing so lends support and meaning to their lives at a time of questioning and anxiety. While support groups for every presenting need can be helpful, they are not for everyone in every case, as Simpson correctly notes:

Not everyone wants to go to a support group or can be helped in a support group, but many can. It is good for husbands, wives and families to be able to get together and share their experiences and support one another. They, as well as the person living with the effects of a brain injury, have a tremendous amount to offer by way of support and insight. It is interesting, for example, to watch two mothers connect. It is interesting to watch two wives and two husbands connect and support one another. If this can be developed into different groups phoning one another, just to talk, then this in itself is support.... The groups also do give some insight...into what it is like to live with the effects of a brain injury, what it is like for families. The groups, if they can work properly, can take away some of the loneliness. A loneliness that leads to many different problems.[39]

Trauma has a terribly isolating effect upon the family that cares for an injured or sick person. Feelings of isolation are a major contributor to high levels of stress. Frequently, they experience deep feelings of loss. Simply knowing that other people also experience the same kinds of challenges is liberating and comforting. It helps people feel a little more "normal" again. Other people understand them—not from a book, a theory, or from a distance—but as insiders. Hearing one another's stories is mutually bonding. It brings huge relief to know that others intuitively feel what one is going through—that they care deeply and truly understand. It is powerfully healing and emotionally life giving. It brings a renewal of hope.

This pattern of meeting in support groups may even suggest a helpful model for pastoral caregiving that brings some spiritual interventions. Leaders of faith communities might consider facilitating support groups, empowering them to be largely lay led. A group leader offers input at key steps along the way either as requested, or invited, or as seems to be appropriate. A key feature is to return ownership of the recovery process to the group of survivors and their families as they experience and express their singularity within areas of common concern, as Rabbi Friedman notes:

The bottom line for clergy visitation, therefore, is that wherever members of the clergy can support or stimulate differentiation in a family emotional system, they stand on the side of systemically affecting the recuperative processes within that family, no matter what the illness, and no matter where the "patient" is located—home, hospital, or hospice. As with other problem areas of family life, sometimes that stimulation is best accomplished by working directly with the ill family member, but sometimes it is best facilitated by coaching his or her relatives.[40]

Soul care and pastoral interventions benefit from this wider angle of vision. The narrow focus upon the identified patient is ultimately misleading.

When a traumatized jailer in the ancient Near East city of Philippi once asked what he must do to be saved, he received an answer about his journey of faith that involved more than himself—it included his whole family, too (Acts 16:31–34). Finding such answers—those that affect the whole family—help to define what sort of pastoral care might be appropriate. This kind of caregiving has a lasting impact upon traumatized families. These kinds of intervention help them to build new—and very different—futures together. It might even help an angry, goose-stepping daughter to learn how to walk beside her father, or help him to make peace with his new limitations. A support group might help them both as they set out on the uncharted journey called recovery.

Marching into unmapped territory is an unnerving experience, a daunting prospect to be sure. At such times, there is a need to exercise spiritual discipline and one kind in particular is helpful—practising the habit of claiming biblical promises as personal grace gifts. It is health giving and faith assuring to claim the personal promise: *There is surely a future hope for you, and your hope will not be cut off* (Proverbs 23:18)—even when circumstances seem to be utterly overwhelming.

Our hope cannot be based upon the denial of pain, for hope is profoundly bound up with it. Were I God—and I thank God I am not—I wouldn't plan it that way, but God has. He has created an unbreakable link between pain and redemption and it finds its focus in the cross of Christ. When I have lost sight of God through the numbing of adverse circumstances, I find Him again when I revisit the sources of my pain, for that is where He is. God waits there to work His redemptive intentions for my life.

In theological terms, the ultimate place of pain is Calvary and the cross—and that is especially where God is to be found. Jürgen Moltmann captures this profound truth when he says:

> The death of Jesus on the cross is the center of all Christian theology. It is not the only theme of theology, but it is in effect the entry to its problems and answers on earth. All Christian statements about God, about creation, about sin and death have their focal point in the crucified Christ. All Christian statements about history, about the church, about faith and sanctification, about the future and about hope stem from the crucified Christ.[41]

I venture to guess that most of us would not design redemption's hope so closely linked to the pain of despair. We might prefer to avoid pain rather than confront it. Avoidance robs us of the possibility for hope in the face of pain. God's design is quite different—he does not shy away from the realities of pain. He does not fudge the issue. He knows that the problem of pain is simple—real pain causes people to really get hurt.

The remedy is not so simple. The price of pain must be paid and He pays it Himself in Christ. And because God confronts it and beats it on the cross of Christ, the ground of our hope is secure and firm, even—and especially—in the face of pain. Even when I was in the most pain—whether physical or while grieving the scars of a wounded spirit—I took comfort from the greater pain of Christ for me at Calvary. He absorbed my pain within His own and made the hope of renewal a possibility. But still ahead of me lay the many times when I would cry out to God for the pain to end, as I ventured out into an uncertain future.

CHAPTER FIFTEEN

Postcards from Kenya

Know also that wisdom is sweet to your soul; if you find it, there is a future hope for you, and your hope will not be cut off (Proverbs 24:14).

By January of 1999, a new urgency drove me on. I desperately attempted to resume my studies, keenly wanting to finish work on a Doctoral programme in Christian Ministry. Fourteen long months had slipped by since our accident and I was anxious to regain my study skills. An earlier attempt had ended in disappointment, for it had all proved too much for me. Wanting to return to the academic challenge, I needed to learn some effective ways that would work for me. I still had some major hurdles to overcome. Whenever I tried to absorb new academic material, poor concentration and faulty recall dogged me.

I had to get back control, regaining a sense of achievement in a life that ran away from me. Nervously I doubted my own abilities in just about everything, and my confidence was gone. Only questions remained: Could I do things anymore—even the simple things—and do them well? No longer could I tell whether any job I was doing was good or bad. It became a puzzle that baffled me. I needed to receive so much positive affirmation, but I wanted people to be honest with me.

As much as I needed it, I feared the cold stab of honesty. It distressed me. Critical comments crippled me at that stage of my emotional recovery. I knew I had to face up to the reality of my current performance, good or bad. That was vital for improving it. What I truly feared, even more than people's honesty, was their well-intentioned flattery. I feared that people might be uncomfortable being straight with me. I hated to think they might praise me to my face saying, *Good job, Paul,* while under their breath be silently adding *for a man with one good leg and half a brain! Yes, Paul, not bad— for a brain-injured person in your position.*

I started in again on studying but it was a long, hard slog. Retaining new, academic information was nearly impossible for me. I would re-read a book I had recently finished only to discover that it sounded brand new to me the second time around, as if I'd never read it. Daunted, almost completely defeated, is a hard place to be—and that is how I felt through the close and careful reading I attempted. That kind of work—and the concentration it demands—is exhausting, like an impossible effort, as I tried to sort, understand, and retain new information for even the shortest time frame.

My habit since the accident was to keep a notebook beside my bed. Frequently in pain, I would awake to be sleepless for long hours; nights dragged interminably slowly. In pained wakefulness I jotted down my scrambled feelings. Sometimes, I wrote furiously into the wee hours. Wild thoughts tumbled out as words on a page, as a shaky hand wrote, guided by flashlight to allow Mary some sleep. It is an exaggeration to call this my "journal," because my entries were too sporadic and often random, but a pressing urgency drove me to inscribe my undisciplined musings. Doing so provided considerable emotional release so that I could roll over and sleep again—for a few brief hours.

Sometimes my thoughts raced back to Kenya—dangerous thoughts, full of pain. I tried to screen them out, but they returned there again and again. I thought often about the many friends we had left there. I saw their faces, heard their voices, vivid and familiar. I recalled people whose lives I'd touched and who, by return of friendship, touched mine deeply. In those recollections I walked with them through the slums and villages, tea fields and sprawling market places. In a cold Canadian winter I basked in the heat of the white sands of a Mombassa beach, watching sapphire waves breaking lazily over white coral, half a mile offshore. I spoke with beach boys from the Kamba tribe selling their wooden carvings, and the Kikuyu mamas displaying their cotton *kangas*—brightly coloured wraparound skirts—from makeshift washing lines stretched along the white sands, onshore breezes turning them into flags. They waved a bright welcome to tourists and visitors to Kenya.

For one of my academic programs I was asked to write about some ministry moments, reflecting on them from theological perspectives. With thoughts turning to Kenya, I relived some vivid events that tugged at me in so many ways, whether physical or emotional. Those ministry moments leave me with questions concerning my own spiritual journey. I will paint them for you now. They are drawn in soft pastels and evocative watercolours. I offer them to you as my personal postcards from Kenya.

The first postcard home concerns the pain of sudden loss—and avoidable suffering.

POSTCARD #1: Halima, an eight-month-old baby girl, fell ill on Wednesday with a fever, diarrhea, and vomiting. On Friday, her condition took a sharp decline. Her young, first-time mom took her to the small local hospital at Tigoni, in the hill country high above Nairobi. My friend, Hal, an American doctor, visited and discovered the hospital had no rehydration fluid. Mixing up a simple solution of salt, sugar, and boiled filtered water, he gave clear instructions on how to administer it.

After he left, the hospital staff preferred to give Halima their preferred remedy of sugar-water, but it lacked the essential electrolytes, which retain fluids in the body. On Sunday night her dehydrated little body finally grew tired, gave up, and she died. Her death, like so many others, was totally preventable.

Together with the other missionaries present, Hal wept openly. He prayed aloud at the simple graveside service we held in the Brook Bond tea fields. We watched the grieving women. In their anguish and pain they staunchly choked back their tears. Bending their backs they raked the rough red dirt into the open grave. Slowly they covered the simple wooden box with soil. At the edge of the tea field, under the shade of the lurina tree, they tenderly laid Halima to rest. Stifling hot tears, the mamas sang songs of faith and hope in Kikuyu, their mother tongue.

Pulling flowers from the bushes around us, we stepped over to the raw red soil. We pushed their stalks into the grave mound. They served as a simple marker for Halima's little life, snuffed out too soon. The birth rate in Kenya is probably the world's highest—yet many children will never see their fifth birthday. The funeral of a child is indescribably painful for us as missionaries—but even more fraught for mothers grieving their lost infants and bereft of hope. The silence of these local people belies their deep distress. Here, you will attend twenty-four funerals for under-fives for each one you might go to in Canada or Britain. Can you imagine the anguish, pain, and sadness that this represents? The pain is thinly masked by the local Christian culture that dictates you shall not weep, for God has done what He wished to do. The women tell me, "God allowed this child to die."

As a missionary teacher how do I begin to allow these hurting people to express their grief? I have a theological mandate for doing so. It is found in the Jesus they worship. By His example He showed us how to weep for a dead friend, Lazarus. He invites us to weep with those who weep. But how can we shed tears in a culture that bought into the Victorian stiff upper lip, gift-wrapped in the culture in which the first missionaries dressed the Gospel they brought. It came prepackaged that way to Kenya.

As a missionary doctor, how can my friend Hal begin to persuade local people that the child could and should have been saved through proper primary health-care protocols? In a culture where people need to learn to let go quickly because so much is so often lost, how can I convey to them that a child's life is so very important? More than that, Halima's little life might be important to a God who loves the very least of us with unremitting love. Will they really believe me when I tell them that His love is stronger than death and deeper than our pain?

POSTCARD #2: My second postcard is painted from a different perspective. Some postcards are poignant, others have a more humorous slant. In the spring of 1996, my wife, Mary, spent four days in the hot Taita Hills near Mombassa. As a Canadian Baptist missionary she went to encourage a group of African pastors' wives. In order to get there, she made the six-hour drive from our home in Nairobi. Her journey took her along what is, arguably, the most dangerous road in Kenya, the Mombassa Highway.

Mary assisted in a school for pastors' wives—a very different concept from anything that we know in the West. The youngest pastor's wife was fifteen and the next youngest, at seventeen, already had an eighteen-month-old baby. That young mother ended the week by making a first-time faith commitment as a follower of Jesus. These upcountry women are unschooled and desperately poor, yet, to be with them is an inspiration.

Each afternoon, Mary taught a sewing class for two hours. She showed the women how to repair tears in their dresses and how to turn around the worn collars on their husbands' shirts. Quick to learn, they were deft with their hands, needing to be shown just once. They also needed to receive some basic sewing equipment. Each woman received from their teacher an old plastic 35mm film canister. It was filled with needles, cotton thread, pins, and a few buttons to serve as a basic sewing kit.

Through the laughter and the chatter during the week, Mary began to get to know these women. Conversations developed easily and quickly around the sewing tasks that occupied them. Towards the close of the day, Mary would lead a short devotional in Swahili. In turn, each lady recited some simple memory verses as Mary listened to them.

The women enjoyed learning and wanted to know all they could. They loved to learn through practical tasks and by reading, writing, and memory work. They talked excitedly together about the new things they learned each day.

Accommodations were simple and frugal for everyone, comprised of a camp cot on the concrete floor of the empty church. The church was a building of rough brick walls made from local red mud, a gray cement floor, and a silver and rust-coloured corrugated iron roof. Each night, the tired women closed their eyes to sounds of bush babies crying on the roof. A hyena howled invisibly somewhere outside in the blackness of the night, its wicked laughter reverberating menacingly in the enveloping darkness.

One evening, Mary quietly crept outside into the night, as the rains began to come strongly. She wore only a thin *kanga*—the distinctive wraparound cloth worn by Kenyan women. Showering in the rain under the African sky is to use the cleanest running water you can find in those parts, and is preferable to the dark brown liquid that glugs red and rusty out of the hose. As they gathered excitedly around Mary, the Kenyan women giggled. They laughed aloud, talking noisily among themselves in their mother tongue. They had never seen a *mzungu*, a Western woman, behave like this and they wanted to check out her credentials. They had to see if she really was white—all over!

Mary felt emotionally low on her return to Nairobi, almost dejected. She was convinced she'd done so little for these women. She reflected that they had laughed a lot, both with her and at her, and they were glad to be able to enjoy their faith together. Delighted to learn new skills, they shared their problems and joys in a happy banter and in more serious conversations together. They had bonded to become an effective informal support group in a culture that does not know that term. But Mary still doubted the real value of what she had been able to do for them.

This postcard raised a number of questions for me as a missionary. I wondered how I might give Mary real encouragement. How could I affirm her as a person—and insist on the significance of her work? That's a challenge when she's convinced that her ministry is small and insignificant. As a husband I have my own concerns for her safety. How do I balance the very real dangers my wife faces when travelling the Mombassa Highway against the spiritual and practical value of her task? From a perspective of spiritual reflection, I wonder if I am able to construct a working theology of missions. And is my practical theology sufficient to explain why a gifted and outgoing person might, or should, reasonably serve in a context where her gifts are so underutilized? Self-doubt can dog you in new and threatening situations, especially in a developing country where the old measures and affirmations of effectiveness and value are quite absent.

POSTCARD #3:The final postcard is a snapshot from our family album. Shortly after arriving in Kenya, we had to live in a one-bedroom cottage for eight months. As a family of seven, this proved to be less than easy. In our cottage, called *Pango*—the Cave—the kitchen doubled as our dining room. The lounge doubled as a bedroom for Mary and me. The boys' bedroom was a corner of the girls' room that had some low partition walls around it that did not reach the ceiling. *Pango* was, at best, inadequate. The lights in the room shone into the boys' section. The chatter of their older sisters disturbed the boys as they tried to get to sleep each night. They soon grew tired and tetchy, impatient and hostile towards one another. We all did.

We were still quite new to Kenya. *Pango* was where we stayed for nine months while studying Swahili at language school. It felt like a cave and became a tense place for us all to be a family. We gave it our best effort while wrestling with a new language, settling into a tropical climate, and experiencing the joys and dangers of a developing country. During that time, we had access to only two pay phones shared by many others. There were two dozen language students, and large groups of guests visiting the adjoining conference centre, as well as the full classes of students at the on-site seminary. We shared the same one hundred acre campus together with seventy local workers and their families.

We longed, of course, to be in our own home. We wanted to be nearer to our children's school. We dreamed of having our own telephone and wanted a link to our folks at home in Canada and Britain. We needed to contact our missionary colleagues in Kenya for work purposes and we missed hearing the voices of friends around the world. We wanted to stay in touch either by voice link or by e-mail through the phone lines.

At that time, the country was in the throes of a three year drought, creating electricity rationing that robbed us of our electric power for six hours a day. In addition, we lost our electricity to frequent and sudden brownouts, power failures or stoppages. We dreamed that we might be connected, one day, to the outside world. Perhaps this would be after language school when we would find a house to rent in Nairobi.

After a long search, we did find a suitable house near our children's school. The owner promised that we would be connected to a phone line in our new home in just a few days—so did the telephone company. They lied. After three weeks we finally got a line. For one week. It broke down—frequently. We visited the local engineers every morning in their forty-foot steel container that housed the local telephone exchange. We drove to the main depot two or three times a week. We spoke sweetly. We spoke harshly. We became bellicose, belligerent, and threatening. No joy. Our phone worked for less than three months during the long thirteen months that we lived there.

The telephones were connected to the local exchange by a mess of wires. These copper wires sagged drunkenly in the heat through the nearby forest, on their way to the local exchange. Sometimes, they sank so low across the road beside our house that they would get tangled or broken in the wheels of passing cars. The precious copper they contained was much prized and sought after as the raw material for making Masai and Kikuyu bracelets or other jewelry. On at least five occasions that our neighbours knew of, the wires had been cut and stolen. Whenever we saw an *mzungu* wearing a copper bracelet we would smile and say to her, "Excuse me, but you seem to be wearing my telephone line. May I have it back, please? I need it to make an urgent call."

During this frustrating time I met a pastor in one of the churches where I was assigned. He offered to effect an introduction for me to a "director" of the phone company. I accepted his kindness. The director promised me a connection to a reliable line within the week. For this service—he wrote a letter on headed paper to another telephone department—he charged me 8,000 Ksh. ($200 Cdn). This was about four months' salary for a full time housekeeper.

I paid my money gladly and waited expectantly. Then I waited impatiently. As I waited...and waited...my impatience turned to anger. Nothing happened. I went to the phone company. They offered me a brand new line if I would simply complete the application form. And pay them 14,000 Ksh. ($450 Cdn). Of course I complied, believing this would expedite the solution to my rather acute problem. Still nothing happened. By now, two men at least were clearly a little richer.

I spoke to a Canadian colleague about my concerns. He was a missionary with another organization. He looked truly surprised. He told me he simply sent one of his house staff to the telephone company with a little *chai*—bribery money—and everything always worked. I told him that I did not feel able to pay a bribe. He replied that I had a choice: either I could continue not to bribe and get nothing done, or I could play the game and get some results—most of the time.

His organization, he told me, administered child and village sponsorship programs all over East Africa. Why, he wondered, should innocent people suffer just because he decided not to "get with the program" and have his office working efficiently?

As a missionary, I wondered if I should get the job done by turning a blind eye to a corrupt system. Should I choose to work within the system in order to achieve some important tasks? What, I agonized, is "the job" anyway? Is it just getting the task done? Or does it involve the relationship I am modelling to the people I serve? Is bribery, I wondered, still bribery when the government pays such low wages that without an extra "payment for service" from me, these workers cannot adequately live?

My moral dilemma was to sort out if it is better to be self-righteous and live without the utilities that ministry requires, or to be somehow tainted but able to complete the task for which I was sent. I constantly wrestled with these kinds of issues. Was I not really dealing with an extra payment for service, rather than a bribe? Could this be properly thought of as something other than a bribe, and if so, what? I answered the question one way at that time, but I wonder whether I would answer it the same way today—maybe not.

I send you these postcards because they are not the usual tourist snaps of an exotic country—not the kind of missionary stories that are commonly heard in church. Instead, they are part of the larger insider puzzle that expats and missionaries face daily. Such questions linger long when you have to live with your answers to them. Maybe you are able to answer them more quickly, more efficiently, and more accurately than I have been able to. Naturally, I hope you can also live comfortably—or like so many expats, uncomfortably—with the answers you finally design for yourself.

Whatever the answers, one thing becomes very clear. Wisdom is required if you are to achieve answers you can really live with—answers that will last for life's long haul. Wisdom alone provides the marathon answers—the ones that can take you the distance into a future with hope. A wise man put it this way: *Know also that wisdom is sweet to your soul; if you find it, there is a future hope for you, and your hope will not be cut off* (Proverbs 24:14).

Africa does not hold the monopoly on a place that requires wise living. That need is part of the human condition—wherever we are. Wisdom is promised to anyone who will ask for it from One who alone can give it. If you want wisdom, it is freely available—and I will join you as together we wait to receive it as a gift from the One who is greater than we are.

CHAPTER SIXTEEN

Into Africa Again

"Oh, that I might have my request,
that God would grant what
I hope for" (Job 6:8).

"Sudden death" has become more than a hockey phrase for me; it is about other things than the end of season playoffs. It is more than skates on a rink; it means a life ebbing away that might too soon be put "on ice" while the *Game Over* sign flashes before my eyes. I was about to find out just how near I had once come to that condition—to having my own body placed on ice.

An unexpected set of circumstances suddenly produced that serendipitous opportunity. Mary and I would find ourselves back in Kenya less than two years after our hurried departure from Nairobi. No words can begin to describe the powerful inner healing this journey brought to us both. This kind of inner health is as necessary as it is wonderful.

We had been ripped away from African friends, our Nairobi

home, and the people we loved and served. We were allowed no time for proper farewells, emotional goodbyes, or those important moments needed to bring healthy closure to our Kenyan experience. Without this, it is more complicated to make healthy new beginnings anywhere else. Instead, you find yourself looking back wistfully over one shoulder. Sometimes memories are accurate; often they are skewed and sentimental. Yet they remain poignant and painful. In a flash, the oddest things will evoke them in all their power and freshness.

Our business in Africa remained unfinished, and we struggled with the feeling that we were emotionally incomplete. We found ourselves in a place of deep grief, mourning sudden losses. We felt that we needed—all seven of us—to get back there and start to make our peace with some of the sources of our pain. But how do you do that? There is no one-size-fits-all answer to that sort of question. One thing becomes clear, however. You begin to make peace with your pain by being intentional, by determining that this is what you really want to do. Then you do nothing—nothing hasty that is. Indeed, the thing you are currently doing could easily be mistaken for nothing because it involves no frantic activity.

Instead, this is an important kind of inactivity. It is a deliberate stillness. You experience it as a centred calm, a peace and poise as you become an attentive listener. "And what do I listen to?" you might ask. Well, you begin to listen to your sources of pain—you listen to yourself, the things you say to yourself. And somewhere within and above it all, you actively listen for the voice of the One who loves you with a love that is deeper than your pain.

That is exactly where I run into problems. It is odd how noisy it can be when you listen in silence. You become aware of all your internal dialogue—and the noise of it is sometimes overwhelming as you try to be centred and still. You hear, at high volume, those inner conversations that you have with yourself. You sometimes conduct them in your mind with other people, and it is usually people who are mixed up in your source of pain. It soon becomes clear, however, that these kinds of conversation do nobody any good. They cannot make you feel better, and they are of no concern anyway to the characters in your angry, animated conversations. For their part, they are quietly unaware that you are trapped in these inner dialogues—fights and feuds—with their imagined voices.

In reality, these people cannot hear you. They do not even know you are talking to them. What is more, they have moved on in their lives beyond the point where you are now stuck reliving old pains to prolong your agony.

As soon as you realize this fact, you start to take your first baby steps. They may be wobbly, painful, and faltering—as you edge along the path from resentment to gratitude, from nursing scars to offering forgiveness. And no, I do not think that this is easy or automatic. It was not that way for me, and it has not been that way for so many people I have spoken to. When people climb a challenging mountain, they do it not for ease but for the adventure and the risk—for the beauty of the view along the way. They climb steep and scary slopes because they would be less than the people they truly are if they did not attempt their climb. And so, like them, we make an honest attempt to traverse a difficult and dangerous route ahead by facing our pain squarely and honestly.

Today, my children still await their opportunity to return to Kenya to make peace with their past—but their waiting is not idle. Instead, they help to create those opportunities by working at part-time jobs and saving their money towards the travel costs. They feel that the frayed endings of their experience in that place still need to be rewoven. Somehow, our children need to place those happenings and happenstances into a reworked purpose and a renewed pattern of meaning for their lives.

The prospect of three full weeks in Kenya suddenly stretched out ahead of Mary and me. Our schedule fell neatly into three tasks, three clear purposes for being there, and I was delighted. Still struggling to put order and shape to our plans, I was relieved to see how neatly our outline schedule had shaped up. We were to go on retreat in Mombassa with colleagues within our mission from across Africa for about a week. We would assist in an in-service teacher enrichment programme for another week. But first, thanks to the foresight and planning of Brian Stelck, a friend and former missionary, we had a whole week of unstructured time for our personal use. We could begin to reconnect with our many Kenyan friends and colleagues—and their welcome and affirmation would begin the serious and joyful business of inner healing for us. There would be joy and sorrow, sobbing and hilarity. But first, this important soul safari would begin with a bumpy car ride.

The journey from Jomo Kenyatta Airport into Nairobi takes the wide-eyed traveller alongside the sun-bleached, yellow grasslands that stretch over the East African plains—a vast expanse of veldt. This is the open country, bearing grass, bushes or shrubs, thinly forested here and there. It is more characteristic of southern Africa rather than the eastern part of the continent.

The grasslands are home to giraffes, antelopes, cheetahs, and lions. Hyenas and jackals will stalk small mammals, stealing the remains of the kill left by the big cats. Wildebeests and Cape buffaloes, elephants and rhinos, wander across this wide and free expanse of grasses. Standing like proud purple shoulders along its edges, as if trying to contain this vast open country, are the Ngong Hills rising up on the near horizon.

Across these open plains wander the Masai tribesmen. They walk tall and fearless, dressed in their red tartan blankets draped stylishly over one shoulder. Their homemade shoes are cut from old car tires and offer scant protection underfoot from the lancing of piercing thorns up to three centimetres long. They carry their deadly *rungu* everywhere. It is a hardwood stick, almost a metre long, selected for its heavy knot of wood at one end. Sometimes they will attach a large metal bolt to it from a big machine. They screw it and glue it firmly and securely into the end of their carefully chosen stick. In the practised hands of these sharp-eyed Masai *morans*—young warriors—the *rungu* becomes an accurate, devastating missile. It will bring down any large animal—or enemy—they might be tracking. It is their protection, together with their spear, as they drive their herds of humpbacked Brahman cattle in search of greener pastures.

You will see them on your drive from the airport into town, these Masai, dotted here and there, moving slowly against the glare of the sun-scorched grass. They will return your cheery wave with a silent stare, their eyes following you as you speed past. They remain unmoved by your attempts to connect with them, just as they are by the threat of wild beasts around them.

On this unique safari into a modern city, you are made aware of a primal connection to a Stone Age lifestyle in the midst of it all. You are reminded of it each time you meet a Masai man carrying his *rungu*. His stretched, pierced ear lobes are pulled up and over the tops of his ears, like a thick piece of spaghetti. The Masai, alone, are permitted to carry their weapons into town.

The uneven potholed road rattles out its own rhythmical sounds to you—a "Welcome to Kenya" as you jog along its bumps. Anticipation bubbles up, and all your nerves stand on end as you grow hypervigilant, trying to take it all in. Your mind is abuzz as you try to interpret the dangers, take in points of interest, and absorb the evident blessings bestowed upon you by this prehistoric place. Clumsily, you juggle contrasting stimuli in a vain effort to process them all and capture everything by holding that moving picture still in your memory.

You are back in Africa. Passing piles of rotting garbage at the roadsides, putrid smells explode in your nostrils in sharp contrast to the smart new industrial buildings that mushroom up along the highway into town. Glass and metal buildings have become glitzy car showrooms, and one is home to a foam mattress factory that does high-volume business. At another building you can rent heavy plant machinery or huge vehicles for road building, civil engineering, and construction projects. Each proud building stands starkly against the dry yellow grasses.

Umbrella thorn trees form a backdrop and picture frame to absorb the harsh glare of these polished buildings. They slowly roast under the hot blue sky as the yellow dust gently begins to dampen their gloss and soften their glitz. It will wear down everything over time, that dry dust.

The African sky here in Kenya becomes the world's largest three-dimensional movie screen. Popular moving pictures are projected onto the life-sized screen of the sky. They are free for all to see. My favourites include two special features: "The Mauve African Sunset" and "Magnificent Southern Stars." They form panoramas to fill the sky above you. Daytime skies are filled with Kenya's more than 1,700 varieties of bird life, disturbed only by the angry African storm that takes us all by surprise. For me, these views become must-see movies projected upon the open sky, available at a glance to all who will take time to gaze in awe.

As you hasten towards Nairobi, dense exhaust—noxious clouds from diesel engines—pours from the tailpipes ahead of you, often blacking out your view completely. Travelling into town at a ground level altitude of 5,500 feet, you will see first-hand why engines are tuned to run so rich. That is the only way to maintain the power to get you up and over those hills as you climb the long, slow slopes in this gently undulating landscape. The cost to your lungs is horribly high as your car strains to reach the low summits.

Dark emissions from your vehicle add to the billowing clouds of exhaust fumes. Drivers ride their horns noisily while loud music blares from colorful *matatus* weaving in all directions across the broken road surface. They constantly engage in some mad escapade that seems to require that they cover every square inch of blacktop with their tire tracks. Sometimes cars wander off the hard surface and onto the soft shoulder at the edge of the road. Yellow dust swirls up high in a fine mist of browns and sepia tones, like an old worn photograph.

Your mouth becomes dry, your nose crusty, and you move your jaw trying to produce a little saliva to break your thirst. But instead you chew on the grit that settles around your teeth. It lodges there as you breathe through your mouth, attempting to avoid the sweet-and-sour smells of equatorial garbage heaps. They grow on waste ground at the street corners. The rhythms of a vast land unfold, and your heartbeat quickens with a sudden adrenaline rush.

You are back in Africa—the untamed continent. You are in places crammed full of unforeseen blessings and many hidden dangers. And you love it and you fear it, all at once.

The speeding traffic rushes lemming-like forward, ever forward. It hastens headlong towards the inevitable bottleneck of road jams to signal your arrival at the edge of downtown Nairobi. Without air conditioning, you wait uncomfortably in the fierce heat, your wet shirt sticking to your seat. You open the window just a crack—enough to let in some air but keep out grasping hands from opportunistic thieves.

Every time your car stops in Nairobi, people will quickly surround you. Young men hawk newspapers and magazines. Tiny street kids plead with you to buy fluted packages of peanuts, holding them out to you with one hand while the other is wrapped tightly around a younger child slung over their hip. A meagre snack, wrapped by small, unwashed fingers, can be yours for only two or three shillings. These little people will take their day's earnings back home to the village or to the slum to help buy food to feed their families. Childhood is just another name for work in this city. These are places of absolute poverty where shelter and clothing, food, medicine, and education are not human rights, for they do not come with this territory. Those privileges remain the preserve of the lucky few.

Young boys, filthy and in rags, will suddenly appear at your car window as you stop at a red light. Mucous rolls down from their nostrils, streaked thick and green over dusty black skin. Their pungent breath betrays them. Behind their backs or hidden in their torn, dirty sleeves they conceal small bottles of glue within brown paper bags used as inhalation masks. They paw at your open window; their dirty fingers curl over the edge of the glass, leaving grease smudges and ugly smears.

215

"Geeve me a sheeling!" they demand incessantly. Oscar-winning performances display a mock anguish with pained expressions on their faces. But their eyes dart back and forth checking out the passengers and the contents of your vehicle. Like magpies they search for anything that glistens in the sunshine. Watches, earrings, necklaces, money, cameras, and jewelry are all at risk in these brief interludes. One child will grab your attention while his accomplice moves around to another open window to grab your belongings. He will snatch whatever might be within his easy reach as the traffic lights abruptly change—and you drive off with a lightened load.

When a thieving child is caught, the angry crowd will beat him. The local people quickly surround him and, as if from nowhere, someone will arrive with an old tire filled with gasoline. Putting it around the thief like a necklace, the child is incinerated right where he is caught, in the open street. The police seem not to notice. This child is a "no-name," one of the faceless poor that roam the earth. Survival is a dangerous game when you are dirt poor.

Blaring music, too distorted to recognize, arrives beside you in the form of a *matatu*. The megabass response sometimes rocks your car with its raw power. The tout—the young man who collects people's fares—sports his collection of ten and twenty shilling bills. He weaves them through the fingers of one hand so that their stubby ends stand out like a makeshift fan. With the other he grips a handrail as he hangs out of the moving vehicle, swinging a leg jauntily into the breeze.

"Beba, beba!"—let's go! He sounds his cry, tapping the roof cornice sharply with a coin or slapping it noisily with a flat hand. With his vehicle alongside you, your world is abruptly filled with music and people, animals and catcalls, as he drums up more business for his deathwish driver.

The street kids, news vendors, and brightly clad mamas busily hawk their wares. Mamas cook delicious *chapattis* on a small fire they set on three rocks under a makeshift wooden shelter called a *duka*. They build their *dukas* at the edge of the sidewalk, back from the road. All of these busy people vie for your attention trying to trade with you. A man stands over a small charcoal brazier. He fans away the smoke from his cooking fire with a flat piece of cardboard. He tries to keep his roasting corncobs from burning. He serves them to you in one of two ways—plain or, if you prefer, spread with cayenne pepper and a squeeze of tart juice from a green lemon. The choice is yours. Either way, you are going to need a cold drink of "soda" to wash down the dry, rubbery corn roast. This meal will be good and chewy. It will fill a hungry space.

Men can be seen standing up against a hedge or wall—or simply turning with their backs to the street—to relieve themselves into the bushes. Women walk by unconcerned by this common sight. They need to concentrate on more pressing matters. Bent over by excessive weight from their heavy burdens, they move along with large bundles of firewood—long and heavy branches tied and bound together on their heads. They balance huge bags of vegetables, baskets, and pots with grace and strength. They may buy them to sell at a small profit, but most vegetables are home grown. They carry them long distances, taking them to and from the markets. They do this while holding and nursing a young child, or even while moving a piece of furniture balanced on their heads or strapped to their backs. Some women may continue to create cushion covers by deftly notching with their crochet hooks as they walk—in addition to carrying a full load. They make brightly coloured chair covers in orange and mauve, and head rest covers in greens and yellows to cheer up their roughly constructed chairs at home.

Wherever there is a patch of grass, it seems you can see men and women stretched out, taking a nap in the noon hour heat. Sometimes, here and there, groups of office workers take a break, sitting on the grass with small Bibles open on their laps. They have a club of some kind for believers, and here they meet under a shady tree to learn, discuss, and pray together. Some sing hymns or worship songs. They sing loudly as they stand clapping, playing tambourines and swaying gently to the beat of the song.

Nearby, the *dukas*—small huts—act as makeshift shops. People walk past those worshippers, sometimes joining in a familiar song. Passersby move towards the *dukas*, wanting to make their small purchases. A hand of sweet bananas purchased here will serve as a healthy and filling snack.

Dukas sell everything from milk and vegetables to combs and newspapers. They dot the landscape, stretched along busy streets and lanes. Goods are exchanged for money through the narrow opening in the wire security screen. This small but sturdy measure prevents needy and greedy fingers from snatching simple treasures. If you want to know something about a neighbourhood, a good place to begin is to ask right there at the *duka*. The mama or the *Mzee* (elder) in charge will likely know all that you need to find out, and more besides.

If you require someone to guard your vehicle as you walk into the slums, that is never a problem. The mama in the nearest *duka* where you have parked will usually be happy to keep her eye on it for you. Scaring off would-be thieves, she will call out to them loudly in the presence of many passersby who will intervene and attack the thieves. A small consideration of twenty shillings—about fifty cents—given to her upon your return is sufficient to repay her care. If you need a reliable young man to walk with you as your guide, she will find you one. He will keep you out of the many danger areas and bring you safely back. A modest payment for his services provides him with the equivalent of an afternoon's employment. These mamas in their *dukas* can be of great assistance as you seek to understand and work with all that is happening around you.

The colour and chaos of moments like these have competing charms—and sometimes horrors—all their own. Life moves along haphazardly in a teeming surge of sun-drenched tints and smells, hot movement and bellicose noise. In such moments you know that you do not control Africa. It is so much bigger than you or your Western ways or your modern superiority. Those moments present a complicated collection of challenging contrasts. They would form the lively context for our arrival again in Kenya, and become our backdrop and stage lights for all we planned to do. So we began our three weeks of re-engagement with the life of Kenyan folks, the people who had become our friends. Our pulses quickened and goosebumps rose on our skin—even in this midday heat –in anticipation of adventure.

Mary and I spoke often of Kenya but had hardly dared hope to return. It all seemed so impossible. Like Job we half thought, half prayed: *"Oh, that I might have my request, that God would grant what I hope for"* (Job 6:8).

Somehow, to our utter surprise and immense joy, God granted our request to one day return. Now we were back and suddenly my perspective changed significantly. I discovered myself to be moving a step further away from resentment and a step closer to gratitude. I found myself in a place that Blaise Pascal encourages us to visit when he says: "Instead of complaining that God has hidden himself, you should render thanks to him that he has revealed so much of himself."[42]

God began to reveal Himself in unmistakable ways on that trip to Kenya. We could not anticipate that He might begin to speak into being so many of our unspoken requests. But He did. And those were our hopes for that trip that we hardly had the courage to voice. We buried them, instead, somewhere deep within us. They emerged as realities over three unfolding weeks and they became unexpected moments of grace—love gifts from God—bonus blessings. In those days, Africa was replete with grace. Those blessings were about to be delivered to us like a string of pearls—gifts that were free for the taking.

CHAPTER SEVENTEEN

Unfold the Adventure

In the future, when your son asks you,
"What is the meaning of the stipulations,
decrees and laws the LORD our God has
commanded you?" tell him: "We were
slaves of Pharaoh in Egypt, but the
LORD brought us out of Egypt with a
mighty hand" (Deuteronomy 6:20–21).

When I worked in London some years ago, I ran a busy department of the London City Mission. My secretaries knew my office rule: today's mail is responded to today. If it requires a complex answer or some fact finding before giving a full reply then an acknowledgement is sent today; a fuller reply goes out tomorrow—or as soon as possible. I was driven by a need for efficiency and purpose. I had to achieve. I wanted results. Delay bothered me.

At home today, the phone will ring and ring—and ring. I get tense and I resent its insistence and incessant noise. I will not answer it. Eventually, after the obligatory five rings the voicemail function kicks in. I relax again. Someone will leave a message—or maybe try again later. I will not scan those messages. Mary listens to them. She will write me a list of callbacks I need to make and later, when I feel able, I will make those calls. I need time, lots of time, to control the stuff—so much stuff—that comes racing at me. It comes thick and fast, cascading over me, and I feel anxiously out of control. I need to slow everything down. I go for many days at a time—and sometimes for weeks—without checking my e-mail. When I feel I have some emotional space and the strength I need, I do it—and I usually reply to all my messages at one sitting. All those messages—I mean those few that I wish to reply to—may demand more energy than I am able to give right now. I will leave them until later, knowing I will likely lose track of them. Then I will expect another, sterner duplicate message from someone who is upset with me. I am upset with me. We are in good company. Most of my replies are, at best, late. At worst, they never happen. I forget them—without trying to—and they disappear. So does the urgency that attends them. It amazes me the number of messages I ignore that never amount to a hill of beans. Nobody bothers to follow through and I wonder how important or urgent they really were. I forget about them. Then all the tension goes and I can relax enough to focus again on the task at hand. Planning ahead is a challenge when you operate in this kind of mild fog. It muffles the noise of haste and the blare of the urgent. It mellows things down, like running slowly and silently through treacle.

Making the detailed plans for our three-week trip to Kenya became an interesting and unusual exercise. It was characterized by alternating bouts of angst and inertia. During moments of angst I ran around like a headless chicken. I achieved no good thing. I generated much heat and little light. I was a pain to live with. During periods of inertia I hid in my bedroom and pretended the world did not exist. I read. I slept. I found busy-work to do on my computer—anything to shield me from the need for action. Decision making—the responsibility of getting it right—was more stress than I could handle. I was not without creative imagination and it was not laziness, irresponsibility, or abandonment of my duty that held me back. The stress of it all made me fearful and very anxious. I had my definite list of things I hoped might happen for us in Kenya. I even wrote them all down on a piece of paper. But it remained just that—a wish list. I did almost nothing to turn my dreams into realities, to make it all happen. I simply did not have the emotional energy to do it. It was all just too much for me.

My wish list related to our first week in the country. This was our precious unstructured time. The other two weeks were already preplanned by other people for us. We just had to fit into their plans. Easy. But there was so much I hoped to squeeze into that first week. There were many people to see—and some emotional places to go. I feared going to those places but I felt compelled to revisit them. I knew I had to do it.

I felt huge gobs of inertia sucking me down, down, down. They took me to enervating places, like falling into a quicksand made of cold porridge and having no energy or appetite to eat my way out of the goo. It held me back, even from thinking for very long about the things I needed to do. Planning those visits, making our special arrangements, setting a firm and fixed schedule, organizing and securing appointments ahead of time—all this was far too much for me. Just the thought of it wore me out. It sapped my strength and drained away my enthusiasm like thick, black espresso coffee pouring from a cracked and broken mug, forming a messy puddle on the pages of my planner.

As I thought about plans, I also thought about faces. I recalled each profile like a portrait filled with a hundred wistful feelings. Each vivid picture of a place was bursting with the faces of people I knew. Recalling different events and situations brought with them their own special and overwhelming feelings. I went through massive bouts of emotional flooding. I would either cry or try to bite back the tears. As I swallowed them back they left me feeling downcast and quite depressed. Anger was always hiding just under the surface. Usually it broke open to fall clumsily on the wrong people— my family. This only added to my deep sense of personal failure that

enveloped me. It pulled me ever lower. I felt a cold fear about returning to face my demons. Part of my inertia was simple avoidance. I
wanted to put off having to face the reality of going back.

Arriving in Kenya, we had many "would-likes" and few definite
plans. The first few days were rescued for us by our friends the
Bartons, a family of white settlers in East Africa going back four
generations or more. Ian and Cathy are born organizers—they do
it well. Wanting to host us in their beautiful character home near
the small town of Limuru, they honoured us with their warm hos-
pitality and generous care. Our Kenyan adventure was getting off
to a perfect start—much better than we could have planned.

Remarkably, as the exploit of our visit unfolded, it got better
with each passing day. Have you ever, I wonder, had the experience
of an afternoon unfolding in a magical kind of way—stretching out
before you in an unplanned format, but with everything you might
hope for just happening along at the right time? I think, too, that
maybe I have had some mornings or even whole days like that. But,
for the first time I can remember, we were about to experience three
solid weeks that would pan out in this astonishing way.

Rough places were being made smooth for us. We had a profound sense that our moments were being filled with special significance for each of us. Healing—the inner kind of healing that enables
the outer sort to happen more easily and more quickly—was happening in abundance. It was going on within us and around us in the
lives of people with whom we wept without restraint as we reconnected deeply. I didn't turn on the tears in some dramatic kind of
way—I just couldn't turn them off. Each time—then and now—that
I meet a person for the first time since the accident, I find myself in
a place where pain and joy link hands. In moments like these I weep
freely. My brokenness feels new and raw, all over again.

We began to meet all kinds of people. People we had longed to
see again, and many we had never planned to encounter. Mulling it
over in my mind, I keep coming back to the new folks we bumped
into. The memory of them causes me to pause. I wonder at how this

visit edged its way forward, unfolding before us to the rhythms of grace. It was filled with nothing less than divine appointments—serendipitous opportunities, like African flowers opening up for us in vivid, meaningful ways. People popped into our consciousness like colourful firecrackers all around us. They turned an organized schedule—like the one I had been unable to arrange for myself—into an avenue of surprises. As we walked along it people stepped out of obscurity, strolling right into our lives. They touched our pain in a hundred healing ways, becoming part of our story.

Let me tell you about some of them. I hope that briefly they will become your friends. The first familiar stranger is an upcountry man in the dry dustbowl of Mitaboni. That small market village is no stranger to drought. It lies in the hot, dry area of the Ukambani, the countryside of the Kamba tribe. The Kamba people are loyal to the government of the day. They make good soldiers and policemen and usually rise to the top of those professions. They are musical by nature and hugely gifted as carvers of wood. They are gatherers of wild honey, harvesting the sweet nectar in large quantities by climbing tall trees, holding a smoking flax to drive away the hostile African bees. Then they can plunder their golden nectar. Those cheerful, courageous workers risk snakebites and fatal falls from high branches.

Late each afternoon, Mary and I walked out in the cool of the day to the local market. We loved to saunter past the colourful stalls, pausing to talk to mamas selling their wares. One evening, we extended our walk to the far side of the market. An older man, an *Mzee*, stepped forward to sell us a live chicken, greeting us in Swahili. He wanted to talk.

"Why," he asked me in Swahili "are you using a walking cane, Bwana?" I started to tell him about our accident. Hardly had I begun when he abruptly put up his hand.

"Stop, Bwana!" he insisted. "I know this story," and he continued telling me the accurate details of my accident to the end of the story as he knew it.

"How do you know my story, Bwana?" I asked him in genuine puzzlement. He replied, "I have heard it many times at my church, Bwana. I have been praying for you." His eyes glistened wetly as he continued, "God has been so gracious to me today," he continued, "He has allowed me to see the answer to my prayers."

Now it was our turn to be wet-eyed as he beamed his huge, warm smile at us and stepped forward to shake our hands vigorously. And I felt God show up in the midst.

The following week, down on the coast, we walked along the beautiful Diani Beach at Mombassa, about a one-hour flight from Nairobi. We were so glad to meet up again with our colleagues and catch up on their news. Sometimes, it was too poignant for me to be able to talk long with the friends who had seen me at my lowest after the accident. It brought back too much pain. On one of these occasions I strolled from our beach hotel over to the hotel next door. Both hotels belonged to the same corporation, so guests had use of either dining facility. They shared swimming and shopping areas, and small neat stores lined the hotel concourse.

One of the hotel's small stores caught my attention with its displays of khaki safari clothing and I wandered in. Nobody was there as I entered, neither servers nor customers, so I quietly tried on a safari vest. Looking at myself in the long mirror, I felt relaxed and unrushed without a shop assistant there to cajole me.

Soon, a female shop worker walked in briskly and we greeted each other in Swahili. We shook hands and Joyce introduced herself by her first name. Continuing in English, she asked what had brought me to Kenya. Explaining that there were many reasons, I told her that one of them was to say a special *thank you* to the doctor who had saved my life, explaining that I had worked as a missionary in Kenya.

I told her briefly about my accident, and recognizing me now to be a believer, she reached down under the counter to pull out a crumpled, dog-eared Bible. That old book was well used. She opened it to the prophecy of Isaiah and put her finger on chapter 54, verse 4. She held it there while she began to tell me her story.

"Bwana, when I was a young woman, a man came into my life and I fell in love. After we were married he went off with other women. He stole my heart. He took it away with him and then he broke it. I was shamed and these many years I have lived as a widow. But since that time God Himself has been my husband. He has never let me go."

Then she looked down at that old book and read: *"Do not be afraid; you will not suffer shame. Do not fear disgrace; you will not be humiliated. You will forget the shame of your youth and remember no more the reproach of your widowhood."*

She looked up as she continued, smiling through glistening tears, "That has been my story, Bwana. He has taken away my reproach. Let me tell you what I have learned, Bwana. God does not waste one of our tears."

Joyce cupped her hands, wanting me to understand. She said, "He gathers them in His hands. And, if we will let Him," she continued, "He will return them to us as the balm of healing and the oil of joy—if we will let him, Bwana."

Fighting my own tears, I held Joyce's hand within my own in a grip of firm friendship. I said, "Today, Joyce, you have been a missionary to me. Thank you, Mama."

Walking along the same beach on another sunny afternoon, Mary and I were dressed for swimming. I asked Mary to help me walk down the beach and into the ocean for a paddle—or maybe even a swim. My walking was lumpy and uneven and my balance was unreliable. Together, we ambled slowly over the hot white sands burning the bottoms of our feet. I could walk no faster. I leaned heavily on Mary's arm as we entered the warm waters of that azure ocean until bobbing waves were deep enough to support my weight, while the cool onshore breezes clackety-clacked through the palm fronds.

Small green monkeys screeched and scooted up into the clumps of coconuts at the top of the palm trees. White-smocked hotel beach attendants took lazy aim at them as they fired off small rocks from their slingshot catapults. I never saw them hit one. The water was warm and welcoming as it washed freshly over us. The waves broke further out, blanching over the coral reef offshore. It felt good to be back in those tropical waters. Exotic fish in abundance flitted and darted around our legs as we peered down into the clear waters to watch them, as if we stood in a large exotic fish tank.

Suddenly conscious of someone approaching on my left, just behind me, I turned to face an attractive blonde, bikini-clad woman about my age.

"Hi!" I said. "Are you on vacation?"

"Yes," she offered, smiling warmly.

"When did you arrive?" I asked.

"About one hour ago, only." Now I was able to catch her strong European accent. It had a pronounced Scandinavian lilt to it.

"I am divorced," she announced abruptly.

"Well, this is my wife, Mary," I said waving my arm towards the place where Mary was swimming, a metre or two distant.

"That is my eighteen-year-old daughter," she said nodding to a young lady splashing in the waves nearby. "And that is my son," she pointed out towards the reef.

"He is twenty and he likes to swim. He is going diving out on the reef for the first time, tomorrow." She said it with a note of anxiety.

"Since my divorce," she continued, "I have had a terrible fear."

"That must be awful," I said, "to be gripped by fear. Tell me, what is your fear?"

"I fear that I will lose my children—that they will die. They will be taken from me." Her voice sounded quite serious and she looked very thoughtful now.

"That is terrible," I said with genuine feeling. "What do you do when you feel this fear?" I asked.

"I pray..." she said

"Whom do you pray to?" I inquired.

"I imagine a very bright light," she said. "As I pray, I see it surrounding my son and my daughter and me. When we are inside that light I know we are safe."

Sometimes we say words that sound strange to our ears. Where do they originate? Those unrehearsed answers will astonish us, catching us off guard—even as we hear our own familiar voice uttering unfamiliar words or ideas. That is how I found myself answering at that moment.

"If that light was in the shape of a human being," I said, "whom would it look like?"

She paused for what seemed a very long time and then said in her heavy accent:

"Je-sus." She almost sang it, inflecting the last syllable in her rising Scandinavian tone.

"Pardon me?" I said. "Where did that come from?"

"No," she continued slowly and deliberately, "no, I am not religious but yes, I think that light would look like Je-sus." She was firm and definite. She had made up her mind. This is who that light would look like.

"Well, tonight," I said, "as you go to bed and you start to pray, that may be a good place to start. Why not," I suggested, "start by asking the light of Christ to surround you and to come upon you. Ask for Him to protect you and those you love."

"Thank you," she smiled, "I will."

So saying, she swam off one way and I paddled along towards Mary. We never saw each other again.

I often think that maybe a third party was part of that conversation, a Visitor in our midst. As a silent guest listening to our conversation that day, perhaps He prompted the words that surprised each of us.

Two tasks pressed in on me as my Kenyan journey continued. A sense of obligation and a deep desire drove me to fulfill both of them. I had to visit the doctor who had saved my life, and I knew that I must go back to the accident site. Intuitively, I felt that the ultimate purpose of the whole trip was, somehow, closely bound up with both of those events—first, dinner with the doctor and then a date with destiny.

Dinner with Dr. Paul Wangai, on our last evening in Kenya, would reveal some details of my accident that I had never heard before. "When you arrived at the hospital," Dr. Paul said, "You were not in good shape. It was very bad. The first three surgeons I called refused to come. They said it was not worth it. You were too far gone. You had broken or displaced bones, sustained two fractures of the skull, and suffered a severe brain injury." A slight pause let the enormity of it all sink in deeper. He seemed to be describing somebody I knew.

"The first anesthetist I called refused to come because our rule of thumb is first we resuscitate and then we operate. Eventually I found a neurosurgeon for your brain, an orthopod for your bones, and a microsurgeon to reattach your right foot. He had to find all the pieces of bone that were in your sock and piece them back together like a puzzle. Each member of your medical team is a believer. They are all followers of Jesus." As Paul spoke I listened without saying a word. I was hearing a story about another person for whom I felt great sympathy. It was an odd feeling to know the person was me.

"We lost you first in X-ray." Paul continued, "Your heart stopped. We lost you again waiting for the operating theatre. We lost you a third time on the operating table. You had a precipitous drop in blood pressure from massive internal bleeding. When we started to work on you, we took one look and knew that it was hopeless. So we gathered around you and we prayed."

Paul looked at me intently. "I believe," he said, "that we began to see God do the things that we could not do for you as we prepared to work on your body." We exchanged meaningful glances in a profound silence. It eloquently spoke of the grace of God whom we both worship, and how He is present to us in times of desperate need.

I sometimes ask the question: With whom would you choose to die? Given the choice, in whose arms would you like to be comforted as you step across the threshold into eternity? Usually, I guess, that would be our life partner. To hear words of comfort from a special person is probably what most want to hear. In a missionary context, where life is frequently at risk in the uncertainties that are so common, you might also want a substitute candidate, maybe a trusted colleague.

I have such a friend. His name is Chuck French. After Mary, there is nobody better I would choose to die with in Africa. Like many a missionary I know, he has paid the price for his service in Kenya. I trust him. I have been confessional before him. He knows me—warts and all—and still he is my friend. So it was only right that I would ask him to come to pray with Mary and with me. But he refused.

"Pardon me?" I said in shocked disbelief.

"No, I cannot come."

"Why?" I asked in horror. I wanted that this significant moment for Mary and for me—revisiting the horror and the pain—should be shared with Chuck.

"No, I don't mean never," he explained, gently, "just not today."

He sat back in his chair and his smile turned slowly down at the edges as he moved into an intense, reflective moment. The tension seemed to gather the corners of his mouth and he puckered his lips.

"It is too important, Paul. We must not rush," he continued. "I want to think it through. Let's do it towards the end of your stay. That will give me the time I need. I want to give it some careful thought, to spend some time praying about it."

I felt very relieved. It was typically caring of Chuck to want to do a fine job for us—the best that he could do.

Our last day in Kenya shone bright and sunny. But it was only later in the afternoon when Chuck drove with us back to the Limuru Road, to the point of impact where two vehicles had once collided. The African sun was already throwing low horizontal rays across the treed landscape, bringing everything to life with new vibrancy. Long shadows created high contrast between light and dark, throwing every shape into sharp relief. The passionate light created feelings that everything around was now somehow painted in an extreme 3-D, making the world seem more intensely real. No longer did you need to touch the things around you; they reached out and touched you in those moments.

Chuck parked his van at the place where our car had finally come to a halt in the aftermath of our tangle with the truck. We looked down into the Roslyn River Valley, standing at the edge of a sharp drop, where the soft shoulder dramatically fell away. It felt very familiar yet so strange; it seemed like we were watching a terrible movie.

Slowly, we started to walk back down the hill the way we had come. We stopped a short distance away, at the point of impact. The army truck struck us there as its extra-wide load crushed our vehicle. Three of us stood there in silence, at the edge of the road, as other big trucks roared past us again, that day.

"How ironic," I thought, "if we were to be taken out by a passing truck today."

At a quieter moment with less traffic, Chuck paced the width of the road at that point with his footsteps—sixteen feet. Too narrow for a wide load of, say, twelve or thirteen feet to let another vehicle pass it safely.

Chuck pulled a small Bible from his pocket and began to read from Psalm 91. When he got to verse thirteen, he read: *You will tread upon the lion and the cobra; you will trample the great lion and the serpent.* By faith, we did exactly that; we trampled underfoot the head of the Serpent, our ancient enemy. We knew that we had to break the power of the curse of that place in our lives.

Thinking back to places of significance that have shaped the pattern of my life, there are places of blessing, and spaces shadowed by a curse. Each kind of place evocatively triggers a rush of connective feelings.

Blessed places are those geographical locations where we have experienced meaningful times in life—times of spiritual insight, of commitment to the truth of God, of witnessing the reality of God's personal love. Places of curse are spaces where we have known miserable moments of great personal failure, moral rebellion, or spiritual ignorance. They are costly places, filled with regret.

The Limuru Road was such a place for Mary and for me. The power of a cursed place lingered in a tightening grip upon us, as the shock waves from our accident continued to resonate in our lives. The defeat of that impact echoed loudly in my life. At times, it deafened me to the songs of love sung by a Saviour who carries my pain as he hangs upon a tree.

But I knew I had to break the vise-grip of that curse upon my life. I understood that it could only be done by prayer—especially here, in a country where putting a curse on people causes them to die, as every *Mganga*—spiritist witchdoctor—can confirm. There is only one thing stronger than a curse upon our lives: the blessing of God. We receive blessing in and through the strong name of Jesus. His name is stronger than any curse.

"Satan is the curse maker, but Jesus is the curse breaker!" said one African to me on one occasion. He breaks the curse and sets us free from the grip of evil on our lives. He replaces the curse with the blessing of His love—a love stronger than death, deeper than the deepest pain.

Chuck finished reading Psalm 91 and said, "Let's pray."

The hardest thing in the world for me to do in those brief moments was to close my eyes. I was utterly fearful of being struck by another passing truck. I had to physically close my eyelids with my hands and needed to batten them down with my fingers firmly pressed over them. As Chuck began his prayer, his voice full of tenderness and care for us both, I was completely overwhelmed with all of the pain I had stored up from the accident.

From somewhere deep within me, great sobs shook my whole body. My shoulders heaved as I tried to hold back the flow. I wept and moaned with a low wailing like a mother in labour. In the midst of it all I seemed to hear words of assurance from God

Himself. As soon as Chuck finished praying, Mary came over to me and said, "As we were praying God spoke to me. He told me that what Satan meant for evil..."

"...God meant for our good." I finished the sentence for her. "Mary, the Lord said the very same thing to me, too."

In those moments, God was visiting with us to confirm that He has a hope and a future for each of us. And this thought continues to feed our trust in Him as we deliberately rest in His care for us.

In those moments, I thought of David, my sixteen-year-old son, desperately wishing that he could be there with us. Shortly after the accident he had asked me, "Dad, if all things work together for good to those who love God and are called according to His purpose, why are we in such deep pain?"

On that occasion I chose not to bat texts back and forth with him. I said, "David, we haven't yet begun to see all that God will do for us, but I am convinced we will. David, just watch this space."

Richard Baxter, the great Puritan pastor, writer, and theologian saw clearly the peculiar benefits of affliction. He chose to see their value in shaping our lives after God's pattern as we move along on our pilgrimage of faith. He said:

> God seldom gives his people so sweet a foretaste of their future rest, as in their deep afflictions. He keeps his most precious cordials for the time of our greatest faintings and dangers. Even the best saints seldom taste of the delights of God's pure, spiritual, unmixed joys, in the time of their prosperity, as they do in their deepest troubles.[43]

Mary and I had tasted our own deep trouble, but on that day with Chuck, beside the Limuru Road, we began to sip a precious cordial—a hope restored. God was beginning to fill the void, that empty space where hope once lived, with the promise of His presence. He was breaking the power of a cursed place in our lives.

The promise is not in vain that we will see God move for us and through us in the most difficult days. He was releasing us from a stuck place in our experience, a place where our lives were still on hold. The Scripture was beginning to be lived out in our own experience and within our personal story: *In the future, when your son asks you, "What is the meaning of the stipulations, decrees and laws the* LORD *our God has commanded you?" tell him: "We were slaves of Pharaoh in Egypt, but the* LORD *brought us out of Egypt with a mighty hand"* (Deuteronomy 6:20–21).

Slowly—but very surely—God was bringing us out of slavery, breaking our bondage to those limitations that the car wreck had imposed upon our lives. He was bringing us into a spacious place of wholeness and into the promise of a future.

Would that future be problem free and untrammeled by pain?— Undoubtedly not. But we could receive it with the assurance of His presence to walk with us and to guide us, if we would let Him. The question is: Would we? Moments of deep spiritual insight are astonishingly easy to forget, and with my compromised memory the answer to that question was by no means easy to predict.

CHAPTER EIGHTEEN

A Boy Called Daniel

Nevertheless, there will be no more
gloom for those who were in distress
(Isaiah 9:1).

In telling you my story, I seek to practice one important princi-ple, a guideline that steers me. An important rule of thumb is to attempt to be inclusive whenever possible. My natural tendency towards self-absorption, however, too often wins, but let me attempt to be less isolationist, and talk in terms of the other per-son's interests.

Of course, I am not yet an expert in doing this. I freely admit it. But, as I stumble along trying to make progress in this area, I rec-ognize that an inclusivistic approach to life helps build community. It links me, if I will let it, back into the lives of other people. It puts heart back into the community of which I am a part, at a time when life here in the West rushes on impersonally with alarming haste. We speed onwards within a single focus, in individuated worlds of isolating self-focus, absorbed in personal business interests and little realizing how deeply our lives impact one another. Africa, by contrast, teaches me that relationships lie at the heart of all that we do. I read it in the Bible, but in Kenya I read it in the lives I touched, and through those who moved me.

As I think, write, and talk about my accident and recovery, I apply a simple but elusive principle of inclusion. People involved in relief and development know it by another name. It is called *impact theory*. Through it, they explore the impact of an event or a relief program upon a community, a nation, and the world. In terms of my accident, the realization hits me that it was never simply *my* accident. It belonged to our whole family. It impacted each one of us.

Horribly often, I hear myself talking about "my accident" as if I were the central pivot of the universe, as though planets, seasons, and events revolve in their discreet orbits around me. But neither was this mishap *ours* alone. Another victim—another family—was involved. He is a boy called Daniel, and they are the Kariuki family—a small family in the backcountry of Kenya, the Kikuyu area of that developing nation. They were as involved—as impacted—and as injured as our own family was by that car wreck. In bleak contrast to people in the West, they lack easy access to all that is necessary to aid their recovery. On that short trip to Kenya we wanted to visit with them, to be with them, deeply desiring to encourage them and talk together as families bonded by a common pain. The painful event of our calamity became a shared reality that blew our worlds apart, and brought our lives together again in lingering aftershock.

Our first week in Kenya was our chance to meet Daniel again. But it wouldn't be straightforward. We had no clear idea of where exactly in Kithogoro village Daniel's house was located. Daniel had been a guest in our home, but never the other way round. We would meet him with his mom each Sunday at church. Our daughter, Leah, was the only member of our family who had been to his house—and that was when she rushed there, breathlessly, to tell

Daniel's mother about the accident that had just happened, that her son was injured. Left to our own efforts, without Leah's navigational help, we faced some fruitless searching before discovering the right shack.

Instead of looking for the proverbial needle in the elephant grass we tried another tack, setting out one hot, sunny afternoon to pay a brief visit to Cheleta Primary School where Daniel attended. The down-at-heel building snuggles into a dusty hollow beside the road, nestling down between the smart New Runda mansions and an old coffee plantation. A cross-section of expats, missionaries, Kenyan politicians, and UN workers occupy large and imposing homes in New Runda. Rich Kenyans grow richer on the high rents levied on their investment homes. The purchase price on just one of these properties far outstrips the lifetime earning capacity of most Kenyans.

We occupied one of these homes ourselves for thirteen months, and that is where we first met Daniel. Oddly, the home was both too big and too small for us. Everything was on a grand scale—the ceilings were twelve feet high and the drapes over the patio doors were made with a drop of nine feet. It was all far bigger than we were comfortable renting, with the feel of a small hotel that was smart, but so impersonal.

That home had one advantage for us. We needed to live close to Roslyn Academy where the children attended school, and this house was close enough for the children to walk there when I worked away from Nairobi using our only vehicle. Though the rooms were generously large, it still had too few of them to allow the children to have their own bedrooms. By adapting the office into an extra bedroom, we created some additional space to do that. Small rooms, but lots of them, would have suited us well, but as grand as it was we did our best to keep it open and welcoming to both *wazungus*—Westerners—and Kenyan guests alike. We made no attempt to impress people; we simply wanted to keep our home welcoming and our hearts open to others by sharing what we had with them.

By contrast to those mansions, Cheleta School's aging white paintwork was consistently rusty and faded, dusted to a dull red by the dry soil of the dirt road in front of it. Whipped into fine clouds by the tires of passing vehicles, it settles dully on all it touches, leaving a blood-red stain of permanent dry dye.

In the rainy season, that dusty road floods, pitted with deep potholes big enough for a man on his bike to be swallowed up to his waist in water. Once, during the rains, we saw it happen as an elderly cyclist made his way gingerly along the waterlogged road. When he hit that submerged pothole, the murky waters rose to a point above the pocket line of his jacket. Teetering for a moment, he finally lost his balance completely. As if in slow motion, he tipped over into the depths. There he thrashed about in the muddied waters for some moments before wading, wet and mud stained, to the road's edge, hoping to find some shallower water there. Slipping and sliding in the mud, he finally managed to haul first himself and then his sopping bike out of the hole and up to the raised bank at the side of the road. Waterlogged and weary, he slowly turned around and resolutely walked back the way he had come, pushing his bike ahead of him through the swirling puddles, ever checking for unseen dangers.

Cheleta School boasts a corrugated tin roof—the locals call it in their native Swahili *mabati*. It always looks rusty—because it is. It offers scant shelter and little protection against the long rains in the spring and the short rainy season in the fall.

In the dry time of drought that coincided with our visit to Cheleta, it would be the availability of water—not heavy rainfall on the leaky roof—that would prove the greatest challenge for the dry-mouthed residents of Nairobi. The absence of that one natural commodity means the stark difference between life and death. In the West, it is impossible to understand this fully—until you have lived through a prolonged period of drought or experienced for yourself the deep privations it causes.

All around the drab school building busy children played in animated small groups, running back and forth to the small *duka* nearby to buy their penny candies. Like school children every-where, their noisy laughter and shrill voices filled the air.

Walking up to a young girl playing with her friends in an alley between the school buildings during recess, we announced: "We're looking for Daniel Kariuki."

Immediately, other children gathered around us to find out what the *wazungu* wanted. "Which way is his classroom?"

"Follow me," she said with a huge smile breaking across her radi-ant face. She ran just ahead of us as we followed hard behind her quick, skipping steps, passing other children in their red gingham school uniforms. Busily, they washed and scoured the stone steps and the soiled, gray concrete walkways and paths. They clutched their small scrubbing brushes and tin pails of brackish water. There seemed to be more water over them than there was in the buckets. The air was alive with their energy and their happy laughter.

Once inside the spartan building, she introduced us to a male teacher who walked briskly with us to the headmaster's office. Invited in, we were offered seats on the sit-up-and-beg wooden chairs—relics from an earlier era. He instructed us to await his senior colleague's arrival. Mary and I started to chat busily together, trying to develop our "Plan B" for use if Daniel couldn't be found there today. After a few short minutes a tall, imposing man in his late thirties entered the room, greeting us both in Swahili and in English.

"How can I help you?" he asked in a refined Kenyan-English accent. We briefly explained that we were searching for Daniel and gave him a quick précis of the misfortune involving Daniel.

"Ah, yes. I remember it." He told us. "Unfortunately, Daniel hasn't been in school for the last eighteen months. But I'll call a boy to help you. He'll take you to Daniel's home in Kithogoro village. He'll take you there, right away."

We couldn't believe our great good fortune. Within minutes we thanked this teacher, and set off on foot behind our young guide. He took us across a pitted path through the old coffee fields, now stripped of coffee bushes, towards Kithogoro. We pondered what the teacher had told us—that Daniel could not afford to continue his schooling. In a system that boasts of free universal education in Kenya, schools are poorly maintained. In order to keep their buildings open and furnished with the fewest of basic supplies, school principals levy their own school fees in a no-pay-no-play system that cruelly penalizes the poorest students.

Continuing talking together, we carefully negotiated a route over dry, bumpy ground. Wondering how we would find Daniel and his mom, I leaned hard on my cane, struggling to walk along the rough dirt trail. It led us into the village, a euphemistic label for this collection of slum huts. Impoverished dwellings, each measures about ten feet by twelve feet, and they extend in rows that form terraces of tin-roofed, mud-walled homes. Large families live together in those cramped and primitive conditions that form some of the drabbest and poorest homes we have seen anywhere in urban Kenya. The hard-packed, red-soil alley separating the terraces matches the dirt floors inside the tin huts. Inside or out, I would not wish to be in either place during the rains. The alleys are awash as the floors turn to mud beneath their leaky tin roofs.

We walked, talking as we went, and were soon surrounded by a small crowd of laughing children. Dirty hands reached out to us in greeting and their dusty faces were dressed in smiles. Clothed in torn and worn old hand-me-downs, they held our hands while stroking our white arms and inspecting our pale skin—and the thin blanket of hair that covers my arms. Giggling, they talked energetically in their Kikuyu mother tongue to each other about us.

As we arrived at Daniel's home we discovered not one, but two homes facing each other across the dry mud alley. Each was positioned almost directly opposite the other. The boys lived in one and Mama and her three girls lived in the other in the customary segregated manner required by Kikuyu—and wider—tribal tradition.

One of Daniel's brothers smiled at us a welcome asking hopefully, with real anticipation:

"Have you come to take Daniel home with you, to Canada?"

How could I deliver a negative reply without killing his hope and disappointing his dreams? The other children around us waited together, watching me, listening carefully to hear my response to his earnest question. I smiled awkwardly, trying to find the right words. But there are no right words—better to be simple and straightforward. Trying to soften the blow would just create false hope and more broken expectations in the end.

"No...not this time," I said gently. Abruptly, he nodded and took off on a rickety old bike over the rough lane that leads to the heart of the village. He was on a quest to find Daniel somewhere in the throng of people strolling up and down the pathways. His younger sister hurried away to find Mama and bring her back home from the small plot of ground where she was working to grow vegetables.

Stepping across the rough threshold of the boys' home we waited for Mama and Daniel to return. The remaining brother entertained us by turning on his portable radio—to an exceptionally loud degree. An old car battery powered it. Behind him, drapes constructed from old black garbage bags hung in loose tucks and folds, acting as makeshift wall coverings in a vain attempt to keep out the wind and the rain. The red dirt floor was black from constant use, pitted and potholed, still waiting to be levelled. I wondered how big the rats were in this part of the village, feeling certain that they regularly visited these poor dwellings to scavenge for food dropped clumsily over the filthy floor.

Daniel's mother arrived first, quite out of breath and visibly excited to see the white people waiting at her door. In a handshake culture, hugging is not so common, but she embraced us in a squeeze tight enough to break three ribs. Laughing and crying all at once, she danced around us in small circles saying again and again *Mungu ni mwema, Mungu ni mwema, sana!*—God is so very, very good! A celebratory moment caught us all in its spiralling joy—an instant to take many pictures to savour the occasion. Through tears we celebrated, each in our own language, sharing together in a common language of love and mutual care.

My thoughts returned to those early days in Vancouver, after the accident, when we received a special letter written in a child's unsure script. As Daniel sat penning those words to us, his heart was very sure. He wrote in his simple way:

Paul,

First of all I greet you in the name of Jesus. I hope you are feeling better today. I want you to know that I am praying for you that God will heal you and comfort you. Hold on to the Lord Jesus because no matter what takes place God loves you so much and has a great plan for your life.

I am sure that he will bring your leg to total healing. Just be assured and you will come back to Kenya. Welcome.

Don't be afraid. When you were born God knew how your life will be and what will happen in your life.

I hope that you arrived there safely and I hope soon you will be okay and you will preach the Gospel how God has done for you.

This is my prayer and love in Jesus. I wish you the best.

Your loving friend,
Daniel Kariuki　　　*Hebrews 13:5*

The letter was written on inexpensive lined notepaper torn from a spiral-bound notebook. It was carefully folded in four. On the outside Daniel wrote in big letters: "WELL COME TO KENYA." It was so very much in character for this young man. He asks us for nothing, but instead he wants to give richly in his relationships. From the material poverty that surrounds him he continues to give all that he has and all that he is. Poverty of substance gave rise to no poverty of spirit in Daniel—empty pockets cannot bind a spirit that is rich and free.

The Scripture text Daniel chose reads: *Keep your lives free from the love of money and be content with what you have, because God has said, "Never will I leave you; never will I forsake you."* This moving verse could have been sent from all our Kenyan brothers and sisters in Christ to the family of disciples at home in North America. In those tender moments when he put the rich thoughts and feelings of his heart into words on paper, Daniel became the missionary's missionary to me.

I keep that letter in a special place, for it is filled brim-full of love for us. Its tenderness softens my heart, prone as it is to shrivelling, squeezed by the pressures of daily life. Recollections of Daniel are like medicine that stops my heart form hardening emotionally. Rich moments fade like fast-receding memories; even when they feel like a Monet masterpiece, captured in words like daubs of impressionistic light filtering through dappled leaves to bathe the whole picture in gentle tones of remembered love and meaning.

Daniel's brother finally rattled back to us, wobbly and breathless on his rickety bike built from discarded bits and pieces.

"Daniel is on his way, coming," he announced with panting excitement.

With rising anticipation we waited for the young man to arrive. Soon, his big-eyed face appeared smiling magnetically, looking so much bigger and older than when we saw him last. Delivering a greeting of hugs and handshakes he looked around the small crowd of children that surrounded us, finally facing the two of us. Unmistakably happy, his first question to us was,

"Have you come to take me home with you to Canada?" Ah, such hope—such disappointment.

Why is Africa so cruel to us all—so raw, so red in tooth and claw? It sinks its talons into your heart. It squeezes until it pierces you, then vampire-like, it draws your blood and drinks its fill. Once gorged, it casts you aside, limp and empty, exhausted and struggling for breath. Africa is a cruel mistress, enchanting and deadly. Like an exotic insect in her deadly mating ritual, she draws your love from you and then leaves you for dead.

And here a boy called Daniel dares to dream of leaving Africa, of coming home—to Canada. Africa will hold him captive to her petulance, a hostage to her fury. But Daniel has a spiritual home that Africa cannot cloy. It is a city not made by hands and to which he moves steadily.

Daniel moves towards it as he makes a vital interior journey, to deeper places within and beyond himself, a journey of faith as he follows the Man from Galilee. The Galilean knows and understands how it feels to be an artisan in a developing country surrounded by poverty, sickness and corruption. He, too, knows—and shows—how to live with a richness of relationships built upon love's solidity, rather than the illusions of false promises offered by material things.

"No, Daniel. We are not able to take you with us to Canada." I said. "Today we have come to greet you, to bless you, to let you know that we remember you often, and we pray for you as often as we think of you."

Why are words so very inadequate at such meaningful times? They make such small gift boxes—hardly able to contain the titanic feelings we want to cram into them. Yet, such feelings must not be allowed to sink without a trace, unspoken. They should be said right here, right now. I pray that they will be understood and received across cultures. I pray that they will bridge the language barriers and generational chasms that separate Daniel from us. And so I started to say a little more to this hopeful, dreaming boy.

"Daniel, look at you. You have grown so big. You are now a man. Perhaps we can try to secure you an apprenticeship. You are clever with your hands. You have made many good toys for Aaron. He sold them for you at his school. Yes, let's do that. We will try to find for you a special apprenticeship."

We gave him our promise. We meant it then, and today we are still trying a number of possibilities, longing to raise some regular financial support for Daniel—and the many young Kenyans he represents. We want to help them learn a trade, a skill to support themselves and their families. Carpentry, woodcarving, furniture or brick making, basketry, and wickerwork are all in the realm of possibility. Some small initial financing would make these dreams a reality for young men like Daniel.

It could be done and maybe it should be done. Imagine Daniel as a skilled worker bringing home enough money to feed and care for his family. He might afford to pay for his siblings to do what Daniel was never permitted to do—to finish up their studies at school.

Oh, Daniel, we left our hearts in part—and in pieces—in Africa. Some pieces are for you and some are for the ones you love. You rarely asked for anything, even when you needed so much. We wanted to give to you then—we still do now.

In Africa, *sustainable development* is a term that is currently in vogue. It refers to particular kinds of development that will continue after you, or your money, have left the country. Training in low-tech crafts and trades—or in business start-up programs that can generate income—is effective and practical in developing countries around the globe. These programs continue long after any initial pump-priming financing has been used up, to become self-sustaining as they begin to generate new income. They provide the necessary seed money for other business enterprises to begin.

If you were to add to these financial dimensions of development some structures of ongoing support through a community of faith, you would build a very strong foundation for some holistic development to emerge. Moreover, such self-sustainable projects are driven by local needs—and appropriate technologies and meaningful methods to achieve the outcomes for which they aim. They are not the oddly-shaped and misfiring imports that too often come out from the West to developing countries.

Ideas for the projects are those of local communities as they negotiate together to identify appropriate places to begin their self-generated, home-planned strategies for development. This community process produces projects that are fully owned by local people, and it is the local community that assists its members, calling them to account for the resources on loan to them.

When this form of development is founded on ethical and spiritual values—in addition to pragmatic considerations—they have a good basis for the Scripture promise to be fulfilled: *Nevertheless, there will be no more gloom for those who were in distress* (Isaiah 9:1). Hope is born—a hope that provides food for the body as well as for the soul.

The Gospel is, after all, good news. It is more than merely the orthodox statements of propositional truth into which the West has made it. It is an incarnational reality, lived out in the glorious messiness of our day-to-day lives. Lived this way, our lives express something of the love that reaches out from God as a suffering servant to his suffering people in servitude to a warped world and its inequalities. Henry Scougal puts it well when he says:

> But lest we think these testimonies of [God's] kindness less considerable, because they are the easy issues of his omnipotent power, and do not put him to any trouble or pain, he has taken a more wonderful method to endear himself to us. He has testified his affection to us by suffering as well as by doing; and because he could not suffer in his own nature, he assumed ours.[44]

That is why the real challenge of the Gospel is for followers of Jesus both to bring and to be that good news to the people they serve. And that involves, as I was to discover, being prepared to suffer.

The Gospel has the power to lift people out of the gloom of their distress. It begins in this lifetime and, beyond that, it offers a hope and a future extending farther than the time-limited experiences of this life. Hope starts now and goes beyond the limitations of time—limitations that I was yet to experience.

CHAPTER NINETEEN

Blueberry Muffins
and Swiss Cheese

Since no man knows the future, who
can tell him what is to come?
(Ecclesiastes 8:7).

The old millennium drew to its tired and unspectacular close. As it did, a certain Dr. Mel Kaushansky stepped briskly and energetically into my story. He brightened it considerably. He would help me to bring my old life (Before the Accident) to some healthy emotional closure. It seemed only fitting at this pivotal hinge in the history of the world that I, too, should turn a significant corner in my own recovery. My mission board had commissioned him to act as an independent neuropsychological assessor to evaluate the losses arising from my brain injury.

In the field of neuropsychology, Mel Kaushansky is considered to have an impressive depth of professional expertise. As a neuropsychologist, he compiles detailed medical-legal reports on people like me, survivors of a TBI. His reports are used in important court cases. He is professional, reliable, accurate—and deeply compassionate. His expert opinions were what we all wanted to tap into and benefit from—our mission, as well as Mary and I.

Mel had set up a day of standardized testing. I steadily worked through twenty-two neuropsychological tests conducted by one of his associates. Mel followed this up with a morning of interviews where he spoke to Mary and me, first together and then individually. He cut to the chase, rapidly touching the core of the issues that faced us. He worked quickly and professionally, engaging both of us fully in the process. He paused often to make a brief check on our responses and emotional reactions, to listen to our questions, to affirm our feelings, or to correct our misapprehensions.

He invited our feedback, and he did it with his zany, Jewish sense of humour—and with deep empathy. We knew at once that he was in touch with the human condition, interpreting it succinctly with rich sensitivity. He made us know that we were cared for, and so we became confident in his accurate and professional judgement. We recognized ourselves in the things he was saying. Unlike other tests we have tried, Mel's profiled us by accurately mirroring to us the people we felt ourselves to be. He talked precisely about our issues. Each time he summarized our discussions up to the point we had reached, he hit the target square on. He was uncomfortably accurate as he invited us to face some issues we would have preferred to quietly ignore or sweep under our emotional mat.

Mel was so concerned about forming a truthful picture that he made international phone calls to England. He wanted to speak with my retired professor, mentor, and friend, Dr. Roy Bell, who was there on an extended visit. Roy has known me closely for more than ten years. Moreover, as a registered psychologist, he is able to offer his own professional assessments, derived through observing me at many points in my recovery process. He has some deep insights regarding my losses, having known me both before the accident, and during my long months and years of rehab.

Every few weeks Roy and I would get together in some of Vancouver's best eateries and finest coffeehouses. In comfortable surroundings he would take me to less than comfortable places in my inner pilgrimage. He would press me, digging deeply to uncover the bedrock issues that challenge me, and would address the stuff that was bothering me that I might prefer quietly to forget. Mel needed to talk to him to get an insider's point of view. So they talked long—measured in both minutes and miles.

A few weeks later, Mel hosted a meeting at his office to present his report to us. You can tell something about a man by his office. Mel's is set in a fine old building downtown, full of large wooden beams, reeking with character and made contemporary by a young designer's flair for some sophisticated pizzazz. That block is home to all kinds of fashionable offices where communications and software companies thrive. It is a happening place to be. The wild variety of young up-and-comers and fashionable business people that we met in the elevator made me feel dowdy and more than slightly passé.

Mary and I stood there, clutching our copy of Mel's report close to our chests. He had sent us a preview copy so we could make our own list of questions. We listened in the elevator to brisk snippets of conversations about cutting-edge computer technologies, advertising contracts, and movies-in-the-making by famous film stars in Vancouver.

We were glad that Roy Bell would be present at our meeting with Mel, to act as my moral support and an encouragement for us both. He prompted me to say a little more whenever he perceived I was retreating from tough topics or failing to express myself as fully as I might. Already, he had keenly observed my habit of simply withdrawing when under pressure and he commented to me about it often. He would never let me off the hook.

Frank Byrne represented our mission in whose employ we remained. He was there to establish both the kinds and intensity of work that I might now be able to accomplish. The goal of our meeting was for each of us to discover what I might competently still be able to achieve. The question was: Could I still be employable and what might I effectively be able to do?

Reaching for a large, coloured chart of the brain, Mel leaned forward. His looks combined those of a latter-day biblical prophet and a rather intense professor of rocket science, all rolled into one. He sat there quietly, chewing his bottom lip. We held our breath, waiting for the word he would bring to us down from the Mount of Wisdom that was his office. As we waited, watching him in rapt attention, his beard stuck out horizontally from his chin, just below his bottom lip. He selected his words carefully. Finally, stabbing his pen at the large chart, he began to speak with words he had chosen with meticulous care.

The mark of a truly clever man is that he can make the complicated things of life sound quite simple. Mel was about to do this for those of us who have not studied the complex mysteries of the human brain.

"This is a picture of the human brain," he announced. "There are many kinds of brain injury, but they fall into two main classifications." He paused for a moment eyeing us deeply, making sure we were still with him.

"Open-head injuries occur with, say, a bullet wound or a penetrating blow that breaks the skull. They are devastating. That is not the kind of injury Paul sustained. No, no, he has had a closed-head injury. First, the frontal impact threw him forward as he hit his face, breaking his nose, jaw, cheekbone, and the orbis around his right eye. This jarring motion caused his brain to be catapulted forward. It struck the two sharp horizontal bone plates inside the skull, above and behind his eyes. It caused a shearing injury to his frontal lobes.

"Next, he received a sharp blow to his right temporal lobe, fracturing his skull behind his eye. This caused his brain to slam against the inside of his skull on the right side. Then his brain bounced back, slamming against the left side of his skull. This caused a reciprocal injury to his left temporal lobe. Finally, he received a blow to the back of his skull where there was a second fracture. The twisting motion may also have broken some strands of his cortex."

Mel looked up at each of us in turn, to ensure we were following his blow-by-blow account. We were. As he spoke, I preferred to imagine he was talking about somebody else—but there was no other "Paul" present in the room that day. Mel's intense glances in my direction confirmed that it was indeed me he was profiling.

"The tests show losses consistent with injuries that have affected his executive functions. These are the jobs performed by the frontal and temporal lobes. They direct our organizing, planning, concentration, and short-term memory functions."

He continued more animatedly: "Well, what does all this mean?" We hung anxiously on his every word. We hoped he wouldn't insist on our taking a quiz before we left his office. Smiling broadly, he sat back in his chair and said: "Well, it means that Paul's injuries are spread throughout his brain. Imagine his brain is a blueberry muffin..."

Personally, I had no problem at all with his analogy. My thought processes frequently seemed to crumble like a muffin falling off a table, hitting the floor, and breaking into pieces.

"Wherever you see a blueberry, that is where there is an injury. If you prefer," said Mel generously, "think of Swiss cheese. Wherever there is a hole, then that is where there is a loss in brain function."

Frankly, I wasn't sure which option I preferred. Swiss cheese or blueberry muffin. Hmm, I mused, let me think about that. Maybe I would rather simply pass on either option, if I were being fully honest with you. Neither of them seemed capable of absorbing and holding much new information—or drawing reliable conclusions from lessons learned in the past.

Mel leaned forward again and said: "I have good news and I have bad news." This was beginning to sound like a familiar Jewish joke—except that now I was the jester's punchline.

"First," he smiled, "the good news. If you take a hundred people and line them up against a wall, Paul is number ninety six." What was Mel talking about, I wondered? Is he thinking of shooting us? "Only four people," he continued, "would score higher than he did on these intelligence tests."

"But," I asked anxiously, "do you mean brain-injured people?"

"No," said Mel, waving his arms animatedly, like a seasoned stage performer, "just ordinary people," he assured us. Bending even further forward he leaned into us, confidentially. He continued in a hushed tone: "What Paul does not know is that three of those tests were intended to catch him out. They were designed to see if he is painting things blacker than they really are. So what did they find, those tests? Was Paul exaggerating? No, he was not. We can trust his word. Yes, we can relax."

We all breathed a sigh of relief. "So what's the bad news?" Mel asked us, and then to answer his own question, he continued: "Well that *is* the bad news. People will look at Paul and say, 'So what's his problem?' Well here is the problem that we identified. When someone is in the ninety-sixth percentile, we would expect that if he drops on a particular test score, he might drop to a score of, say, seventy-five percent. But on three tests Paul dropped right off the bottom of the scale. That is where we believe his real losses have occurred. These tests measured his short-term memory, his focus and concentration. And don't forget the tests were done in laboratory conditions of silence and without interruptions. They were not done at home with five teenagers and their friends in the house, with music blaring or the telephone ringing, or someone coming to the door, or the host of other interruptions that we all have to deal with so many times each day. This means that while there may be a dozen different things that Paul can do—and do very well—he cannot do two of them at once. His ability to multitask is impaired. This is new for him. It is not how he was. Before the accident he was a high-functioning person. Now, if he were a construction labourer, for example, he might find no real impairment in his performance. But in his many roles in public ministry he will continue to demand of himself the same high standards of performance as before. He will become frustrated and cast down when he fails his own high expectations for himself. So what does that mean as far as his work is concerned? Well, one thing it means," Mel concluded, "is that Paul cannot be a senior pastor."

Only the previous day I had visited a large church about an hour-and-a-half away from my home. It enjoys glorious mountain views in Abbotsford, set in a the beautiful Fraser Valley area of British Columbia. They had asked me to visit because they were searching for a new senior pastor. I told Mel where I had been.

"Abbotsford, Shlabbotsford!" he exploded, waving both arms down towards the floor in a dismissive and defiant gesture. "I have asked Roy Bell here if a pastor can be allowed to do just one job, these days. He tells me that some churches in the past might have let a pastor be just the preaching pastor—but not these days. So, I look at what my rabbi does," Mel pierced me with his focused gaze, "and frankly I don't think you could do it."

He slapped his knees. "It's the life cycle issues that will kill you, Paul. Sure, you can preach a good sermon, maybe even a great sermon from time to time. But people don't see the three weeks it now takes you to prepare it, or the three days of recovery you need from the exhaustion of preaching that message. They don't see your inner turmoil when, in the middle of preaching, you can't remember the next point you were going to make. You were a high achiever and it drives you crazy. It is at these times of preparation and recovery that there will be births and deaths and marriages in your church. There will be suicides and hospital visits and political infighting at all the wrong times for you. And that is what will fry your brain, Paul. I will give you just ten days, maximum, in a senior pastor's job—and then you will be completely done in."

I winced at him. My quiet look pleaded with Mel for another kind of answer. Mel, however, wasn't going to budge. He was stubborn and intransigent. "The tests show," he continued in his matter-of-fact tone, "they show that you are currently suffering mild to moderate depression. What does that mean? It means that the claws of depression are not yet gouging your back. If, however, you go into a senior pastor's job, you might crash and burn in public. Just think how much more depressed you will feel then. You will have failed in front of everybody. Besides," said Mel, sounding a little more conciliatory in tone, "how many kids do you have in school right now?"

"Three, at the moment," I said.

"Three!" Mel exclaimed in triumph. "Three kids at school. They don't want to shlep up to Shlabbotsford. They want to stay right home where they can enjoy some stability. If you want to shlep, *you* shlep. You shlep all by yourself the hour-and-a-half up to Abbotsford and the hour-and-a-half back again. You wanna shlep—YOU shlep. But I don't think you are ready to shlep anywhere! So, no shlepping!"

Mel waved both hands from far above one shoulder in a downwards, sweeping action towards the opposite foot. His gesture said it eloquently and definitively. Shlepping was quite definitely out of the question. "Besides," Mel continued in full stride, "before you take on a job in the future, I want to be on the interviewing committee—to keep them straight. There are some things they may need to know."

Frank Byrne, the man from my mission, leaned forward to ask: "So, what can Paul do effectively? Could he, for example, do some deputation work for us around Canada on behalf of our mission, speaking about his service in Kenya?"

"Yes," said Mel, without hesitation, "especially if he can use the same kind of material in different places, but not if he has to prepare a new talk in every place."

"That's fine." said Frank.

"What about teaching?" Roy Bell interposed. "Could he, maybe, teach at a theological college?"

"Yes," Mel said, quickly adding, "but if most professors teach seven courses, Paul teaches three. If they supervise four doctoral students, Paul takes none. If they sit on six committees, Paul sits on none. We keep him focused and we keep him part-time only. Then, each year we review his ability to multitask, and then we make appropriate recommendations and some adjustments to his schedule, accordingly."

"Mel," I asked hopefully, "will my short-term memory heal? Will I be able to continue with my academic studies, and will I eventually be able to multitask again? And what about the fatigue that blights me so that I have to rest most afternoons? Are these temporary problems or are they permanent?"

"Likely they will be permanent." Mel said flatly. "They will require that you learn to put into practice those compensatory strategies you have learned in rehab. They will help you overcome the worst effects of your losses. Now," he said, calling us all to full attention, "you ask me if you will be able to finish your doctorate. Here is my honest answer..." He started to speak quite slowly now, and very deliberately.

"My honest answer is: *I—don't—know!* If you were twenty-three years old, Paul, and you had made the amount of recovery that you have enjoyed to date, I would say without a doubt you will finish it with no problem. But you are not twenty-three years old—you are forty-seven. The brain gets slower as we get older. If you were somebody else I would maybe tell you to go out and prove me wrong. But that is your problem, Paul. You are already trying to prove everybody wrong. And who suffers? I will tell you who suffers. Your family suffers, that's who suffers! So, just relax. Stop trying so hard. Live a happier life and let your family live a happy life and a less driven life, too."

Frank and Roy smirked with a satisfied "whaddid-I-tellya?" kind of expression smeared across their faces. Mary looked triumphantly radiant. I asked myself: *Can it be possible that they agree with Mel?*

"Paul," Mel added, "take time for yourself. How much holy space—sacred time—do have in your life?"

"Well," I hesitated, fumbling the question. "I enjoy some quiet time each evening."

"Not enough!" Mel said forcefully. "You need bookends for the beginning and at the ending of each day. These are special times for making holy space. Take time to pray and to quietly meditate on Scripture, to read good books, listen to quality music, and to centre down in the depths of your being, and to know your God. Your faith is a medically accepted aid to your recovery."

In those moments, I profoundly knew that Mel was right—as profoundly as I felt these things to be absent from my life in the quantities that I needed and longed for. "Thank God for my Jewish neuropsychologist," I thought. "He is able to tell this pastor the things he knows I need to hear."

Some weeks later, Frank wrote me with an outline of his suggested plan of action. It would involve six months in which I would travel across Canada for ten days at a time to speak on behalf of the mission. I relished the thought of doing something—anything—purposeful again. I would speak at churches and in people's homes about our work in Kenya—and about our spiritual journey in these bumpy days of recovery. From the depths of my own pain I could speak into the pain of others.

From the hard lessons I was learning through my own recovery, I would be able to share something of the gift I had received—the assurance of a renewed hope and a future. Hope was a gift I could not tap dance into existence through my own clever footwork. I could not stage-manage it into being through a positive mental attitude, by applying some clever time management techniques, or by employing the latest pop-psychology fad. This gift was mine, but only as I freely received it day by day from One greater than myself. That is all I could do, receive it freely. It spoke of grace.

I am discovering that this kind of gift grows as you share it freely with others. Far from taking you into emotional or spiritual overdraft, the more you spend it by giving hope away to others, the more interest accrues. You simply cannot get into an overspend situation that way.

By contrast, however, hope seems to wither and fade whenever I choose to keep it under lock and key, hiding it away for myself alone. It seems that some gifts are simply meant to be shared. Hope is one of those gifts that you need to give away. It concentrates on what lies beyond one's present vision to focus, instead, on a future that fulfills one's deepest desires. Hope surpasses the narrow limits of our mean imaginations.

A wise man once asked: *Since no man knows the future, who can tell him what is to come?* (Ecclesiastes 8:7). Of course, nobody can. The reply of silence that follows that question in the Scriptures strongly implies this answer. Nobody can tell us. At first, we are tempted to hear this as a hostile answer—a statement of abandonment. But as we listen longer, it sounds more like an invitation to rest and to trust. Only the One who holds the future knows the future. And His great gift to us is that He cloaks the future—with all its terrors and fears—keeping it from our view. We do not know what it holds until, in the fullness of time, we must pass through it, as we tread the deep waters of affliction.

In trying times, we do not walk alone. If we let Him, He will walk ahead of us to make rough places smooth for us. If we let Him, He will walk beside us, assuring us of His deep and personal love for each one of us. If we let Him, He will walk behind us as our rearguard and shield for our vulnerabilities, keeping our weak spots safe from attack.

John Bunyan wrote the classic description of the journey of faith in his *Pilgrim's Progress*. He understood the pilgrim's journey to be long and hard, fraught with many dangers and pitfalls. But he also understood that we do not journey alone. At many points along our journey we know the company of God at our right hand. Bunyan describes one such awareness thus:

> Now Christian was afraid, and was minded to turn around and
> go back with the others. For he was sure that nothing but death
> lay before him. But the porter at the lodge whose name is

Watchful, perceiving that Christian had halted as if he would go back, called out to him, "Is your strength so small? Don't be afraid of the lions; they are chained and they are placed there for the trial of faith where it exists, and for the discovering of those who have none. Keep in the middle of the path and no harm will come to you."

Then I saw that Christian went on, trembling for fear of the lions but taking good heed to the directions of the porter. He heard the lions roar, but they did not harm him. Then he clapped his hands and went on till he stood before the gate where the porter was. He said to the porter, "Sir, what house is this and may I lodge here tonight?"

The porter answered, "This house was built by the Lord of the hill, and he built it for the relief and security of pilgrims."[45]

For Bunyan, it is clear that on the journey from the City of Destruction towards Mount Zion, the route of our journey of faith, lions abound—but so do places of safety. They are put there for us by a loving power greater than we are. They are there for our relief and for our security along the way. They foreshadow the ultimate place of safety that is the final destination for all pilgrims like Christian. And this gives us hope along our travel, especially on difficult days when the future—that vast unmapped ocean—seems unsure and unstructured and subject to sudden storms that terrify and trouble us.

So who can tell us what is to come? Nobody. There is none to tell us—no man, woman, or child knows the future. At first hearing, this sounds alarming to our ears. Yet, the One who holds the future in the gentle grip of His strong love gives to each of us a promise that is not offered in vain. He assures us—despite all that our eyes may tell us to the contrary—that we have a firm hope and a solid future.

We can make this hope our own as we learn to lean hard upon Him. This hope and future embraces the present moment and confronts the realities of this day in history. Hope challenges each day—

even those that present us with sudden horrors or overwhelming challenges. We receive hope as a gift and we hold it in trust.

Hope carries us forward into a future that lies beyond the short tenure of our brief days, our time-limited and tentative lease on life. Hope takes us forward from our own City of Destruction—whatever that might look like for each of us—towards God's promised Mount Zion, the place where there shall be no more tears or pain or sorrow.

But that kind of confidence in the future still lay a little way off for me, as we walked that day from Mel Kaushanky's office and into the glare of sunshine. We moved forward with less confidence to face the harsher realities of the present moment. I prayed that the prognosis Mel had offered would be so different. I wanted to be normal again.

CHAPTER TWENTY

The Forward Glance

Why are you downcast, O my soul?
Why so disturbed within me? Put
your hope in God, for I will yet
praise him, my Savior and my God
(Psalm 43:5).

"What are your long-term plans, Paul?" I sometimes hear that question with dread. For months, Mary and I preferred to joke that our long-term plans revolve around the onerous question of what are we having for dinner tonight? Part of the challenge of answering questions about our future plans is that we simply have no firm or easy answers.

A deeper emotional dimension is involved when facing the future—and it contributes to the massive inertia I feel when trying to answer that question. When pain shakes your self-confidence badly, you sometimes fear you may not be able to do anything worthwhile, ever again. Suffering and pain can set you off on a steep, downward spiral.

The sudden helter-skelter of your emotions, like widening

concentric circles, can put you on a journey where hope is altogether jettisoned. You finally come down with a bump, landing painfully in a horribly dark and frightfully lonely place.

It is too deep, this place of darkness. Alienated and afraid, you cannot clamber out of a trap where there is no light and the walls feel greased and slippery. It is at such times that you know yourself to be completely stuck. You begin to sink in the emotional sludge that pain produces. You might hear your own voice—as if it belonged to somebody else—crying out for help. And then you begin to ask yourself how you ever got to be in a place like this. How did you lose your steady confidence, your hope based on a real assessment of who you are within this challenging environment?

As a growing child, your self-confidence grew up with you. Over many years, your self-assurance expanded as you tried your hand, at various times, at hundreds of different activities. Even now, as you attempt a variety of challenges, you achieve varying degrees of success. This becomes the pattern, the routine, for most of us. With these accumulated experiences you build a large database of information, and you store it in your memory. From your growing database you draw your insights and understandings. Intuitively, you know the sorts of things that you can do well. You can also make accurate judgements about the kinds of activities that really are not within your particular strengths.

You might occasionally, or even repeatedly, bump up against your own limitations as you constantly try out new activities. In this way you begin, perhaps, to learn that your limitations are as important to understand—and to accept—as your abilities and successes. No less than your strengths, your weaknesses and challenges define the person you have become. Boundaries of ability form the personal parameters that provide you with a clear outline definition—they describe the shape of the person you have come to be.

An important part of this database is your skill at evaluation. Your ability to accurately grade your own performances is vital for any activity you may choose to undertake. "Am I doing well? Is this an okay level of performance that I'm achieving? Have I done a good enough job here? Have I met the reasonable expectations of others doing this kind of activity? Can I perform consistently at this level, or was it just a one-off, some kind of fluke?"

Those are important questions. If we so choose, we can normally answer them candidly, honestly and accurately. We can answer them independently without the need to hear it from others. Usually, we are able to clearly and persuasively verbalize our answers to others—except after a brain injury.

I discovered, after mine, that I had lost my baseline—all the "givens" to which we refer and against which we measure ourselves in different situations. I could no longer trust my ability to know what were the basic requirements expected of me when I did a job. I found it hard to know if I was really hitting the right target. I felt I was awash—all at sea in a tropical storm, sinking fast in a leaky boat. How do you lose your steady confidence, your hope based on a real assessment of who you are, in this kind of challenging environment? It's horribly easy—just removing the baseline of understanding your own abilities produces a loss that will remove any hope that you have any abilities, at all.

This kind of challenge led to a massive loss of confidence for me, and a lack of trust in my own abilities. It fed my old habit of discounting the work that I do. I felt my achievements to be trivial, of poor quality, or irrelevant. And soon I began to feel that way about myself. "I do not really like myself," I told Maribeth, my psychotherapist in the Acquired Brain Injury programme.

"Given that I could choose anyone in the world to spend an afternoon with," I said, "it would not be me. I do not like my own company." Today, I am not yet sure that I've come to like the imposter I see in my bathroom mirror. He looks and sounds like me but he performs quite differently now from the days before the accident. He is slower—more angular and a bit obtuse in his responses since the accident. He frequently embarrasses my family, and me. I think he burns out old friendships, these days, and dismally fails to make new ones. I have a hard time loving him. I fear that others do, too.

Part of this tendency is surely a disposition to be overly self-critical and it predates my accident. But the habit seems to have been horribly intensified through the accident and the consequential losses that I have suffered. So what is the way out for me and for people like me?

Part of the answer for me was to attempt to perform again at a high level. Brian Stelck, president of Carey Theological College, patiently provided the safe environment that I needed. His insightful guidance and interventions allowed me to begin to work on narrow, single-focus projects. I began them singly, doing just one kind of activity at a time. That was about as big a challenge as I could handle.

I often feel overwhelmed by it all, however, and I become anxious and hypervigilant. I might do a task three or four times, terrified lest I get something wrong. Every small detail cries out to me at the same high volume as the really big features in a task. Those important, big themes become easily blurred, enmeshed with the minor details—the small embellishments of the task. I struggle to distinguish them clearly and deal with them discreetly. I fight to handle them differently and put them in some kind of appropriate priority order. Everything assumes the importance of a major item that must be done now.

Brian carefully and deliberately ensured that each project led into a further project. There was an orderly sequencing and progression to the activities he assigned me. While moving forward, I attempted to refer to the previous project, trying to rehearse those old skills while practising the new ones demanded by the project in hand. This back-and-forth pattern began to develop my ability to return again to some limited form of doing multitasking activities.

The process was slow. Painfully slow. Criticism from others would decimate me. My mistakes, when even gently pointed out, caused me to be flooded with feelings of utter inadequacy and depressing hopelessness. Social interactions and encounters with colleagues proved to be horribly embarrassing and difficult for me—and probably for them, too—especially when I was fatigued or anxious. That seemed to happen desperately frequently.

By the time of our meeting with Mel Kaushansky, I had worked on various college projects from time to time for about a year. By then, I had spoken in public at many meetings and lots of church services. I felt myself to be much improved, and others have commented to me about the good job I was doing at different times and in various places. I smiled as I heard their kind comments—and then, of course, I dismissed them as being empty flattery or misguided hyperbole. Despite it all, I began to feel that I might slowly be starting to build a new baseline of competency. I was establishing a new reference point against which to assess my own performances, once again. I felt that with each activity successfully completed, I was passing another important milestone on an uneven road to recovery.

Frank Byrne, from my mission, had responded positively to our meeting together with Mel. His suggested work schedule closely followed Mel's recommendations. The plan, over the next six months, was that I would travel across Canada, ten days at a time, to speak to churches about our work in Kenya. Following that, I would be granted a study leave for one academic year to enable me to finish my Doctoral program.

At last, a long-term plan was set in motion. I felt relieved and somewhat daunted. Would I be up to the task? I wasn't sure. I feared the worst while hoping for the best. As I write, I am coming to the end of those speaking tours. For me, as I now look back on them, they have—as far as I can tell—gone well. Some Doctoral research and thesis writing still lies ahead. The sense of threat looms large. Will I be up to the task? Not sure. I simply want to do my best—and to enjoy the process as much as my uncertainties and my insecurities will allow.

"What are your future long-term plans, Paul?" As I hear the question I hear the difference between "future" as a statement about career choices and "future" as a journey of faith. And a faith journey has its own distinct insights and challenges. The question echoes and reverberates again and again, like a voice calling my name into a dark and empty cave.

"Don't you know that I find it hard to plan ahead?" I want to reply defensively. "Can't you see that I still resist answering the telephone, fearful that I might forget to note your call in my planner?" I want to explain it all to you. I want to tell you now while I am calm and can put it all into words. I frequently forget, so I feel anxious that you will invite me to do something for you. I dread messing up, making double bookings—but I also find it hard to say *no*. I rarely have the presence of mind to say, "Let me think about that and I will get back to you." And if I did say that to you, I would fear that my forgetfulness would rob me of the sense of insistent immediacy that prompts me to do what I said I would.

You see, I want to feel and to sound *normal*—normal enough to make plans and to follow through on them, to make good on my word, to honour my commitments. I want to do what I used to do and be the way I once was. So I find that I usually accede to your request—and that very commitment puts me into yet another minor panic. Minor it may be, but it is panic more than I need or want. Sometimes, the feelings of overwhelming anxiety are strong enough to make me pull out of a firm arrangement at the very last moment.

But your question about my long-term plans continues to echo. It repeats again and again. Why? Because there is a deeper level of inquiry embedded within it. At this deeper level it is about more than the personal agenda of my schedule bookings, my wish lists, and shopping plans. It has more to it than my ability to create an impressive wall chart of appointments or to keep an effective desk planner. Its deeper dimension has to do with the purpose of my life—its very significance.

Significance is not about status. It is about how I answer the question I often ask myself: "What does my life *signify*?" That question unnerves me—and I hear it echoed in your inquiry about my "long-term plans." Somehow, those plans express and hint at the value of my life—what it all signifies. For me to tell you simply—and honestly—that I have no plans feels like I am admitting that, after all, I have no significance. I feel my life adds up to nothing very much, after all. To tell you I am engaged in some small-scale activities here and there feels like saying my life is all just trivial pursuit. I feel like a one-legged man with half a brain trying to catch the mist.

Yet there is another reality—a counter-reality—at work here. This is an authenticity of the spirit, ploughing its straight furrow against the flow of emotional landslides filled with spiritual rocks and mental debris that are the residues of a wounded spirit. The counter-reality deals with this fallout by crushing it, composting it into soil that has a healthy crumb structure. Spirituality, that is *spiritual reality*, deals with uncertainty, pulling some solidity from it like a conjuror pulling rabbits from an empty hat. And this kind of honest spirituality happens in the place where I reside, and in the realities where I pitch my tent.

I currently reside in a space called *I Don't Know*. It is a good place to rest awhile, but maybe only for a short time because it becomes awkward and uncomfortable very quickly. *I Don't Know* looks, at first glance, like a dark place of ignorance and inability, a chaotic place where planning cannot happen. It is full of problem people—people who simply don't have the ability to get things done. And it is a place that is full of me.

At a deeper level, perhaps we are all stuck in this place called *I Don't Know*—however good we may be at dreaming dreams, plotting plans, and working hard to make them happen. If each day truly is a gift—and my accident persuades me that it is—then none of us knows tomorrow, anyway.

We cannot pull tomorrow down faster, or squeeze it into the plans we have made for it. We cannot live in tomorrow; we can only live in today. And today requires of us that we live it well. To do so makes tomorrow go a little better, too. Regardless of all the plans we have written into our schedule, they may never happen after all. Or, the future may happen in ways that are stubbornly different from how we programmed it all to be, or to develop, or to grow for us. That is one of life's great frustrations. It is also one of life's last great wonders.

To watch the way life pans out, shapes up, and moves on with so many unexpected twists and turns, is to watch an amazing mystery unfold. Astoundingly, all this unplanned stuff takes little or no regard for what I may once have written in my planner. And so, for me, this place called *I Don't Know* remains a place of inscrutability and a place of utter wonderment. It fills me with a quiet sense of reverence and a growing anticipation. It is beyond my grasp and gloriously out of my control.

I stand in silent awe, watching like a fascinated child peering into a kaleidoscope, as things fall apart before me, and then fall quietly back into a balanced and ordered sense of place. They form and reform in unexpected ways. If I can just let go, for a moment, releasing my tight grasp on my anticipated outcomes, I might enjoy the show. More than that, I will be caught up in it, instead of fighting against it.

Ultimately, it feels that these things—the kinetic parts of an unfolding future—are moved by a hand greater than mine. This is no mechanistic kind of fatalism. It is not a theology of *que sera, sera,* whatever will be, will be. Rather, it is recognition that the One who is greater than I is in control—and an admission that I am not. He calls me to play my part and to play it well. For me to do so will help shape outcomes, but God is the author of my days.

In this place called *I Don't Know* I hear a voice that calls to me as deep calls unto deep. It calls me to attention, to be present in the moment, to be fully attentive as I walk, to watch, and to listen, and to expect. There is something of the feeling of prayer about it all, a communion with the Father of Lights, the Giver of Insight. Rhythms of grace are alive within my journey, moving me along it, swaying me gently forward. Purpose and significance are given—

not grabbed—in this place called *I Don't Know*. They are not self-ish possessions for me to keep for my benefit alone, for they are loaned to me for sharing with others. Purpose is to be stewarded, and significance to be invested wisely to the end that I spend myself in others. I am not sure, any longer, that I want to limit the possibilities of my life to the mean and narrow plans of my own making—even if I were still able to effectively plan in this way.

I may bumble along inefficiently these days but I find myself singing as I go. I sing a jazz theme now. Jazz is what is left when the normal orchestrations of life have crumbled and broken down. I am attentive to that still, small voice of interior jazz, of spirituality, of the Master Jazz Singer. He calls and I answer. The busy noise of planning—the crashing and grinding inside my head as I force myself to plan and to rehabilitate my impaired executive functions—that busy noise all becomes a clatter and a din.

A small voice can easily be dimmed by so loud a cacophony. It can be drowned out by it, completely. But the small voice is there, still, unmoved like the calm in the eye of the storm. If I stop my frantic activity for moment, I can hear it. I can join it, if I choose, and together with this small voice I, too, can be still. I can learn to sing a quiet song, a simple jazz tune.

Perhaps sacred time begins when we pause briefly—even for a moment—against the onward rush of schedules. Noisy activity always seeks to kill the silence and fill the space. Without the pauses, those in-between times, we rush breathlessly forward like lemmings about to leap. Maybe holy space is carved out of the crush and press of the clutter that seeks to invade our private space, our personal zone.

This place called *I Don't Know* may, after all, be a perfect space—one that is empty of schedules and anxiety and full of time to be squandered. In such a place, time can be exuberantly wasted in wonder and awe. It becomes a viewing point from which to watch the kaleidoscope of life falling into place around me.

I find my corner, discovering my place in it all, and sit there within all of this falling-into-placeness. I find myself falling, out of control, falling into place, into my space, a place of significance, caught and held by a Hand of perfect control. And something new begins to happen for me. In my life, a renewed sense of purpose and significance starts to unfold before my astonished gaze. Matter and meaningfulness emerge once more, gently and slowly. All of this happens free of hurry, as balance settles and a peaceful symmetry arises. They grow out of the chaos—that painful imbalance and gross asymmetry—of my accident.

What does all of this say to me? Even now, I have so few plans. My schedules are empty and I can produce no concrete answers for you about my long-term future. But all of this tells me that a hope and a future are realities, after all, for me. They take shape before my eyes in ways that I cannot stage-manage. I dare not. If I vainly try to take control, I fear I might end up settling for less than I could or should become.

I wait and I watch and I listen—again and again—for a still small voice, hoping that this voice will bring me news of a strong love, God's love-gift of hope for me. I long to hear this voice whispering a love that is deeper than my fear. I need to hear it and then speak it into being in my daily life and situation. So did the psalmist as he pleaded with God. And that is something of what I think God is doing—speaking strongly and softly.

The psalmist discovers it is hard to form a forward glance when your head is craned back to take a long look over one shoulder. You cannot receive your future until you have released your vise-grip on the past—even when the past resonates with pain. He asks himself that terrible *why?* question. It haunts us all at critical moments in our lives. He says, *Why are you downcast, O my soul? Why so disturbed within me?* (Psalm 43:5). His head is bowed as he looks down, down, down. He focused on the pain of his past, failures that dog him. He has, for the moment, lost any sense of a hope and a future.

Just as he sinks deeper into a sticky inertia, he manages to pull away enough to spark some action. And what is the significant

272

thing he does? He continues to talk sense to himself. He recognizes both the truth of his desperation, and the lies that it tells him.

We all tell lies to ourselves. We persuade our spirits that we are worth less than we are. It is naysaying in the face of challenging circumstances that has brought the writer of the psalm to a downcast place. Now he chooses to rise above the realities of a cloyed and knotted mess. He takes, instead, a radically new perspective. He chooses to view his life from God's vantage point. He replies to his broken spirit by speaking into his quiet despair some words of hope. He instructs his wounded spirit: *Put your hope in God, for I will yet praise him, my Savior and my God* (Psalm 43:5).

His hope is not groundless. It is no mere wishful thinking springing from an overactive, positive mental attitude. Nor is this the idle daydreaming of someone who has finally lost touch with reality. This is no escape from reason. The psalmist's hope is built on confidence beyond that of his own making. He trusts, instead, a hand that is greater than his own. It is a hand that steers his future, moving him from this place called *I Don't Know* towards a place called *A Hope And A Future*.

In his *Journal*, George Fox, the early Quaker, wrote about the restoration of hope and how it transformed his own life. He says:

Then the Lord gently led me along, and let me see his love, which was endless and eternal, surpassing all the knowledge that men have in their natural state, or can obtain from history or books; and that love let me see myself, as I was without him. When I myself was in the deep, shut up under all, I could not believe that I should ever overcome. My troubles, my sorrows, my temptations were so great that I thought many times that I should have despaired, I was so tempted.

But when Christ opened to me how he was tempted by the same devil, and overcame him and bruised his head, and through him and his power, light, grace and Spirit, I should overcome also, I had confidence in him. So it was that opened to me when I was shut up and had no hope, nor faith. Christ, who had enlightened me, gave me his light to believe in. He gave me hope, which he himself revealed in me and he gave me his Spirit and grace, which I found sufficient in the deeps and in weakness.[46]

The psalmist, too, moves from a place of distress to a place of praise. But praise is more than a place—it forms part of the person he is. Praise becomes central to the essential person of faith that he has become.

I once met a Jamaican woman, a person of faith, in one of those serendipitous moments that come into our lives from time to time. It was a brief meeting where our spirits touched in a glancing blow of blessing that sparked with meaning. She said to me at this intersection of our lives: "Worship is what we do but praise is what we become." Of course she is right, for what she said echoes the psalmist's instruction: *Put your hope in God, for I will yet praise him, my Savior and my God* (Psalm 43:5).

God, Saviour, hope, and praise are linked to form a solid reality when other promised realities crumble. They are a real reason for hope and a sure promise of a future, especially in those darker days of overwhelming pain. The final destination of every journey of faith is hope restored. It takes us from time towards eternity— one in which hope becomes a relationship with the One who promises it to us, and turns hope from being a mere possibility into a lived experience of joy.

AFTERWORD

*He has delivered us from such a
deadly peril, and he will deliver us.
On him we have set our hope that he
will continue to deliver us, as you
help us by your prayers. Then many
will give thanks on our behalf for the
gracious favor granted us in answer
to the prayers of many*
(2 Corinthians 1:10–11).

"So, Paul, how is your recovery going?" a friend asked me recently. "Are you a hundred percent now?"

"No, not a hundred percent yet. I still have some challenges," I replied. Then I saw his look of perplexity. I looked absolutely fine to him. I was walking without my cane and my pronounced limp of a few months earlier had become almost unnoticeable for most of each day.

So what is my problem? Am I just malingering? I could see him wonder about me and ask himself whether I was milking the problem for all it might be worth. I almost heard his thoughts even before they reached his lips, they were so loud.

How could I reply? I did not have the energy to even begin explaining it all to him. We were together among other people at a wedding reception, and his question was asked as we passed each other on the way to and from the large glass bowl of fruit punch. Besides, I feared that if I did attempt a fuller answer, I would only appear to be making some transparently self-justifying statements. I wanted to tell him that most of my challenges are unseen and that most of my disabilities are hidden from his view. The pain at night, the sleeplessness and the fatigue it produces—how could I begin to explain? What could I tell him about the swelling of my feet after too much exercise or a lot of standing or sitting for too long? What about the fog that returns to my mind when I am tired, my fear of phones, my habit of double-booking myself for preaching engagements, my difficulty in planning ahead or in doing two things at once? And so the list continues.

The assumption behind his question is that either I have returned or that I will return to "normal"—to the Paul he once knew. Medically—according to my doctors, at least—that will not happen. But there is slowly emerging now a new kind of "normal." Already, it is beginning to happen for me. It is a return to a very great measure of functional ability—despite the ongoing challenges that are there.

The large amount of recovery I have enjoyed and that I currently experience surprises me and troubles me. It surprises me because so many doctors have told me frankly that it would not happen. Maybe they genuinely believed what they told me based upon their medical experience—or perhaps they were simply guarding their backs in this litigious age in which they ply their trade. At least if they warn me about the worst potential outcomes, then I can have no grounds for suing them for nondisclosure about my condition. Whatever the reasons, I am surprised at the wonderful measure of recovery I've received to date—and I am so thankful.

But I am also troubled. It is not that I am ungrateful, you understand. It is that I still long to see other wounded people make similar gains. I feel badly for them when I do not see it happen—even after praying. I am puzzled. Of course, I know that God is sovereign, He is in control. He can heal and He can also—and often does—withhold healing. But why would He grant such a generous amount of recovery to me? I simply do not understand. I almost feel embarrassed by it. I want to show you my scars all over again to prove to you that I really was as badly injured as I have claimed. I almost feel guilty.

Yet, mixed with this is a profound sense of reverential awe at God's remarkable goodness to me. So, together with the psalmist, I also want to affirm: *I will praise you forever for what you have done; in your name I will hope, for your name is good. I will praise you in the presence of your saints* (Psalm 52:9).

The praise I bring is neither cheap nor easy. At the bottom of it lies many unanswered questions and a large slice of survivor's guilt. But I will give Him praise because I feel so very thankful for all that He has done for me. I will be glad and rejoice, without denying my questions.

What about a hope and a future, those precious commodities that evaporated completely at one dark point along my journey? Have they returned? I will be honest with you. I am not trying to impress you or sell you the party line, whatever that might be.

As I search my soul today, I find that this hope and renewed sense of a future are right there, no longer hidden from sight but in full view. Are they there because of a stretching program, or yoga, or a positive mental attitude, or my stellar will to live, or some technique or system? As helpful as some of those things might be, I have to tell you they have nothing to do with my spiritual journey of faith and my recovery of a hope and future.

There is nothing I can claim credit for as I move forward along this recovery journey. The real heroes of the piece are my family members, my children, and especially my wife, Mary. Other significant players are the small army of people around the world, people of faith, those followers of Jesus who prayed for me, and still pray for us as family. I meet people today who tell me, "We pray every day for you." And I believe them when they say that. They remember us each day, and have done so since the day of our accident.

I don't really understand the mechanics of prayer. But I know it to be true that God hears and answers our prayers—and I am grateful. God is central to my story and I hope that you sense it as you read it. He is central to my story because he is central to my *life*. As I look ahead, I watch and wait for God to show up for me. Someone once put it this way: *But as for me, I watch in hope for the LORD, I wait for God my Savior; my God will hear me* (Micah 7:7).

The biblical writer experienced this for himself, and so have I. I know that if He will do this for me—and for the people in my life whom I love and who are important to me—then He will do it no less for you as you also learn to lean hard upon Him. He will show His love to you and to those you are concerned for—the ones you are close to and whom you love.

You don't have to take my word for it. You can simply talk to God. You can tell Him what concerns, angers or puzzles you. You can pray in ordinary words, from the depths of your being, and you can do it in the strong name of Jesus, as His Spirit empowers you. You can do it expectantly, knowing that He hears you. And then you can actively and intentionally look for His answers as they enter your experience. Madame Guyon, the French mystic, spoke about the importance of prayer in all of our lives. She said:

> Everybody is capable of prayer, and it is a dreadful misfortune that almost all the world has conceived the idea that it is not called to prayer. We are called to prayer as we are called to salvation.
>
> Prayer is nothing but the application of the heart to God and the internal exercise of love. St. Paul has said, "Pray without ceasing," and our Lord bids us watch and pray. All therefore may and ought to practice prayer.[47]

If you choose to pray in this way, God may surprise you, just as He surprised me. Sometimes there simply are no great or flashy firework displays in our walk of faith—only the deep assurance of His great love for you. And that confidence is enough and more. It restores you to your hope and your future.

As you continue on your journey of faith you may find it helpful to keep a journal, a kind of journey-of-faith travelogue, or some other meaningful way for you to record your faith experiences. It is both wonderful and important to be able to mark those milestones—to commemorate and to celebrate God's goodness to you at special times when He meets you in unusual moments of grace.

I have shared some of my own milestones with you through telling my story. My wish is that you may also know the reality of His rich blessings as you journey on in your faith. As you follow in His footsteps, tracing them in every path where your own journey leads you, may you find His love holding you close, especially when you are called to carry pain.

And after everything has gone, may even the darkness fall away from you. As the dawn's early light appears again, pale on the horizon of faith, may you know your hope restored, and with it a new assurance of a future that is promised, held firm and secure for you.

CITATIONS

[1] Frederick Buechner, *A Room Called Remember* (San Francisco: Harper and Row, 1984).

[2] Robert Rasmussen, *Safe in His Sanctuary* (Sisters, Oregon: Multnomah Publishers, 1999).

[3] Claudia Osborn, *Over My Head* (Kansas City: Andrews McMeel Publishing, 1998), p. xi & p. 64.

[4] Glenn Tinder, *The Fabric of Hope, An Essay* (Atlanta, Georgia: Scholars Press, 1999), p. 15.

[5] Ibid., p. 13.

[6] David Aikman, *Hope—The Heart's Great Quest* (Ann Arbor, Michigan: Servant Publications, 1995), p. 13.

[7] Henri J.M. Nouwen, *With Open Hands* (Notre Dame, Indiana: Ave Maria, 1972), p. 76.

[8] Ken Gire, *The Reflective Life* (Colorado Springs: Chariot Victor Publishing, 1998), p. 116.

[9] Václav Havel, *Disturbing the Peace* (New York: Vintage Books, 1990), p. 181.

[10] Philip Yancey, *Where Is God When It Hurts?* (Grand Rapids, Michigan: Zondervan Publishing House, 1990 edition), p. 210.

[11] Wolfhart Pannenberg, from his article "The Future and Unity" quoted in *Hope and the Future of Man,* by Ewert H. Cousins, ed. (Philadelphia: Fortress Press, 1972), p. 74.

[12] Jürgen Moltmann, *The Experiment Hope,* edited and translated by M. Douglas Meeks (Philadelphia: Fortress Press, 1975), p. 89.

[13] Eugene Peterson, *A Long Obedience in the Same Direction* (Downer's Grove, Illinois: InterVarsity Press, 1980), p. 131.

[14] Jacques Ellul, *Hope in an Age of Abandonment* (New York: The Seabury Press, 1973), p. 190.

[15] Walter Holden Capps, *Hope Against Hope* (Philadelphia: Fortress Press, 1976), pp. 33–34.

[16] Gerhard Ebeling, *The Nature of Faith*, translated by Ronald Gregor Smith (Philadelphia: Muhlenberg Press, 1961), p. 181, quoted by Carl E. Bratten in his article "The Significance of the Future" in *Hope and the Future of Man*, by Ewert H. Cousins, ed. (Philadelphia: Fortress Press, 1972), p. 54.

[17] Jürgen Moltmann, *The Experiment Hope*, p. 188.

[18] Jürgen Moltmann, *Theology of Hope: On the Grounds and Implications of a Christian Eschatology* (New York: Harper & Row, 1965), p. 20.

[19] Eugene Peterson (1980).

[20] Walter Breuggeman.

[21] J. I. Packer, *A Quest for Godliness: The Puritan Vision of the Christian Life* (Wheaton, Illinois: Crossway, 1990), p. 233.

[22] Philip Yancey, *The Jesus I Never Knew* (Grand Rapids, Michigan: Zondervan Publishing House, 1995), p. 219.

[23] Patrick Hirschi, Claudia Berwald and Rick Brown, "Couple Issues After a Brain Injury" in *Living With Brain Injury* by Sonia Acorn and Penny Offer (Toronto: University of Toronto Press, 1998), p. 101.

[24] Brain Injury Association of Minnesota web site (www.braininjurymn.org).

[25] John Goldingay, "On Being Human" in *Theology, News and Notes*, Fuller Seminary, Dec. 1998, p. 6.

[26] Edwin H. Friedman, *Generation to Generation* (New York, The Guildford Press, 1985), p. 15.

[27] Ibid., p.15.

[28] Ibid., pp. 17–18.

[29] Ibid., p. 18.

[30] Ibid., pp. 19–20.

[31] Ibid., p. 21.

[32] Ibid., p. 22.

[33] N. D. McNair MD, *Traumatic Brain Injury*, Nurs Clin North Am 1999 Sept; 34 (3):637–59: National Library of Medicine web site (www.nlm.nih.gov).

34 JAMA 1999 Sep 8;282 (10):974–83 PubMed Query web site (www.pubmedcentral.nih.gov).

35 Salvador Minuchin & H. Charles Fishman, *Family Therapy Techniques* (Cambridge, Massachusetts: Harvard University Press, 1981), p. 67.

36 Mike Strand, *My Closest Friend*, Brain Injury Association of Minnesota web site, Sept. 1999. (www.braininjurymn.org).

37 Craig Morrison, *My Date With Fate*, Brain Injury Association of Minnesota web site Sept. 1999 (www.braininjurymn.org).

38 M. John Simpson, *Difficulties Faced By Survivors and the Families of Survivors After Brain Injury and Ideas to Help* (Simpson Rehab Management, Chilliwack, BC: 1998), p. 37.

39 Simpson, pp. 34–35.

40 Friedman, p. 136.

41 Jürgen Moltmann, from *The Crucified God,* quoted by Walter Holden Capps, in *Hope Against Hope* (Philadelphia: Fortress Press, 1976), p. 140.

42 Blaise Pascal, *Pensees*, (438), quoted in *Exploring the Spiritual Life*, edited by Sherwood Eliot Wirt (Tring, Herts: Lion Publishing, 1983), p. 18.

43 Richard Baxter, *The Saints Everlasting Rest*, quoted in *Exploring the Spiritual Life*, edited by Sherwood Eliot Wirt (Tring, Herts: Lion Publishing, 1983), p. 83.

44 Henry Scougal, *The Life of God in the Soul of Man*, quoted in *Exploring the Spiritual Life*, edited by Sherwood Eliot Wirt (Tring, Herts: Lion Publishing, 1983), p. 59.

45 John Bunyan, *Pilgrim's Progress,* quoted in *Exploring the Spiritual Life*, edited by Sherwood Eliot Wirt (Tring, Herts: Lion Publishing, 1983), p. 129.

46 George Fox, *The Journal of George Fox*, quoted in *Exploring the Spiritual Life*, edited by Sherwood Eliot Wirt (Tring, Herts: Lion Publishing, 1983), p. 138.

47 Madame Guyon, *A Short and Very Easy Method of Prayer,* quoted in *Exploring the Spiritual Life*, edited by Sherwood Eliot Wirt (Tring, Herts: Lion Publishing, 1983), p. 138.

ABOUT THE AUTHOR

Paul Beckingham's award-winning articles in the Christian press focus upon key issues confronting believers, as they attempt to read the text of their lived experience through the text of Scripture. Spiritual formation, integrity, and healing are themes that drive his writing.

Paul holds degrees from London University, England, and Regent College and Carey Theological College, Vancouver, Canada. He gained the Carey Prize for Pastoral Care and the Leighton Ford Award for Leadership in Evangelism.

In Christian ministry, Paul has served as the youth director of the London City Mission in England, pastor of Marineview Chapel, Vancouver, and as a missionary with Canadian Baptist Ministries in Nairobi, Kenya, together with Mary and their five children. They worked among two different tribal groups, the Kikuyu and the Akamba peoples.

In their third year in Kenya, their missionary service was cut short in October, 1997, when they were driving a small car with their son Aaron, and Daniel, a young Kenyan boy, on their way to a slum village on the northern edge of Nairobi. They were struck head-on by a large military truck—a Kenyan Army military tank transporter, hauling an extra-wide load. Despite serious injuries, miraculously, they all survived.

In the years that followed, they found themselves to be on a slow journey of recovery in which they had to face the terrible loss of hope that a life-threatening event can bring. Yet, they also experienced love, assistance, and prayerful support from family and friends around the world. Through times of pain and anguish they have discovered their hope being gently restored. As a family together and as individuals they continue along their pathways of faith in a story that is still to be finished.

For the Beckinghams, hope in a time of pain, grace in a time of brokenness, has become their companion theme. They speak about their experiences to churches and support groups. Their goal and prayer is for God's hope to be restored to others who experience the pain of loss and the anguish of a broken spirit.

Together with his wife, Mary, and their five children, the Beckinghams make their home in Vancouver, while travelling to speak or teach in Europe, North America, and Africa.